THE PAINTER'S SECRET GEOMETRY

THE PAINTER'S
SECRET GEOMETRY

A Study of Composition in Art

CHARLES BOULEAU

with a Preface by JACQUES VILLON

A HELEN AND KURT WOLFF BOOK

HARCOURT, BRACE & WORLD, INC.　　NEW YORK

Translated from the French by Jonathan Griffin

CONTENTS

PREFACE

In the artistic chaos of these last years, when the absolute liberation of the individual instinct has brought it to the point of frenzy, an attempt to identify the harmonic disciplines that have secretly, in every period, served as foundations for painting might well seem folly.

But this folly is in fact wisdom. It is the way to a kind of knowledge essential for whoever wants to paint. Essential, too, for whoever wants to look at pictures. The framework of a work of art is also its most secret and its deepest poetry.

But this study—so important that it is strange it should have been left so long unattempted—was not an easy undertaking. It is a dangerous quest, one in which the seeker's mind must be always on guard against itself. Charles Bouleau has had need of a great deal of humility; he has taught himself to abandon many of his initial ideas, to renounce various seductive hypotheses that had given this or that branch of his researches its first direction, in his determination always to be true to the reality of the work of art before him.

The aesthetic theories which he expounds in this book are never arbitrary ones. They are those of the period under discussion: they have always a firm historical basis. Charles Bouleau does not single any of them out for partisanship. Advancing step by step through the vast mass of work produced by the painters, he has had the skill to separate out the new contribution of each period and each artist. He has carried his analysis through with strict method, seeking, in the case of each work studied, to recreate the intellectual atmosphere of its time.

The result of such long and scrupulous reflection is a book that is often highly original. Though, for example, numerous writers before him have discussed the golden number, Charles Bouleau's study of the Renaissance use of musical proportions in the composition of pictures will come as a revelation to many readers.

In a word, this book goes a long way towards recovering the spirit of geometry as Piero della Francesca understood it; it is an attempt to reveal that secret geometry in a painting, which has been for the artists of every period one of the essential components of beauty; and the examples which the author offers from among the works of modern painters, of Mondrian for instance, are a striking proof of his objectivity.

Jacques Villon.

INTRODUCTION

After gazing for a long time at the *Death of Sardanapalus* in the Louvre and making some notes on its composition, I was rash enough to pursue this line, turning to the *Entry of the Crusaders into Constantinople*, the *Massacre of Scio*, the *Women of Algiers*. This research and the pleasure it yields had taken hold of me. After Delacroix came Poussin and Cézanne; then David and Seurat... It was the beginning of five years spent in questioning hundreds of artists through thousands of canvases.

This book is not a treatise on painting. It is a study of the internal construction of works of art, a search for the formulae that have guided, over the centuries, the distribution of the various plastic elements. The framework of a painting or carving, like that of the human body or that of a building, is discreet; sometimes, indeed, it makes one forget its existence; but it cannot be absent, for it is what gives a work of art those 'principal lines' of which Delacroix speaks in his *Journal*.

Throughout the book I shall always try to look at the paintings in question in my capacity as a painter. I shall be searching for the genesis of the work rather than for the secrets of its *formal beauty*. I shall try always to resist the temptation to find the criterion of aesthetic value by applying some favoured formula; not being either a mathematician or a philosopher, I shall never attempt to prove that a work of art is a paragon of beauty simply because it may fit some highly exacting and scientific schema.

Nor is this book a *history* of composition. I shall take certain liberties with the time sequence. Due weight must be given to certain resemblances, resulting from affinities between artists of different periods: as in the case of Cézanne, Delacroix and Rubens. Conversely, in order to follow the use of geometrical figures (or of some other compositional device) through the centuries, I shall be obliged to treat certain painters in several chapters, under different headings. In spite of all this, the chronological order will often come to the fore, reflecting as it does the movement of ideas and the fact that every artist is at the start a pupil.

We shall find, as we go along, that there are many valid solutions to the problem of the distribution of forms within a work; we shall recognize, too, that artists like change, follow fashions and are subject to currents of taste.

In the midst of all these fluctuations we shall come across fixed points: the books on painting. The venerable treatises by Cennino Cennini, Piero della Francesca, Leonardo da Vinci, Alberti, Dürer and Lomazzo, the relevant passages in the writings of Delacroix and others less well known, will guide us in our search and will steady us, forcing us constantly to put the artist back into the atmosphere of his own time.

What is the art of composing a picture, and why, as a student, was one told so little about it? Is it a matter of instinct and flair? Some people assure us, nonetheless, that an extremely subtle and secret mathematical science lurks underneath the apparent spontaneity of the masters. Others, it is true, state that it is only a false science, a few tricks, a kind of *savoir-faire* which the budding artist must make haste to acquire. I found that these questions, when I tried to answer them, led far afield.

To begin with, the complexity of the subject is great: the organization of plastic ideas is a response to needs that are not confined to the domain of painting. The requirements of monumental art have to be taken into account in any work of large dimensions, in painting and in decorative sculpture as in architecture. Then there is the effect of the picture-frame on its contents—an effect which, though it remains very general, has a determining influence on the way the painted surface is organized, engendering in it geometrical figures that are often highly complex.

The evolution of ideas and forms in the course of time plays a greater part than the quite abstract requirements just mentioned. There is a geometry of the Middle Ages. It has its own peculiar features, and it disappears with the civilization that was expressed in it. The more and more complicated figures traced with the compasses are in due course abandoned, and at the beginning of the Renaissance an aspiration towards simplicity and an intense dislike of overloading create the conditions favourable to a new enthusiasm—the enthusiasm for applying to the plastic arts relationships of musical origin, whose philosophical beauty had already been praised by Plato in the *Timaeus*. These relationships were first studied by theorists and then applied by architects; but the painters were not slow to lay hold on them; and they constitute an essential element in the style of the Italian Renaissance. There is more than one way, however, of using musical relationships: starting from them, one can create a disequilibrium, a swinging movement which, much admired during the Baroque period, gave them a new life at the very moment when they were about to fall into disuse. But the Middle Ages were not completely dead—not everywhere. The taste for geometry persisted, though simplified; circles and arcs of circles, even the golden section, were still used; and the simple but imperious action of the rectangular shape of the picture continued to exercise its effect through changing fashions and styles. This form, of itself, creates a division of the contents, which may be either a discreet indication or a rigid discipline.

A painting is not simply a plane surface; it undertakes the conquest of space, and the different stages of its conquest are bound, in their turn, to be expressed in the composition: there is the conquest by means of geometry in three dimensions, and also the conquest by means of light and shade. The progress of this leads to a plastic art of illusion obeying the same laws of stability and weight as the real.

It is characteristic of contemporary painting that in it each one of these methods of composition triumphs in its own right, as though all that till now was jumbled together were suddenly revealed in its pure state.

And to this analytical activity in painting today a book like the present one surely, in its way, bears witness.

I MONUMENTAL ART

First let us look at the artist, whether painter or sculptor, who works within the framework of a monument, under the direction of an architect; he is not free to imagine and organize his work as he would do in his studio. To decorate a monument involves accepting servitudes that are bound to affect profoundly the distribution of the parts, their proportions, in fact the whole composition. This is my reason for studying first the characteristics which monumental art imposes on plastic art.

The monument is that which is bigger than a man, that which dominates him by its dimensions and mass—and which in consequence calls for an attitude very different from the simple perception of an object. A monumental work is bound up with the space which surrounds us. Seen from outside and as a whole, it is part of the landscape; seen from inside, it is a closed world in which we grow and move about. Monumental art requires not only vision but movement. A movement of withdrawal, in order to get a view of the work as a whole in the midst of its surroundings and to appreciate its unity; and a movement of walking about, so as to go round it and enter into its various parts. Though monumental art is no monopoly of architecture, it is closely bound up with it: a statue, in itself, is a work of architecture; decorative sculpture or mural painting contributes to a monument its completeness, accentuates or enriches certain points in it, but must never be detrimental to it.

Monumental art is therefore always bound up with space, and with a space larger than a man. The movements it imposes, those of withdrawal and of walking about, give it its distinctive characteristics and produce its main problems.

A monument looked at from a distance takes on a somewhat unreal appearance: it cannot be touched; it is hard to judge in relation to oneself; and the first problem to arise is: how can one know the building's real dimensions? Is it very large, or is it quite small?

On the other hand, when one walks through a monument, its forms are constantly changing: some points of view show it at its best, or better, others are unfavourable. The artist must always be placing himself in the position of the visitor, of the user; the place where he will be most inclined to stop is the sensitive point which demands his utmost care;

Church of Saint-Savin-sur-Gartempe: God and Noah. *God the Father with the features of Christ appears many times in the Saint-Savin frescoes; he is always made appreciably larger than the figures who are close to him and whom he is addressing. (Archives photographiques)*

it is from there that the forms of the monument must exert their full power over the imagination. This brings us to the second problem, that of monumental perspective.

The monumental scale

It is on the architectural elements devised for human use, and, above all, on the representations of figures (statues, frescoes...) that it normally falls to indicate the dimensions of a building by making possible the comparison with what is called the human scale.

Man refers everything to himself. Everything exists merely through this relationship. Primitive man observes the phenomena surrounding him, judges them to be useful or harmful, and loads them with metaphysics. The art that has come down to us from remote times is always magical; it is the expression of what is weaker than man or of forces that surpass him.

In the art of the great political communities, man is still the measure. The gods are represented by giants. In Egypt the Pharaoh, because he sees himself as of divine origin, has statues made of him that are ten times, or fifty times, larger than life.

One must go to Greek civilization to find an art in which the figure keeps the same size whether a man or a god is being represented. The artist identifies the divine form with his own. He gives the gods his tastes, his passions and his beauty. Only in exceptional cases does he dedicate colossal statues to them. He seeks in his own body the secret of divine beauty and has the courage, in face of the powers of nature, to proclaim the greatness of man.

The Romans had seen the work of the Greeks, but also of the Egyptians. From the Greeks they retained the sense of the human, but the Egyptian colossi excited their vanity as conquerors. They enlarged the Greek models and made colossal statues of gods or of the Emperor. Then came Christianity. The God of the Jews had been a terrible God: Jewish law, understandably, forbade his representation. But Christianity is God made man: the scenes from the life of Jesus return to the normal stature; only the Pantocrator, in the apsidal recess or in the zenith of the dome, retains the majestic figure of the giant god.

At that moment Mediterranean civilization suffered inundation by new and very strange forces. This was no revenge on the part of the Near East, no return to the feeling for the colossal, but the advent of fresh concepts which came from the depths of Asia. The human figure lost its proud domination. Yet a new humanism was soon to be born in the West; and on almost every conceivable part of the religious buildings there appeared astonishing people—new dwarfs, new giants—whose subtle relationship with the monument we shall shortly see.

Chartres Cathedral: a Queen of Juda. *The statue-column arises in obedience to architecture. Its small head, narrow verticality and fluted folds make it the image of the column: it clothes the column, confirms its dimensions but does not, like a caryatid, replace it. (Archives photographiques)*

14

Saint-Nectaire, capital: Resurrection of St Nectaire. *In the Romanesque period sculpture and painting adapted themselves strictly to architecture. Here the relatively small dimensions of the capital are purposely stressed by the stockiness of the figures and their large heads. (Archives photographiques)*

Rouault: *from* Divertissement. *Rouault, in his book illustrations, sometimes takes up again the old Romanesque method. A work of art can be a microcosm, laying open an imaginary world; but here, on the contrary, the figure with the huge head forcibly reminds the reader of the dimensions of the page. (Ed. Tériade. Photo Y. Chevalier)*

We reckon that an object, or a figure, is on the human scale in so far as it appears to match man taken as a unit. As I have said, man feels the need to refer everything to himself. It is characteristic of our intelligence, that faculty of synthesis and order, that it brings the diverse into unity and measures it against models, the most immediate of which is the self. By a phenomenon of *optical intelligence*[1], man takes hold of the figures which he sees some way off upon a monument, and brings them back to the unity of the self or—more exactly—to his own dimensions. Optical intelligence takes the form of a rapid, immediate act: we are not conscious of its working; as soon as we have stood back a little, it reduces for us the size of any colossal figure so that, whatever the artist may wish, we can no longer see it as a giant; and in the same way a small figure is enlarged, so that we shall never take it for a dwarf. The cherubs holding holy water stoups in St Peter's, Rome, do not do justice to the immensity of the nave. It is astonishing to see how a worshipper approaching them seems quite small, revealing with violent suddenness their colossal dimensions[2]. The Paul Delaroche frieze at the Ecole des Beaux-Arts consists of huge figures which we 'read' from a distance as men of lifesize, and so they diminish the huge semicircle. What follows? *How does one combat the illusions of optical intelligence? How can an artist convey size, convey smallness? How can he make exceptional dimensions felt? Briefly, how can he reconstitute the true dimensions of the monument?*

There are two means of doing so: either to put large and small figures together on the same monument, colossi together with figures of our own stature; or to alter the proportions of the human body.

The Egyptians used the first method. In their frescoes and bas-reliefs there is always a crowd of small people surrounding the Pharaoh. Even the Sphinx appears huge only if one can see the temple nestling between its paws, a building on our own scale, the elements of which are made for man. When this temple was buried, it was impossible to estimate the size of the Sphinx in any engraving where the artist had not taken the precaution of inserting some Bedouin or traveller.

In the Middle Ages, the second method was the one used for conveying greatness or smallness and for making the exceptional dimensions of any figure (and in consequence, of its frame) felt by us; and this was the period when respect for the dimensions of the monument became most strict.

In Romanesque sculpture the human figure displays a docility that has always astonished observers. Where else, except perhaps in the Far East, would one find such a willingness on the part of the human image to submit to distortion at the artist's sweet will? Baltrusaitis, in his masterly thesis, has shown once and for all that these transformations are dictated

1. Or by a perceptive mechanism that is prior to intelligence but prepares the way for it and tends in the same direction.

2. Sculpture in the open air to some extent escapes from this law, in the first place because the light eats into the forms, and then because, as soon as they reach a certain dimension, the belittling distortions of perspective make themselves felt. While a statue with a height of three metres can be made ten heads tall, it would be absurd to give one of six metres a height of twenty heads.

not by caprices but by highly precise requirements[3]; the human figure has not a fixed form but yields humbly, like the other elements of the building, to the internal laws of ornament and external laws of architecture[4].

The ideas brought out by these analyses have now become current; but what perhaps has not been sufficiently stressed—it emerges from the experience of the fresco painter who was up against the same problems—is that, while the figure obeys a more or less complex geometry, it also obeys, and just as strictly, the dictates of a respect for the dimensions of the monument and for the relationship of these to the human. It does so by an extremely simple means, which strikes the optical intelligence at once: by a modification of the canon of human proportions, a modification that has to do chiefly with the importance given to the heads and the hands. *Seen on a monument and from some way off, a human figure with a large head looks small, and one with a small head looks big.* If two figures are, both of them, more or less lifesize, the one with a small head will seem considerably larger than life and will, in consequence, give grandeur and elegance to the element that encloses it. A huge head will produce the contrary effect.

The representation of man risks deceiving us as to the true dimensions of the monument. The representation of a deformed man, on the contrary, emphasizes these dimensions, and brings us to what is called the canon of human proportions, of the interrelation between the dimensions of all the parts of the body. Since these proportions, as observed from life, are extremely varied, artists have always sought a norm for them, have tried to extract not an average but a canon—which is a very different thing, for a canon implies the idea of beauty. This conception, though it may seem abstract and refined, has been current among men from the remotest Antiquity. The Egyptian canon was remarkably stable; it was modified only three or four times in the course of thirty centuries. The Greek canon was codified in a still more dogmatic way, since its measures were not confined to studio practice but acquired a philosophic value; yet each master had his own idea about it, and the canon retained a considerable flexibility. The artists, adopting a convenient unit of measurement, said that a man was six, seven or eight 'heads' tall.

With the barbarian invasions, all idea of a canon disappeared. Man himself, as an isolated being, as a 'person', often disappeared, becoming no more than a sequence in a rhythm, an element in a wavy palm-leaf. And yet, whenever he is recognizable, whenever we see him in action in a scene that is definitely human, we reconstitute him and imagine him as a large or a small figure according to his appearance. This at once makes us modify our judgment of the dimensions of the element that supports him. To the artists of the Middle Ages this human figure, as pliable as soft wax in their hands, with a form no longer regulated by despotic canons and yet still always striking us as human, was a marvellous instrument of suggestion. They used it with an astonishing cleverness, especially up to the thirteenth century. On the capitals of the Auvergne churches and

3. J. Baltrusaitis, *La Stylistique ornementale dans la sculpture romane*, Paris, 1931.
4. Cf. also: H. Focillon, *L'Art d'Occident*, Paris, 1938.

Picasso: War and Peace, *detail. Picasso subjects his figures to the boldest, most violent distortions. Here the two great figures of War and Peace have small heads, which makes them seem even larger. They are contrasted with the warriors and with the horses, whose proportions are more normal. By this contrast Picasso, who has always a most exact sense of scale, respects the dimensions of his canvas. (Vallauris. Photo* Cercle d'Art)

in friezes, figures smaller than lifesize are four or five heads tall; on certain archstones in south-west France they are three heads tall, and the narrow dimensions of their frame are thereby accentuated. On the huge tympana the figures are elongated to as many as twelve or fifteen heads: they seem to us truly immense, far larger than life, and so guarantee to the part of the architecture which they adorn the full feeling of its real size. In addition, the Romanesque artists, being true people of the Mediterranean who, to understand the feelings of the person they are talking with, pay as much attention to his hands as to his face, attach in their work a great value to the hands as means of expression. These are living, they mime the scenes that are represented—in the Saint-Savin frescoes as well as on the Auvergne capitals. The Romanesque artists rely as much on the hands as on the heads for their power of reminding us constantly of the scale of a figure, and the dimension of the hands, as of the heads, remains more or less the same whatever the length of the body.

In the thirteenth century, admiration for the ancient sarcophagi and a more constant observation of reality made the 'extravagances' of the preceding age seem shocking[5]. The distortions became more timid, but did not altogether disappear; as a general rule, the small figures on the

5. Of these two reasons, the first was the more powerful, for observation from life had been practised all the time. What can be more natural, better captured from life, than the little men on the Auvergne capitals? And where else does one see the costumes of the time represented with more exactitude? People find in nature what they are looking for; in the thirteenth century they looked for elegant calm figures in noble drapery. It was the first classicism.

Dufy: La Fée Electricité, *detail. In this vast composition (10 m. by 60 m.) Raoul Dufy has managed to preserve the full monumental grandeur of his wall space. All his figures are about lifesize as they are in the detail here shown. In the centre of the panel, high up, they are slightly larger, this being necessary in order to make up for the distortions of perspective. (Musée de la Ville de Paris. Photo Seuil)*

arching of the cathedral porches are four or five heads tall, those on the lintels five or six, while the very large statues, with their suggestion of columns, are seven or eight[6]. In this way we are given a direct feeling of the narrowness of some frieze or section of an arch whose purposely modest rôle is that of an accent, of the compact cubic volume of some capital, or of the soaring of the great verticals. Thanks to the suggestive power of the parts bearing figures, the architecture has constantly the exact effect which the *maître d'œuvre* intended.

The wide liberty enjoyed in the Romanesque period has been recovered in our time. Now, as at the beginning of the Middle Ages, the canons carry no weight, the forms burst their restraints and a man will be what an artist chooses to make him. Yet the artist must not forget to take account of the human spectator, whose imagination reconstitutes, indeed recreates, the work of art in his own way, and whose optical intelligence brings any known form, as soon as it is identified, back to the norm.

Thus all the great moderns who have really had a feeling for the wall as such have always paid attention, whether by instinct or reflectively, to the technique of the Egyptians as well as of the Romanesque artists. Raoul Dufy, in his *La Fée Electricité*, associates two very large figures with a multitude of lifesize ones; and we see at a glance the size of Matisse's *St Dominic* in the chapel at Vence because small figures are set against him. Picasso manages to make all his monumental works fit in with the architecture, the more easily because he is not afraid to disarticulate, to break up the human form; sometimes he takes huge figures, as elongated as those on the Burgundian tympana, and finishes them off with small circular heads, surrounding them also, like the Burgundians, with more stocky figures. On the other hand, one is bound to note that Fernand Léger lacked respect for architecture and so diminished the scale of the monument by introducing massive figures, huge hands and even certain abstract but obviously plastic elements which remind us of tool-handles and other familiar objects. But Rouault, in his *Miserere*, is continually bringing us face to face again with the real scale of the book by his figures with their large heads (cf. p. 233).

The Greeks would never have employed such means to make the scale of the monument felt; their spirit could not stand distortion. The figures in their friezes are never very small, nor are their caryatids ever very tall. The measure of man is always kept in mind; it is for this reason that the Parthenon could not be made larger or smaller without destroying its harmony. Note, however, that the Parthenon frieze is one metre high. The Romanesque artists would have introduced into it figures of a stature

6. Viollet-le-Duc (*Dictionnaire*, article on *Proportion*, p. 557) was the first to see this clearly. He admires the medieval architects for subjecting the elements of their buildings not to a module but to the 'human scale, that is to say to the dimensions of a man... this was a way of presenting to the eyes the true dimensions of a monument, because in this way an exact relationship with man was established in all its parts.' But his observation, true and new though it was, was applied to the bases, capitals and diameters of columns, never to the representation of figures.

of four of five heads, and we should then have known precisely the dimensions of the monument. Phidias's people look lifesize to us, and the monument appears slightly larger than it is[7].

With the Renaissance it again became very difficult for the artist to modify human proportions as he liked: the general admiration for the sculpture of Antiquity forbade these fantasies. But the Renaissance theorists attacked the problem of the canon of human proportions in a different spirit from that of Antiquity. The Middle Ages, with their mysticism of symbols and correspondences, were still weighing on them: for proportions to be beautiful, it was not enough that they should be agreeable and rational—the numbers which governed them must have a metaphysical resonance. The men of the Renaissance, though modelling themselves on Vitruvius, their revered master, retained in spite of themselves the heritage of the Middle Ages, which had made man into the microcosm, the image of the whole world: their desire was to establish human proportions on a basis of simple relationships with a very general application.

Without going now into the details of those relations based on the small numbers, a subject which will be treated with some fullness later, it may be remarked here that the Renaissance masters were tentative in establishing their rules, and that their teachings led to a considerable variety in practice. It was, in fact, recognized that the canon of human proportions was subject to variation. On this point it was no longer possible to submit to a rigid dogmatism. The theorists tried hard to persuade the artists

Matisse: Chapelle du Rosaire, Vence. *Beside the huge figures of St Dominic and of the Virgin, Matisse has placed the small figures of his Stations of the Cross. By means of this contrast he has remained faithful to the laws of scale and allowed the chapel to convey the dimensions which the architect had given it. (Photo Hélène Adant)*

Fernand Léger: Façade of the Musée Fernand Léger, Biot. *Fernand Léger originally meant this composition for the stadium at Hanover; there it would perhaps have been carried out on a smaller scale. But these enormous hands and this colossal figure, which looks stocky because of its huge head, make it hard to realize, at a certain distance, that the wall is 16 metres high. By a failure to respect the scale a monumental work has been transformed into a fairground booth. (Photo Jacques Mer)*

to return to rules, but they did not agree among themselves and their rules were never applied strictly. The artist no longer had fixed bases; he observed nature and interpreted it according to his genius.

Perhaps the first to attempt to lay down laws was Alberti. Da Vinci and Dürer then showed that there were not one, but several possible rules. All these men were trying to find the ancient canon of Vitruvius who, as an architect-mathematician, had adopted the canon of Lysippus (eight 'heads') and tried to incorporate it into a system that was very much his own, bringing the human body, geometry, architectural orders and, in fact, all beauty together into a single play of relationships. This return to Vitruvius in an attempt to find a key to human proportions was to prove extremely important; it was responsible for the enthusiasm which the painters felt for mathematical relations and harmonic proportions. But it must be noted that Vitruvius's canon was already a departure from that of Polykleitos (the *Doryphoros:* seven 'heads'); and the Renaissance

7. Already, therefore, in the Parthenon we can see that the human scale may be a remarkable means of suggestion. It is not always there to remind us of the truth, but sometimes to produce illusion. Even in periods when artists cannot allow themselves any distortion, they are able to make clever use of the human scale. The most striking and immediately perceptible difference between seventeenth-century and eighteenth-century decoration, between Baroque and Rococo, is that in the latter period the human figures become diminutive. As rooms become smaller, optical intelligence still comes into play to give the illusion of size.

21

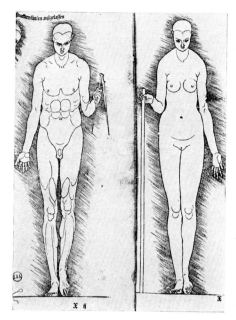

Albrecht Dürer: Figures. *Dürer made many studies of the varying dimensions of the parts of the human body from childhood to maturity, not omitting such factors as thinness or obesity, but the aim of these researches was clearly to arrive at a type of ideal beauty.* (Vier Bücher von menschlicher Proportion, *Nuremberg,* 1525)

masters in their turn modified it, almost without meaning to do so, by each presenting his own interpretation of it. This is especially striking if one compares the images put forward by their pupils at the end of the sixteenth century. Jean Cousin claimed to be following Vitruvius strictly, but the example he gives of the ideal human figure is an elongated, sinuous creature who can only get into the prescribed mould by twisting, and his female figures are so many Dianas of Anet[8].

Thus the canon of human proportions retained some of the adaptability inherited from the Middle Ages. This adaptability often lost its *raison d'être;* it was now not always at the service of the monumental laws[9], but it remains like some tenacious residue and resists every attempt to impose a norm. This is because the artist has given it a new purpose, has endowed it with a new power: expressive value. The Mannerists taper their figures, depict them with long spindle legs and swan necks, not in order to render the large expanse of a wall evident to us, but for the sake of the charm, of the languorous grace which we in fact enjoy in these forms.

In this way an imperious law of monumental composition produced certain necessary distortions and then, no longer understood or remembered, disappeared, leaving behind it a habit whose origin was forgotten and which was capable, one day, of serving other purposes[10].

Monumental perspective

Let us now consider another obstacle to the artist's freedom of fantasy: a discipline imposed by architecture, by the monument of which the work is destined to form part and which, like the respect enforced by the dimensions of the frame, will have a direct effect on the composition. This is monumental perspective.

It is not with perspective in itself that we are here concerned. True, the problems which that raises for artists are often closely related to those of composition, and the two kinds of research may be compared to two

8. *Livre de pourtraicture* by Maistre Jean Cousin, Paris, 1571.

9. Lomazzo, however, had retained the feeling for the wall and for its laws: 'In the great subjects,' he says, 'the figures must be judiciously enlarged to a little beyond natural beauty, for the sake of their congruity...' (*Trattato dell'arte della pittura,* 1584, Bk VI, ch. 2).

10. Cf. Focillon: 'A syntax has created its vocabulary and the vocabulary survived the syntax.' (*L'Art d'Occident,* p. 126.)

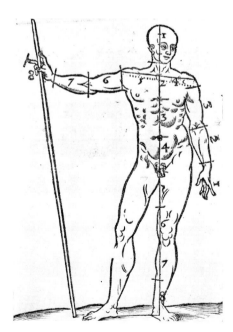

Figure by Jean Cousin, *from* Livre de pourtraicture *(Paris,* 1571*). Jean Cousin imagined he was going back to Vitruvius, but his figures are much more elongated than those of the Ancients. (Photo Giraudon)

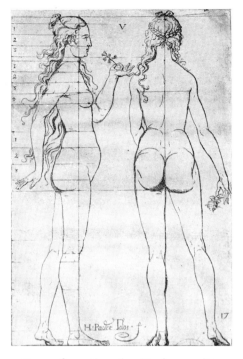

Figure from the 1649 Toulouse edition of Lomazzo's 'Trattato dell'arte della pittura'. *The Toulouse painter, Hilaire Pader, in illustrating Lomazzo, gives as his example of the canon of seven and a half heads a figure that is more Mannerist than Greek. (Photo Giraudon)*

roads that sometimes cross or even coincide (so that we shall often encounter perspective in our course). But the two fields are distinct, nonetheless, and the study of the various sorts of perspective as solutions of the problem of representing space can have no place here.

Monumental perspective is the system of congruity imposed on a work of sculpture or painting by the place it occupies in a monument. There must be not discord but harmony between the *representational work*, whether historiated or not, and the *monument*, which is also a work of art. The monument has the right to insist that respect be shown for its walls and its proportions, just as we have already seen it insisting on respect for its scale. The paintings must not, by the illusions they create, destroy the mural surface; and on the other hand, the foreshortenings produced by their position must not harm the effect of the paintings themselves. A relief carving or a fresco placed high up under the cornice cannot be conceived in the same way as it would be if it were low down, at eye level.

Let us now, therefore, come closer to the monument, hitherto considered as a whole, and take our stand in the middle of the church, at the foot of those fresco-covered walls... The forms shift, they take on different configurations at every step we take, and then they come to a standstill when we stop where one should stop, at the place where the artist foresaw we would raise our eyes to them. The foreshortened view of the high walls distorts the subjects that are represented; this does no harm in the case of Byzantine or medieval works, which keep the same frontal power when looked at from far off or close to[11]; nor are these multiple points of view unfavourable to the archaic frescoes, in which the purely descriptive false perspectives make no attempt to produce illusion, but decorate the wall like a tapestry, without penetrating the surface[12].

But the problem became a difficult one when artists began to be obsessed by the search for an exact perspective that would give the illusion of reality—that is to say, from the beginning of the Quattrocento onwards. The canniest of them, those who had the feeling for the monument and for monumental sculpture, like Piero della Francesca, Andrea del Castagno

11. The Byzantine artists were, however, preoccupied with the distortion and dwindling due to perspective. The problem was either to enlarge the head, in which case the person represented would lose his stature, or to retain the canon that had been adopted, with the danger that the head would practically disappear because of its height. I was lucky enough to work for many months in the Church of Saint-Savin, which gave me the chance to study those masterly paintings at my leisure and see how the twelfth-century masters had solved these problems. They knew that a spot of bright colour on a dark ground seems larger than it really is; hence the coloured haloes behind the heads—of which there are examples already in S. Clemente, at Ravenna and in Santa Maria Antiqua. The stained-glass artists of Chartres had not forgotten this.

12. Giotto had his own solution for the problem of telling a story on a wall without penetrating the surface. No doubt because he himself was an architect, Giotto loved the wall and had the greatest respect for its density. Hence he suggests, in his frescoes, a restricted space, limited by a smooth vertical surface from which a few architectural elements emerge; and his people move and have their being on a shallow stage in front of this backdrop.

or Mantegna[13], soon saw that perspective with a normal vanishing point made any painting placed above the spectator appear to lean forward. They therefore adopted, in such cases, very low vanishing points, level with the ankles of the persons represented[14].

Italian logic was destined to go much further and to establish on the wall a true perspective precisely related to the height of the painted scene above the spectator's eyes. Under the people in the paintings, and even sometimes hiding their feet from view, there were to be jutting cornices, completely realistic.

After this, it did not take long to arrive at the *trompe-l'œil*. In S. Ignazio at Rome, as soon as you leave the central point for which the perspective was devised and from which it achieves illusion, everything around you caves in in a sort of cataclysm. A world of fantasy, absolutely unreal, is built up and then destroys itself. It is the world—at once false and so exciting to the imagination—of stage scenery. Here the *trompe-l'œil* is pushed to the point of absurdity; yet too much fun has been made of these ingenious methods of the late Baroque; it must be recognized that the *trompe-l'œil* does, for the benefit of a certain point of view, restore the balance of the architecture and set the figures in their proper positions in space, instead of breaking up the wall into unrelated pictures, each with its own horizon line—easel pictures that completely mask the monument and transform the wall into a wretched dado.

In absolute opposition to this lineage of logical, rational mathematicians of perspective, who draw us into their world of probable illusion with the virtuosity of jugglers, Veronese takes his stand, with his dislocated perspective which does away with the vanishing point. Does this mean that he is a belated primitive? No; his works are highly satisfying to the most classical turn of mind. But let us look at them more closely than usual, taking the whole series of his *Biblical Feasts*. Let us follow the lines of the tables, then those of the pavement, then finally those of the cornices; we shall have the surprise of finding lower and lower vanishing points, all of them, it seems, close to the central vertical axis of the picture. Let us examine them still more thoroughly; these *fabbriche*[15], which in the distance are always shown parallel with the plane of the picture, have their vanishing points sometimes to the right, sometimes to the left of the central axis.

What does this mean? There are several vanishing points, or rather there is a *vanishing area* situated near the centre of the picture but slightly

13. Cf., on this subject, the interesting passage from Sebastiano Serlio's preface to Book II of his *Architecture* (*The second Booke of Architecture, made by Sebastian Serley, entreating of Perspective...*, English translation, London, 1611): '... it is requisite that the Horison should stand even with your eyes... but... (in some cases) a man must take upon him to place the Horison somewhat higher, by the advice of some skilful workman, which maketh histories or other things upon houses, thirtie or fortie feet high above a mans sight, which is unfittingly.'

14. Cf. p. 93.

15. *Fabbriche*: an old Italian term used by the landscape painters for buildings and fragments of buildings in a picture.

below and covering the space of several square metres[16]. Veronese manipulates the spectator's eye as he wishes, placing it to the left, to the right, higher or lower, according to his fancy; or, more exactly, he transforms the spectator into an Argus with a hundred eyes that roam over the canvas in all directions at once. This does not mean that he goes back to the primitives, whose method is to raise the horizon line as much as possible in order to portray a multitude in detail (as Pinturicchio was still doing in the sixteenth century). On the contrary, Veronese's vanishing area, in which the lines of the perspective come to an end, gives the same impression as a backdrop behind a shallow stage: Veronese is, in fact, nearer to the monumental conception of Giotto, who placed his people, like a sculptor, in front of a closed background. Veronese's world is not closed—on the contrary, it is vast, airy and luminous; but it never makes a hole in the wall; and this astonishing result is due to his multiple perspective—to his way of, so to speak, breaking up perspective and rendering it inoffensive. This is very striking if one compares Veronese's *Biblical Feasts* with a picture on a similar subject such as Bassano's *Marriage at Cana* in the Louvre, a work constructed according to a spatial perspective whose oblique and violent vanishing point digs into the picture like a wedge.

The final extreme of the *trompe-l'œil*, its *tour de force*, is to be found in the ceiling perspectives, the domes that seem to open into the sky.

The Byzantine domes and apses were entirely occupied by the bust of the Pantocrator. That enormous, massive, dominating head might seem to contradict the law of monumental scale, but really confirms it. For if we imagine the figure entire, then its feet touch the ground and its proportions become those of the tallest medieval figures. At other times the cupolas were decorated with a frieze of figures that went right round; but these never lost contact with the cornice and never created an imaginary space. The first ceiling figures proper are those painted by Mantegna in 1470 in the Camera degli Sposi at Mantua. Here the ceiling no longer exists; individuals in perspective, leaning on a circular balustrade, are seen against the sky.

Perhaps the first flying figures are those of the *Creation* on the Sistine Chapel ceiling. But the whole of that ceiling is a system of painted architecture, solidly resting on the walls, with some of the coffers in it open, leaving holes through which one can see the sky. Scarcely ten years later Correggio went much further. His cupola paintings are so bold that nothing more astonishing was achieved even at the high tide of Baroque decoration. That of the Church of St John the Evangelist at Parma, less well known and earlier by a few years than the breathtaking cupola of the cathedral in that city, already utters the challenge with the greatest clearness; at its centre, exactly above our heads, ascends the risen Christ, alone,

16. Guadet (*Cours de perspective*, 1929, p. 191) has counted six vanishing points in the *Marriage at Cana*, but, he says: 'The horizon line of course remains constant.' Emanaud (*Géométrie perspective*, 1921, p. 351) recognizes that the horizon line is not clear in this picture and that in the *Feast in the House of Levi* 'the solution is a bad one'.

Veronese: Marriage at Cana. *A study in perspective. The so-called classical perspective makes all lines perpendicular to the plane of the picture converge at a single point: Veronese, on the contrary, aims them at several different points grouped together in the central zone of his canvas. In this way he opens space up, instead of limiting it. (Paris, Louvre. Archives photographiques)*

in the sky. In the cathedral the eddying world of angels about the Virgin, with its quantity of varied and ingenious foreshortened figures melting one after the other into the light, set going a wild enthusiasm among the artists, who were also stimulated by the stupefaction of the public.

After this, not only was it impossible to decorate a ceiling except in *trompe-l'œil*, or to adorn a cupola without making it into a gaping hole, but—what is more curious—these foreshortened figures, seen from below or from above, invaded easel painting. Correggio himself, having shown himself so clever in a *genre* which he had made the fashion, was unable to give it up. His figures are seen from above in the *Virtues* (Louvre) and *Ganymede* (Vienna), from below in the *St George Madonna* (Dresden), which is the strangest example of a quite unnecessary ceiling perspective: in it the Virgin, the principal subject, is quite small and foreshortened, while the outstretched legs of the saints occupy much of the foreground. The Venetians in the sixteenth century followed this example, as for instance Veronese in his *Adoration of the Magi* at Munich, and Tintoretto in his *Presentation of the Virgin*; then came Baroque painting. This somewhat artificial effect of a teetering perspective is due simply to a displacement of the horizon line, which slides to a position far above or far below

Correggio, in some of his frescoes, aims at plunging views or soaring ones: the horizon is moved upwards in his picture, the Virtues, *in the Louvre, and downwards in the* St George

Madonna. *The breathtaking monumental perspective of his ceiling paintings led, in Correggio and the next generation of artists, to a predilection for foreshortenings.*

Correggio: St George Madonna *(Dresden Gallery. Photo Alinari)*

Correggio: Virtues. *(Paris, Louvre. Archives photographiques)*

eye level, or even moves right outside the frame. Here again, as in the distortions of the human canon, we are face to face with a persistence, in easel paintings, of habits acquired in monumental art, from which they had their *raison d'être*.

One finds in modern art creators of mirage who are related to the Baroque illusionists. Let us take one case, that of Fernand Léger. We have criticized him for not respecting the true dimensions of the surface that was to be decorated. But his aim was rather to transform architecture and turn it into something else; in interiors he tried, by the play of colours, to *'changer les murs de place'*; and on the outsides of buildings he made the surfaces undulate and sometimes vanish[17].

Thus the principle of suggestion dominates all monumental art. The forms which the artist attaches to the wall are seen by us not with our eye but with our mind. Whether it be optical intelligence or a creation of our imagination, there is always a spontaneous judgment triggered off in us

17. 'The exterior volume of a piece of architecture, its sensible weight, and its distance, can be diminished or increased according to the colours chosen.' (F. Léger, quoted by A. Verdet, *Fernand Léger*, Geneva, 1955.)

and transposing reality; and this subjective vision, by the grandeur or the intimacy it gives to the monument, by the magic of the real or false lines which our gaze follows, stamps its character on the architecture as a whole[18].

18. Some time ago Charles Blanc observed, though without analyzing how it came about, that 'decorative painting enlarges or reduces a building, moves it away or brings it nearer..., diminishes its defects or exaggerates them. It raises the vaults higher at will or brings them closer to the eye, extends the surfaces or narrows them.' (*Grammaire des arts décoratifs*, Paris, 1882.)

II THE FRAME

And now, detaching ourselves gradually from architecture, from the domination of an art which subordinates whatever collaborates with it, we shall gradually define the problems proper to painting, isolate painting from contingent forces and concentrate our attention on it alone.

A painting acquires its unity even before it is a picture—as soon as it is separated from its surroundings by a frame. As soon as this frame exists, and even if it is an architectural one, closely bound up with the forms of the monument, it imposes its stamp on its contents and gives them a form. This influence of the frame is exerted on a carving in relief just as much as on a painting, so that we have not yet to do with a law proper to painting: indeed, it is in the field of sculpture that the most striking examples are to be found[1]; but, general though it still is, this fact already begins to define the problem and brings us nearer to easel painting.

Friezes

In a frieze that unrolls across a wall like a ribbon, the parallel horizontal limits exert pressure on the contents, though letting them escape to right and left. So a frieze is already a frame, but a frame that is open on two sides, a frame that holds the forms above and below only; and the freedom it gives them at the sides is, as it were, an invitation to movement. It is not by chance that the themes chosen for friezes are so often a procession or a march-past. The figures advance, sometimes converging towards the choir of a church or towards the axis of a monument; sometimes also they run the whole length of a wall or of several walls, inviting us to follow them; we march beside them, their suggested movement becomes our movement, and the figures succeed one another in time as well as in space. If not a march-past it is a story, and the order of its events, transposed on to the wall, is again temporal as well as spatial, since we pass at short intervals from one scene to another.

Thus the frieze engenders a movement which takes place in duration as well as in extension, and this notion of duration, a new one for the

Ghirlandaio: Adoration of the Magi. *Of the regular geometrical figures, the circle is one of the most perfect. The various possibilities that arise from it will be studied in this chapter. In the picture here illustrated, Ghirlandaio inscribes in the circle two squares, and its centre is clearly marked by the hand of the Child Jesus. (Florence, Uffizi. Photo Alinari)*

1. Romanesque capitals and tympana.

cresc.

Parthenon: East side frieze. *The elements in a frieze are seen successively: they present themselves in time as well as in space. In the Parthenon the figures are sometimes arranged in compact groups, sometimes with more distance between them, so that they take their places in accordance with a musical rhythm. (Composite picture, from marbles and casts in the British Museum. At the beginning and the end, four figure drawings attributed to J. Carrey. From* Le Parthénon, *by Gustave Fougères, Ed. A. Morancé)*

plastic arts, brings us closer to the arts of time, to music and poetry. The frieze, in fact, has rhythm rather than composition. Like music, it will present a succession of different values, slow or quick, semibreves followed by crotchets or quavers. Like poetry, it would be scanned in longs and shorts, in unequal accents, in a regular recurrence of rhyming syllables.

Let us take a few examples. Some of the most ancient monuments of painting are the Egyptian friezes, painted on the flat or on low relief. Most often they are bands arranged horizontally, showing a succession of scenes: servants are marching, all in one direction, towards the important person, a god or a pharaoh. In some exceptional cases the movement may be vertical and horizontal, as in the *Nocturnal Navigation* framed by the body of Nūt, goddess of the sky; but always there is one direction, a continuous movement towards an objective. From this arises the rhythm. In places the small figures crowd together, bend, press close against one another; the gods, occupying several levels, contribute the areas of repose.

The most perfect example of a melodic composition is the Panathenaic frieze of the Parthenon. It is here, perhaps, that plastic art comes nearest

f   *din*

to music: not only is the rhythm evident, scanned, and balanced with exquisite delicacy, but it is like a song that rises to a climax, a symphony that develops in all the fullness of its complexity. To be convinced of this, one must put the fragments back into their order. Here, as Charles Picard remarks, is to be found, for the first time in a Greek temple, unity and convergence. The figures start from the back and separate into two parallel processions traversing the whole length of the long walls, in which the groups of horsemen answer one another symmetrically, contributing their jerky gallop, their series of rapid notes followed by the vibrant mass of the chariots.

But it is above all on the façade wall, where the two processions come to rest face to face before the gods, that the music reaches its ultimate refinement. Here the movements are much more complex: on the left, bearers of offerings are moving rightwards in a rhythm that is at first unequal, then equal and more close-packed, then again loose and unequal, initiating a sort of grand *crescendo* that culminates at the six seated divinities, who turn their backs on it with a noble and smiling indifference. From the right there is a free repetition of the same rhythm, with still more grace in the grouping of the figures in twos or fours; while in the

centre, between the two clusters of gods, at the place where the contrary movements are broken and a sort of dead point is established, five isolated personages appear to move in their stillness and to be continuing the secret thread of the melody.

Never again has the art of the frieze achieved such heights. In it we truly feel what is meant by the classicism of Phidias—equalled, in its easy grace, by that of Mozart.

What, compared to this, are the archers of Susa—a work in which the artist, like a tom-tom player, has intoxicated himself with monotony?

S. Apollinare Nuovo: Mosaics in the nave. *The spectacle of these women carrying crowns in their nearly identical repetition reminds one of the progress of a litany. (Ravenna. Photo Alinari)*

At Ravenna, those splendid women carrying crowns repeat the same gesture insistently; but a slight tilt of the head, a variation in the robe or drapery, gives them a mysterious life. Already the Byzantine mosaics are painting. And in the same way it is painting—a marvellous art of painting in coloured wools—that we find in the Bayeux Tapestry.

Celebrated as it is, this exceptional piece has been little studied, or at any rate more as an historical document than as a work of art; and yet in the arts of design the early Middle Ages produced nothing as considerable as this.

This time we have to do with an historical frieze: in it time is reconstituted materially, so to speak, as in the successive images of a film. Starting from the left we move slowly towards the right in an irresistible motion governed by the epic story—governed also, as we shall see, by the lines of the composition. We move, but with pauses—a primary rhythm imposed on us by the recurrent direction of certain episodes. The scenes, separated from one another by small trees with interlaced branches and sometimes by a tower, are now short, now long. The short ones extend for about two metres, the long ones for about twice that. They are independent strophes, composed for their own sakes and centering on a principal character to whom our attention is unmistakably drawn. But the movement keeps on from left to right, though with sudden fragments of scenes that, going the opposite way, pull us up and make us, for a short space, go back in time. These illogicalities, as some have considered them, prove on analysis to be only apparently illogical. The *trouvère* sings

to us of the adventures of a hero who is before us; when some messengers arrive they are suddenly there, and only afterwards we see where they have come from. The news of the death of King Edward bursts on us, we pull up in surprise, and then we follow his funeral procession back to its source, the scene of his last will and testament.

This rhythm, already imposed upon us simply by our 'reading' of the Bayeux Tapestry, casts an even more binding spell if we look at the forms. With tenacious insistence these all tend in the same direction, rising towards the right: horses at the gallop, lances, veils, groups of people, slanting terraces of buildings score the long ribbon with sloping lines, which are echoed in the border; and, as in the border also, the movement is now and then abruptly reversed. If we pay closer attention, we notice that these long oblique lines often come up against a vertical—a tree, a person standing upright, archers arranged above one another, or a rearing

NT·FLVMEN·COSNONIS·ETVENERVNT AD DOL·ET CONAN FVGA VER TIT· HIC MILITE
AROLD·DVX·TRAHEBAT·EOS· RED NES
DEARENA

Bayeux Tapestry, *detail:* William's Army besieging Dinan. *The battle scenes, as for instance the charges of William's knights, follow a rising line from left to right, then descend vertically, then begin a fresh rise: a saw-tooth movement. In contrast, the scenes of negotiation and discussion tend to be constructed on the basis of vertical lines. The whole of this long epic is divided up by trees or towers into separate scenes, some short, some long, some between the two. (Archives photographiques)*

horse—forming a succession of longs and shorts that are the very web of the poem.

So, just as in the *Chanson de Roland* with its story of the treason of Ganelon, the poem of the treason of Harold is divided into strophes and scanned in lines.

The *Danses macabres*, likewise, are continuous friezes, farandoles out of a ballet illustrating a sermon upon death. Their rhythm is very simple: a dead man, a living man, a dead man... and both at the Chaise-Dieu, and in the Paris Cemetery of the Innocents (the memory of which has possibly been preserved for us by the Guy Marchand book of 1485), in spite of a general movement to the right as in reading, the dead always lead the living towards the left *(in sinistrum)*.

Friezes sometimes extend over several bands, and it must be noted that they then lose some of their energy. They spread out, and the movement slackens. Even so, a direction still makes itself felt. At Saint-Savin three of the four bands of frieze in the vault ask to be read in the direction of the choir; one, for some unknown reason, moves back the other way.

And lastly, many medieval and later works are only apparently friezes. The hangings that used to be displayed in the choirs of churches, as for instance the Angers *Apocalypse* and the Cluny *Life of St Stephen*, offer a series of scenes firmly separated from each other by vertical borders. The frescoes of Giotto and of all the Italian Trecento are arranged in the same way. The frieze is broken up, the frame closes in, already forming squares or rectangles that arrest the movement of the forms.

Closed frames

At Assisi, in the lower church, the great rib-vault above the altar forms four triangular segments adorned with frescoes by a pupil of Giotto. The scenes, devoted to the glory of the saint and his virtues, are ordered like a Romanesque tympanum and associated in the same way with the

architectural forms. The centre is occupied by the principal persons; about them the lesser lights are grouped in close-packed ranks, with their robes swept inwards by the borders of the triangles, their bodies gently bent by the curve of the vault and their feet sliding into the corners. It is clear that the elements of these huge scenes are unable to spread out freely, that a limit curbs their impulsiveness—a limit to which they adhere willingly, lending themselves to its design.

So the frame acts as a mould, giving its contents a certain form. Simple though this discipline may be, it already is one, and is therefore already a principle of composition. When the frame is more complicated, the discipline becomes more despotic: this is what happens in the Gothic period. The architectural frames of that time are highly varied; circles, lancets, multifoils. They reign supreme in the stained glass, imposing their forms on the many scenes of the great windows. They also escape from architecture, to adorn with their graceful curves, sensitively traced with the compasses, tapestries or the panels of altarpieces; and they even introduce themselves, reduced to a miniature scale, into the pages of the books. Certain thirteenth-century polyptychs, certain miniatures, are so prettily divided up by arcading that any attempt at composition would be useless. This network is one, and suffices.

Later the frames grow simpler and less various, but certain forms persist more stubbornly than others. The circle is one of these: it goes back to the most ancient times, is found throughout the Roman and Byzantine mosaics and the textiles of Egypt and the Near East, and then takes on a new life in Renaissance Italy. A *tondo* (circular picture) is nearly always a simple and charming picture, with supple forms enclosed in a ring; and at a time when a monotonous rigidity dominated the altarpieces, it offered from the very first its slightly precious grace, freed from symmetry. Originating in Tuscany from the twelve-sided dishes, whose subjects were secular, it was soon reserved, by preference, for the Virgin and Child. Botticelli and his pupils had a special predilection for it. One can see in this example the whole history of the frame, and trace the part it has played in composition. Sometimes the scene is densely packed and the

1.

2.

3.

1. Signorelli: Madonna and St Joseph. *Here the frame is a limit which the figures cannot overflow; they huddle within the circle and fill it completely with their inclined bodies. (Florence, Uffizi. Photo Anderson)*

2. Piero di Cosimo: Holy Family. *The circle is capable of containing other geometrical figures In this picture the figures are clearly arranged within a square standing on its point. The two trees to the right and left reveal the presence of another square standing on its side. (Dresden Gallery. Photo Giraudon)*

3. Raphael: Madonna of the Chair. *Here Raphael adds to the density of the forms a kind of whirling movement about the centre, a rotatory movement suggested by a network of curves. (Florence, Pitti Palace. Photo Anderson)*

4. Botticini: Adoration of the Magi. *(Chicago Art Institute)*

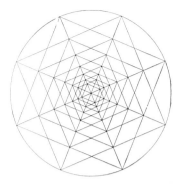

people crowd together in the space reserved for them: in these cases we have the frame as a mere limit. At other times the heads are bent, the arms curve in, following the line of the rim: here the limit is also a design.

One way or the other, a clearly external force is still, in these cases, exerting itself on the forms in the picture; but organization can go much further. The idea of a circle involves that of a centre. This will sometimes isolate itself from the mass, in the form of an empty space or of a full one. The centre and the circumference can even suggest a movement of rotation, a sort of whirlpool, of which the most curious example is that most famous *tondo* of all, Raphael's *Madonna of the Chair*. But the centre of a circle is not a blob, it is a point; the point of intersection of the diameters. This brings us to a quite new conception of the frame. It now creates not merely a limit but a plane geometrical figure that asks to be organized. The circle has diameters and a centre. In it one may also inscribe a triangle. It is curious to compare the *tondo* by Botticini, here illustrated, with its model, Botticelli's *Adoration of the Magi*. The master had grouped his figures in accordance with the discreetly suggested lines of a triangle, which remained secret, at the heart of the forms. In the imitator we find a strictness that is more dry, and at the same time a greater quantity of decorative detail; everything is traced with the compass point, and the lines of perspective follow the diameters and intersect at the centre of the circle, realizing in a striking fashion that identification of perspective with composition which is so frequent at this period, and of which we shall have more to say. The figures have been made very small so as to fit into this complicated network—the scene has lost its ease.

5, Botticelli: Adoration of the Magi. *The principle of this composition is the inscribed square. A succession of receding squares secretly distributes the forms within the circle. This combination of squares inscribed within one another scoops out the surface and produces an irresistible feeling of depth; but since in the axial position it would be too obvious, Botticelli and his imitator use it more subtly by placing two upper corners on opposite sides of the vertical axis. Thus the angles of the two groups of squares obtained in this way serve to establish the architecture and perspective. (London, National Gallery)*

4.

5.

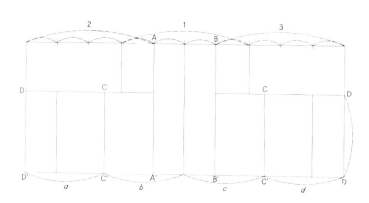

Roger van der Weyden: Last Judgment. *(Beaune, Hospice. Photo Bulloz)* The structure of the polyptych is based on squares. These squares are obtained either by starting from its height (1), or from its breadth (2).

1) *The artist makes a first square (square 1) from the whole formed by the centre and its two small wings. This construction clearly gives the proportions of the central panel as one to two* (AB/AA'). *From each side of the central panel he produces the same square (squares 2 and 3); the breadth of the two small wings at the far ends being known from*

that of the central panel which they must cover, that of the large wings is now fixed (their shared hinges, on the right and on the left, CC′, fall naturally at one-fourth of the total breadth). At the same time the height of these wings is also established by the square: a square is constructed from the hinge to the outer edge (CC′ DD″), dividing the lower part into four squares folding two by two.

2) The painter could also have started from the total breadth, a dimension which was perhaps imposed on him. In that case he divided it, on the one hand, into four—making

four squares (squares a, b, c, d) which gave him the height of the wing panels; and on the other hand into ten, so that the middle two-tenths fix the breadth of the central panel, whose height is given by the square constructed on the four-tenths remaining on either side.

The composition, with its flexible symmetry, follows first the armature of the total rectangle: the oblique lines joining its lower corners to the points on its sides that divide these into six establish the positions of the two rows of saints, right and left, govern the inclination of the beam of the balance, and

separate Heaven from earth. At the same time use is made of the diagonals belonging to the upright rectangles which form the panels, so as to create a play of triangular groups of lines which order the figures on either side. It is the intersection of these shafts with the long slanting lines of the armature of the total rectangle that determines the position of the Virgin, the Apostles and the saints. The movement of the resurrected human bodies likewise obeys oblique lines drawn from the lowest point of the central axis. The distance from the centre of the rainbow to the top of the picture is equal to the height of the side panels.

41

Bronzino: Allegory of Love. *The willingness of the figures to bend in accordance with the demands of the frame is here brought into evidence. They even seem to double the frame, to reproduce it within the picture by forming a rectangle and strongly marking its diagonal. (London, National Gallery. Photo Anderson)*

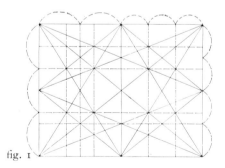

fig. 1

Armature of the rectangle. *This figure is important: the divisions which it involves (on the left we have shown the division of the half rectangle into three, on the right into two) will prove to be among those most frequently encountered in the course of this book.*

The circle has a centre and diameters, the square and the rectangle insist on their diagonals. In some pictures these essential elements are stressed with great frankness and naïveté. Bronzino's *Allegory of Love* (London, National Gallery) adheres to the rectangular frame (frame as limit), and at the same time undergoes the attraction of the diagonal. Similarly Annibale Carracci's *Hercules at the Crossroads* in the Naples Museum.

But the rectangle—the usual shape for the frame of an easel picture, and the one to which most of the other shapes can be reduced[2]—offers the painter not only its diagonals but also a series of regular sections that can be traced quite simply, using the diagonals as starting points, without need of compasses or measures; the point of intersection of the diagonals gives, by lines drawn through it perpendicular to the sides, the middle points of these. The surface may then be divided into four quarters, and the diagonals of the halves, and then of the quarters, of the total rectangle, may be traced. These are the constituent lines of the rectangle, from which the artist can derive all those he may need. In fact, the points of intersection of the diagonals of the quarters supply the division of the sides into four equal parts, while the points of intersection between these same diagonals of the quarters and the diagonals of the halves give us a division of each half-side into three, and so of each side into six, and this naturally allows of the division of the sides themselves into three (fig. 1). By joining these points of division to each other, one obtains various systems, of which the chief ones are shown in figures 2, 3 and 4: division of the sides into four (fig. 2) or into six (fig. 3). The excessively dense network of figure 3 is often simplified as in figure 4, which in fact gives us a division of each side of the frame into three. Sometimes the diagonals disappear entirely from a composition, which has its axes based only on secondary lines issuing from the points of intersection.

These simple divisions of the surface of circle or rectangle are not in themselves a composition. Each is a network, or less than that, a convenience, a sort of stock of constituent lines for a given geometrical figure. Here, if I may, I will venture a comparison. Just as the musician must, if he wishes to remain within a given tonality, respect its sharps and flats, that is to say the accidentals which are the 'armature' or key signature of the particular key, so the painter, face to face with a particular form, will be unable to neglect certain divisions which it imposes on him—or which, in any case, cannot be ignored. These interior lines depend on the form circumscribed by the frame, and they express it. I shall call them the 'armature' of that form, because they exist independently of the painter, and because he makes more or less use of them according to his taste—and this in pictures as different in period, style and composition as two sonatas can be, which have nothing in common except that both of them are in D major.

2. One side may be arched; or the rectangle may be subdivided into the panels of a polyptych.

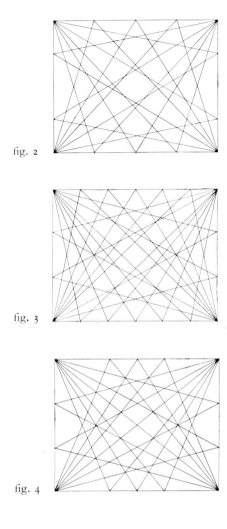

fig. 2

fig. 3

fig. 4

To make this idea quite clear, I will choose a few examples from different periods, paying most attention to one of the essential masterpieces of painting, Roger van der Weyden's *Last Judgment* at Beaune, that great polyptych in nine strictly organized parts.

The dimensions of these parts obey not only the necessity that the small panels should fold exactly over the centre and the large panels over one another: they also obey a construction based on squares, as shown in the illustration.

But there is more still; in this polyptych, contrary to what happens in most of the works in this *genre*, the nine parts form a single great composition. Even in the *Mystic Lamb* of the Van Eycks, that prototype from which Roger surely drew his inspiration, while there is certainly an evident unity of subject, the upper part is clearly separated from the great frieze in the lower part, and is itself broken up into distinct scenes. Here, on the contrary, all the elements are fused together; the painter has ignored the limits of the panels in order to bind to the centre the great divine figures and then, in their turn, the frieze of adoring saints and the predella of the resurrected (the *Mystic Lamb* had also a predella under the altarpiece, but it was quite separate and distinct and has disappeared[3]). It is for this reason that the Beaune *Last Judgment*, that vast work conceived as a whole, is organized not only on the basis of the squares, but also on the armature of the single rectangle that contains the nine elements of the picture. The oblique lines which join the lower angles of this rectangle to the divisions of its sides into six establish the positions of the two rows of saints on either flank of the Archangel St Michael; they also fix the exact angle of the beam of the scales; and lastly, the first two of these sloping lines serve as the frontier between Heaven and earth. This armature has been a guide to the artist in the arrangement of his groups, large or small; it appears again in the triangular form of the Virgin and of St John, and in the angular rhythm of the resurrected, who follow the directions of the oblique lines exactly.

Another way of constructing a picture, derived with equal naturalness from the rectangle, is 'rabatment', or rotation, of the short sides upon the long. We shall later study the use made in the Middle Ages of a square inscribed in an upright rectangle. When they placed the rectangle horizontally, the painters were obliged, for reasons of balance, to arrange a square to the right and another to the left, and these naturally overlapped in part, so that in this very simple scheme there are, inscribed in the frame, two squares which overlap more or less according as to whether the rectangle is more or less elongated. These squares in turn make their diagonals felt, and the crossing of these creates at the centre a small square standing

To understand clearly what is meant by the armature of the rectangle, it should be noted that the presence of the diagonals does not in every picture leap to the eye. Far from it: it is enough that their points of intersection, or the horizontals or verticals drawn through these to the sides of the picture should supply the construction of the picture with its foundations. When the points have been chosen in this way, the painter withdraws these diagonals, as the builder his scaffolding.

3. P. Coremans, *L'Agneau mystique au laboratoire*, les *Primitifs flamands*, III, 2, Antwerp, 1953, p. 35 (n⁰, 10).

Unknown master, Antwerp, 16th century: Crucifixion *(central part of triptych).* *This is an example of the armature of the rectangle. Of the division into six horizontal bands only the upper and lower bands have been used; by their intersections with the diagonals of the rectangle, with the diagonals of the horizontal and vertical halves and with the diagonals of the quarters, they have determined the cadence of the verticals in the picture. In this way the network of the armature serves also directly for the placing of certain figures: the Virgin, for instance, is on one of the diagonals of the quarters. (Tournai, Seminary. Photo J. Messiaen)*

on one of its corners, its size varying in proportion to the overlapping of the two large squares. The combinations resulting from this procedure differ very widely, as the figures show[4].

Sometimes the lines of construction vanish, giving place to the verticals and horizontals drawn through the corners of the small central square, which may by themselves establish a whole composition; sometimes, again, these verticals and horizontals create fresh lines of construction by their intersection with the diagonals of the squares.

Finally, this scheme can be superimposed on the diagonals of the rectangle whose intersection with the diagonals of the squares introduces still further variants.

4. When the short sides of a rectangle are rabatted (slewed over on to the longer), the lines drawn perpendicular to the four sides from the points where the diagonals of the squares thus obtained intersect the diagonals of the rectangle are not in the golden ratio, except in the case of the Euclidean golden rectangle, as shown in the figure; and this is logical, since in this rectangle all the diagonals and obliques intersect in this ratio.

In the cases of all other rectangles, even $\sqrt{2}$ and $\sqrt{3}$, the points of intersection are not according to the golden ratio.

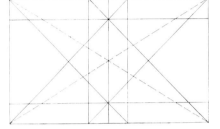

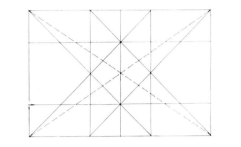

Two examples of this type of construction are given here, one of them rather simple (Giotto's *St Francis before the Sultan*), the other more concealed and more complex (Poussin's *Finding of Moses*); we shall often return to it, for, alongside principles of composition that are more subtle and more closely linked with the thought of a given period, these types of construction with their close relation to the shape of the frame turn up again and again in the work of all sorts of painters and in almost every period.

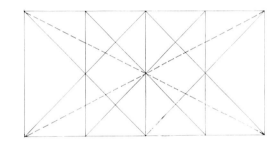

Rabatment of the shorter sides. *This is another essential diagram, for we shall meet with it in various forms. Every time the framework of a rectangular picture includes the small central square standing on one of its corners, there has been a 'rabatment' of the shorter sides of the rectangle. But here again it should be made clear that the sides of the squares obtained by rabatment, their diagonals and the tops of the central square standing on its corner are not necessarily visible in the design; it is enough that they should have supplied the construction of the picture with the points on which it will be built.*

Giotto: St Francis before the Sultan. *The rabatment (rotation) of the shorter sides of the rectangle on to the longer is here used in its simplest form. Clearly this strict scheme has made it possible to fix not only the sides of the throne but also its base and the height of the partition in the background. (Florence, Santa Croce. Photo Anderson)*

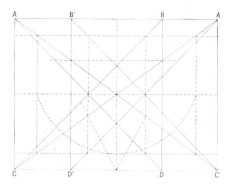

Poussin: Finding of Moses. *The partial superimposition of the two squares ABCD and A'B'C'D' gives, by virtue of the variable dimensions of the rectangle, a greater suppleness to the armature. The diagonals of the squares (AD, BC, B'C', A'D'), by crossing, form at the centre a small square standing on one of its corners; from its four corners it is possible to drop perpendiculars to the sides, and these in their turn will intersect the diagonals of the squares and those of the rectangle, providing several possibilities for construction. In this case Poussin uses them to frame his group of figures. The top corner of the small central square provides the centre of the arc of the circle that forms the base of the composition. (Paris, Louvre. Photo Bulloz.)*

In spite of the possibilities it offers, artists sometimes find the rectangular frame, that most convenient of shapes, an embarrassment. It is not always easy to get into it the scenes that have first been sketched freely on paper. The artist's habit of drawing without cease (every occasion being a good one for noting down a form or an observation of detail, without any definite aim) is bound to suggest ideas that he will wish to preserve; and this fact, from the sixteenth century onwards, led to a complete change in the usual way of creating a work of art and therefore in the artist's attitude to the frame. Paradoxical as it may seem, the painter sometimes even decides on the shape or size of the frame when the sketch of the composition is done. When we study the drawings of the masters we find many examples of this way of proceeding: the artist tries to define his thought with pencil or pen, treats the subject as a whole, groups the

46

Cigoli: Sheet of Studies. *Clearly the framing lines with which Cigoli shuts off some of his drawings form the sketch for what will be the composition of the picture. Till then the sketches had been merely studies of groups. As soon as Cigoli encloses them in a rectangle or in a square, the problems of distribution are raised. (Vienna, Albertina Collection)*

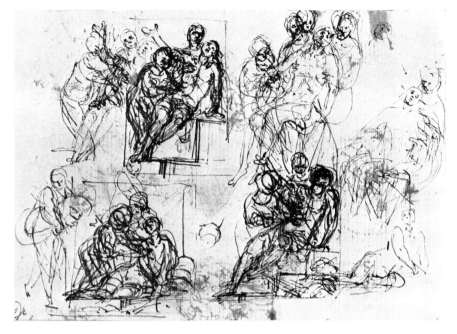

figures, and then tries various rectangular frames that cut into or block out certain parts of it. This technique is indeed recommended by Paillot de Montabert[5], who advises making sketches on materials that can then be either cut down or enlarged by the addition of pieces. It is only after all these experiments that the composition establishes itself within the frame. Sometimes it takes its place without any trouble, as though at ease, making use of the axes offered to it by geometry; at others it seems to be trying to get out of the frame, to break that prison. And so we get two very different types of composition which are allied to Wölfflin's *open* and *closed* compositions.

5. *Traité complet de la peinture*, Paris, 1829.

Manet: Study for a portrait of a woman. *To Bonnard this procedure of experimenting with framing became the means of introducing a still greater element of the unexpected; he went even further than Manet and did not hesitate to cut pieces off his picture. What artists before him did at the moment of the preparatory drawing, Bonnard did after painting the picture, with the canvas itself. (London, Courtauld Institute)*

47

III GEOMETRICAL COMPOSITIONS
IN THE MIDDLE AGES

Symmetry

In the Middle Ages the commonest altarpieces were those with wings, their simplest form being the triptych—a central panel flanked by lateral wingpieces half as broad, so as to join when folded over it. We have already seen how this principle can be elaborated almost infinitely. The wingpieces are multiplied, and sometimes they display sculptures as well as paintings; very often the side pieces are not real wings; they do not fold over, they may even prolong the central part with a descending line. But the more the architecture of the altarpieces is broken up and intersected, the more simply the scenes on the painted panels will be arranged: a complicated frame imposes a rudimentary composition. Hence only certain artists of real independence manage to get away, in the altarpieces, from a somewhat monotonous naïveté and—this is the essential point —from the strictest symmetry.

What is symmetry? The etymology of the word (συν μετρον: with measure) takes us back to its accepted meaning in Antiquity, to Vitruvius's definition: 'a proper accord of the members with one another, each part related to the whole'. Referring to this in his *Dictionary*[1], Viollet-le-Duc expresses regret that artists have lost sight of this true sense of the word and, in the name of symmetry, no longer look for more than a trifling repetition of identical elements. And in fact the usual sense of the word is much more limited than that which emerges from Vitruvius's rather vague and entirely aesthetic conception. While symmetry, generally speaking, means an arrangement of similar parts similarly placed within a whole, the idea it evokes in ordinary life is the simpler one of an axis of symmetry with, on either side of it, two shapes that would coincide if folded over.

This brings us to a curious fact: in the figurative arts there is practically only one kind of symmetry—symmetry in relation to a vertical axis or plane. Why? Various elements seem to have converged to produce an entirely instinctive choice.

Psalter of St Louis and Blanche of Castille. Clerk, Astronomer and Recorder: *With his astrolabe the astronomer is checking the bearings which enable him to establish the solar cycle upon which the reckoner relies in calculating the dates of the movable feasts. Thus the painting which introduces the calendar section of the Psalter is a homage to astronomy and to mathematics. (Paris, Bibliothèque de l'Arsenal)*

1. *Dictionnaire raisonné de l'architecture française du XIe au XVIe siècle*, Paris, 1858-68, article on *Symétrie*, p. 105.

49

First and foremost, man. As we noted at the beginning of this book, man refers everything to himself: this is the principle of that optical intelligence which we have tried to define. Here too man realized that his own body was constructed approximately (and outwardly) on either side of a vertical axis of symmetry. He observed the same thing in animals and in most of the forms he met with in vegetation. The only case presented to him of symmetry in relation to a horizontal plane was that of the reflections in the clear waters of pools.

But if a tree is symmetrical like the human body, though more crudely, this is for reasons of balance, and here we come to the real, if unconscious, cause of this artistic predilection: weight. It is on weight or gravity that the principle of the scales is based, and a pair of scales held even is the best image for the stability of the parts of a complex whole laid out on a single plane—which is what a painting is.

Chinese or East Persian Brocade, 5th or 6th century. *The two birds, facing one another and joined together by the device of doubling, become a single decorative pattern in the form of a heart. (Danzig, Church of Our Lady)*

To return to the altarpieces: it is the central part of the triptych that acts as the axis of symmetry, sometimes as a whole if it represents one subject only, such as a Madonna adored with identical gestures by the saints on the wingpieces, and sometimes by means of its own axial figure if the centre itself represents several people. But the altarpiece-composition is the naïvest and poorest expression of symmetry—poor because lacking in creative force. No force binds together the parts of this purely static whole to make of them a new work.

If, on the contrary, the axis of symmetry is in the middle of a single panel, hidden in the midst of forms instead of asserting itself heavily in a central *motif* cut off by wingpieces, then the two symmetrical images are directly juxtaposed and their close connection turns their duality into a unity.

In an unpublished thesis on *Les thèmes dédoublés dans les tissus du Haut Moyen Age*[2] there is this passage: 'When doubling occurs, two faces of the same *motif* are grouped together by our gaze, are made to be viewed together: they combine and become a single new form... and this constitutes a real act of creation. This form, which we suddenly discover, surprises us because it defines itself powerfully by characteristics not possessed by the elements of which it is made up... Any *motif*, a flower or a bird, is transformed by this doubling into a purely abstract, regular figure, whose geometrical arabesque exerts its effect on our imagination.'

This strict doubling, so frequent in the genesis of ornament and in its decorative variations, is never met with in a picture. There, when the *motif* is reversed, there is always some detail that differs from its fellow, and these small changes modulate the repetition. At other times the symmetry remains so hidden at the heart of the forms that a person who is simply reading the story told by the picture may be unaware of it. To feel it, one must not *read* the design as a story, one must *look:* the symmetry exerts its effect on the person who looks, and then immediately that abstract geometrical figure already mentioned, more or less intended by the artist, makes its appearance.

2. W. Rabaud, thesis for the *Diplôme d'études supérieures*, at the Sorbonne, 1929.

Silk Embroidery, Central Asia, 6th or 7th century. *Here the doubling serves to construct the chariot and give it geometrical form: a square is inscribed in the circle.* (*Brussels, Musée du Cinquantenaire*)

It is enough that the people on the wings of an altarpiece should lean towards the central figure, instead of remaining monotonously vertical as in a Tuscan *pala*[3], and already, in spite of the separation of the central *motif*, the beginnings of a triangular form are seen. Let us suppress the centre; let us join together the two symmetrical sides, giving the direction of the *motifs* the suppleness of a curve in place of the stiffness of a straight line, and the single figure created by their union becomes a decorative pattern, the equivalent of a regular palmette.

This procedure was quite familiar to the artists of the Middle Ages. It was part of their decorative language; we find it already in the textiles of the seventh century, as the thesis just quoted observes, and it was a ruling principle throughout Romanesque sculpture.

Some styles recur periodically, brought back by the ebb and flow in the life of societies or of forms. The Renaissance in its decline witnessed a reappearance of this taste for linear pattern, for the harmonious curve that is beautiful in itself. Let us imagine a medieval artist irrupting into that Mannerist circle—he would undoubtedly have felt at home. That indeed is what happened to El Greco, who came from the land of icons where the Middle Ages survived their own death. He then, with the lyricism that was all his own, developed patterns on a vast scale covering the walls, huge palmettes formed out of bodies leaning towards one another, and out of floating draperies[4].

But the hidden symmetry that is so frequent in painting is for the most part bound up with a far more complex kind of composition, and we are then faced with a geometrical scheme of which symmetry is one of the qualities and not the chief one. Symmetry in its pure state, so to speak, and sought for its own sake, is rare. We have already seen that, in any case, the representation of a subject cannot be fitted into a strict repetition on either side of an axis of symmetry. Not only will certain details be different, but it will be a case, usually, of an unsymmetrical symmetry like that of a face: everyone knows that, if a photograph is made up from one side of a face reproduced twice, the result is a curious image in which it is hard to recognize the original, for the two sides of a human face, though apparently symmetrical, are not so in reality.

Let us take as one of the most refined examples of unsymmetrical symmetry, Signorelli's *Pan and the Shepherds*[5]. On either side of the hieratic figure of Pan with his hooves curiously crossed to form an X, there stand two beautiful symmetrical yet supple figures, a bright one on the right and a dark one on the left; at the sides of the picture two other figures also correspond, a dark one on the right and a bright one on the left. A recumbent figure in the foreground binds these two extremes harmoniously together. In this way the regular alternation of brights and darks tempers

3. *Pala d'altare*: altar painting.
4. Cf. the *Burial of Count Orgaz*, the *Pentecost*, the *Ascension*, the *Feast in the House of Simon the Pharisee*, etc., and cf. p. 151.
5. Picture destroyed.

Signorelli: Pan and the Shepherds. *This picture, unfortunately lost, is an allegory with a somewhat elaborate composition, of which only the symmetry is here studied. This is broken by several alternations: a brightly lit figure is opposed to a dark one, a young man to an old man, etc. The shepherd lying down in the foreground breaks the vertical axis and binds the figures together. (Picture burnt during the war, formerly in the Berlin Museum. Photo Giraudon)*

Bramantino: Philemon and Baucis. *The obvious, indeed naïve, symmetry has several features that are extremely rare. It includes a horizontal axis—a phenomenon which in nature is exemplified only by reflections in water. The lower branches of the tree form this axis, and the triangle of the gable finds, as it were, its reflection in the folds of the tablecloth. (Cologne Museum)*

the rigour of the symmetry, which is also given suppleness by another means: the two outer figures occupy symmetrical positions but could really be superimposed if they were slid together, and this subtly breaks the monotony of a too mechanical arrangement.

Compared with these refinements, the Bramantino in the Cologne Museum seems so naïve that it raises a smile. It is, after all, not an altarpiece, and the symmetry it demands is a hidden one; but with its central figure, its regular-branched tree and its triangles, all superimposed along the axis, with its main features imperturbably doubled on either side and even minor decorative detail repeated, the picture seems as if designed by some neophyte of the Cult of Geometry.

Gauguin: Jour de Dieu. *An example of symmetry with its axis not in the centre of the picture, and with the figures twisted so that some are seen full-face and others from the back. (Chicago Art Institute)*

It is curious to find how, even in this business of symmetry, the frame leaves its mark, and how strong a hold it has on the content. The triptych form of frame is the most imperiously symmetrical because it folds; but all frames lead in practice to symmetry, and to enclose a work of art in a frame has proved, in the West, to be a definite need, which may even have a philosophical basis[6]. As soon as the artist is no longer subject to an architectural frame, he imposes on himself an artificial frame of a regular form that may be divided into two, so that the surface enclosed is cut into two identical halves. This need is not felt in the Middle East or in Asia; Egyptian painting, for instance, is practically without frames, whereas in Europe even wall paintings, which could perfectly well extend freely over large surfaces, most often impose on themselves regular limits. We have seen how friezes turn into false friezes, breaking themselves up into rectangles; in them the musical rhythm is chopped up and replaced by the action of the frame. Vaults, too, are divided into compartments, as in the Sistine Chapel.

A decoration that seems to escape from this rule is that of Benozzo Gozzoli in the Palazzo Riccardi, where he unrolls his sumptuous processions on the walls like an oriental carpet. Here, apparently, there are no regular bands or frames. But let us look more attentively: each panel forms a rectangle with limits that are invisible but very real, within whose architecture the artist, still attached to the habits of his race and of his time, feels free to compose his scenes with their multitudinous characters. These large rectangles permit—and impose—a symmetrical ordering of the contents: an axis of symmetry is traced by means of a huge cypress with an absolutely straight trunk (cf. p. 91).

In any case symmetry—sometimes supple and alive like that of a plant, sometimes more rigorous—draws us into that world of secret geometry which has governed the arts of design for centuries.

6. The very process of our thought is involved. To us the work of art, like the concept, is defined by its limits only.

Codex amiatinus: a Scribe. *On a small scale, this page of a manuscript is a complete picture, thanks to the Graeco-Roman influence. Its perspective and its colours reconstitute the atmosphere of a library. (Florence, Bibliotheca Laurentiana)*

Geometry in the Middle Ages

On one page of the *Lindisfarne Gospels* (Northumbrian, early eighth century; British Museum), St Matthew sits writing in a great book that lies open on his knees. What may be the prototype of this, or a copy of another on which it was modelled, is to be found in a manuscript in Florence[7]: it shows a scribe who sits in his library writing, with other books arranged on shelves. The painterly qualities of this small picture and the sense of depth it conveys make it still a Graeco-Latin work, and a most delightful one. The English *St Matthew* is treated in a quite different spirit: here the image has become a rectangle cut by a diagonal. The saint, though still in the same position and carrying out the same design, is treated in a linear fashion and is strictly inscribed within the geometrical frame.

The whole of medieval art is already there, in that contrast. A Roman painting is a poetic evocation: it tries to suggest some scene from life, either indoors or perhaps in a garden, and this by means of every sort of artifice: colour contrasts, the play of perspective, illusionism... At the beginning of the Middle Ages, on the contrary, suggestion becomes secondary to the symbol and evocation to writing. The theme, nailed down by a decorative or geometrical tracing, becomes a sign. The image is inscribed within a frame which subjects it to its laws, and this happens in the earliest of the illuminated books, well before the appearance of paintings on wood panels.

Carolingian and Ottonian and, above all, English miniature painting, of which there is an extravagant wealth from the first centuries of the Middle Ages, supplies us with many examples of simple divisions of the rectangle. The diagonal that governs the Lindisfarne *St Matthew* often recurs[8]. The rectangle placed upright may form two squares or may contain a square in its lower part, as in the curious *Pietà* at Oxford[9]. This square in turn naturally imposes its own diagonals: indeed this is the most common formula, and we shall see it become general at the moment when research into space gained prominence, for the edge of the square will be identified with the horizon line and its diagonals with the perspective. As examples here let us take merely the *Annunciation*[10] and *Otho on His Throne*, two miniatures at Chantilly and at Bamberg respectively.

The circle inscribed within a rectangle, or fitting naturally into a semicircular arch, is frequently found in quite early medieval works of art. Does there exist a purer diagram than that which governs *Charles the*

7. Codex amiatinus, Florence, Bibliotheca Laurentiana. On the date and origin of this painting cf. M. Rickert, *Painting in Britain, the Middle Ages*, London, 1954, plate 7 and notes pp. 15, 29.

8. *St Albans Apocalypse*, New York, Pierpont Morgan Library, and *Canterbury Apocalypse*, London, Lambeth Library. Rickert, *op. cit.*, pp. 112-113.

9. From a *Book of Hours* attributed to Herman Scheerre, Rickert, *op. cit.*, p. 169.

10. The *Aethelwold Benedictional*, Chatsworth, Rickert, *op. cit.*, p. 26.

Lindisfarne Gospels: St Matthew. *Here St Matthew has the same attitude as that of the Florentine scribe, but the spirit is quite different. The form is here only a sign, strictly inscribed along the diagonal of the rectangle. (London, British Museum)*

Bible of Charles the Bald: The King and his Court. *Two intersecting circles determine the position and dimensions of the figures. The distance between the two upper points from which the curtain is suspended is equal to the radius of the circles. (Paris, Bibliothèque Nationale)*

Bald on his throne surrounded by his court[11]? The figures conform faithfully to the design, which consists of two equal circles intersecting, one of which fits into the arch, and the radius of these circles is given by the two points at which the curtain is attached.

Having reached this example, the most astonishing of all in its utter clarity, let us give some thought to the method thus strangely revealed and to the state of mind and preoccupations of which it is the expression. A man, Cennino Cennini tells us[12], has proportions, while as for a woman,

11. The *Bible of Charles the Bald*, Paris, Bibl. Nationale, Latin 1, fol. 423.
12. Cennino Cennini, *Il libro dell'arte* (1437 or earlier); text edited by Daniel V. Thompson Jr., Yale, 1932; English translation by the same *(The Craftsman's Handbook)*, Yale, 1933, pp. 48, 49.

Psalter of Blanche of Castille: Clerk, Astronomer and Recorder *(Folio I verso). Constructed on the internal lines of a hexagon drawn inside a large circle whose diameter is determined by the height of the picture. (Paris, Bibliothèque de l' Arsenal)*

'she does not have any set proportion', and 'I will not tell you about irrational animals, because you will never discover any system of proportion in them'. Why are perfect proportions reserved for men? Because man is created in the image of God. This naïve passage from the old painter's treatise reflects the philosophy of the Middle Ages and makes us understand the veneration felt by the men of that time for the whole numbers and simple relationships that are the expression of perfection, and therefore of the divine.

And yet those men had only a very rudimentary knowledge of mathematics. Their touching veneration had no very solid basis. It was merely an abstract idea, a philosophy of numbers, the pale heritage of Plato and Pythagoras handed on by St Augustine. The admirers of his *City of God* found in it—absorbed and transposed by Christian thought—the concepts of the more spiritual among the ancients, their effort to discover in mathematics a bridge between the earthly and the divine.

These ideas were to expand in the fifteenth century with the development of the exact sciences and the direct study of the ancients themselves; but they were already a stimulant to the artists of the preceding centuries and constituted the basis of their conception of art.

Though not advanced in mathematics, the men of the Middle Ages knew how to use compasses, and it was by geometry that they tried to attain their ideal. Geometry, practised by the Arabs, had quickly made its way into the West and was currently taught in the thirteenth century. It then permeated decorative art, whether on the large or on the small scale; purely geometrical designs derived from arabesques, intersecting arcs and polygons[13] took the place of the decorative patterns or extremely simple sections that we have seen the Romanesque artists using.

A book whose exalted origin has made it an object of particular veneration takes pride of place at the beginning of the new art: the *Sainte Chapelle Psalter of Blanche of Castille*[14]. It is supposed to date from the time when this princess was young, that is to say from the very beginning of the thirteenth century. Gothic art had passed its earliest stages: it had already yielded a fine harvest of cathedrals in the Ile-de-France and was sure of itself, of its youthful strength, of its new secrets. And it was then, and then only, that it penetrated and brought fresh life to the closed and traditional world of the illuminators.

Perhaps a little earlier than this book and closer to the exact join between Romanesque and Gothic and yet already highly original, the *Ingeburge Psalter*[15] gave evidence of a determination to wipe the slate clean of the Romanesque principles of composition; and the artist, in his bewilderment, clung to the idea of imitating the new sculpture. The result was a book with a character of its own, austere and simple, with an exceptional gran-

13. Cf. Friedrich Hoffstadt, *Gothisches A.B.C. Buch, das ist Grundregeln des Gothischen Styls für Künstler und Werkleute;* Frankfurt a. M., 1840 [-45]. (In it may be found all the Gothic elevations and ornaments, traced with the compasses.)

14. Paris, Bibliothèque de l'Arsenal, no. 1186.

15. Musée de Chantilly.

deur. But this spare art was only a stage. Having abandoned the magic world of the interlacing arabesque, illuminators felt compelled to understand and adopt the laws of the new art.

With the *Psalter of Blanche of Castille* this was accomplished. In that period of extraordinary energy (at least in the Royal estates), of youthfulness and of creative impulse, it took little time to run through all the stages. Between the queen's book and that of the princess royal there is a whole world. It was the moment of that explosion of astounding novelty, the windows of Chartres, which opened, before the transformed art of monumental painting, the way already shown by architecture and sculpture. Taking the work of these great glass-painters as his model, the master illuminator of the *Psalter of Blanche of Castille* assimilated the inner secrets of Gothic composition, made use of them with absolute strictness and established them in the art of book illumination for centuries to come.

Apart from some fine initials and calendar vignettes, the illustrations of the *Psalter* include full-page miniatures and a series of medallions arranged two by two. If we leave aside certain pages where the influence of the stained-glass windows is too obvious, such as the *Crucifixion* and the *Tree of Jesse*, there remain four large miniatures. The first, which is the most famous for its beauty and for the originality of its iconography, depicts the *Astronomer* holding up the astrolabe to show the reckoner the elements of his calculations. Is this not, first and foremost, a homage to mathematics? This perfectly balanced picture should be the first to reveal to us its secret. Let us trace out the circle whose diameter is the longer axis of the picture. The sky is an arc with the same radius. The constituent lines of the hexagon inscribed in that circle establish the point from which the astrolabe is suspended, the direction of the ruler, the height of the steps, the folds of the garments and the edges of the heads. The astrolabe falls exactly down the central axis. The other pictures, especially the *Creation of Eve*, seem to be organized according to the same scheme.

Turning to the medallions, we notice at once that, on each page, two circles are slightly engaged in each other. In these, eight scenes from the Old Testament, twenty-four from the New Testament are enclosed, with a natural and charming grace that seems reckless of any boundary: from time to time, negligently, a foot comes over the border... But under this apparent spontaneity the strictness of the composition very soon makes itself felt, and its secret is easy to find. The circles intersect along an eighth of their circumference, and the cord of intersection yields the side of the octagon which, together with the square inscribed in it, serves to establish the composition of all the scenes in all the medallions. There is one variation only: sometimes the octagon is stood on one of its sides, sometimes (and most often) on a point. The objects that go over the border—feet, trees, etc.—nearly always mark the corners of the square. They are landmarks, the vestiges of the rubbed-out diagram. To analyse all the thirty-two medallions would be tedious, but let us mention, as among the most striking, these: *Noah's Ark* (octagon on a side), *Adam and Eve Expelled from Paradise*, the *Nativity*, the *Temptation of Christ* (octagons on a point). Sometimes the scheme slants slightly, in one direction or the other.

Diagram of medallion. *Group of thirty-two medallions constructed on an octagon. In each case, the circumference of the circle is cut at eight points, and the chords joining these points form the sides of the octagon, which serves as the basis of all the scenes. Only variation: the octagon sometimes rests on a side, sometimes (and most often) on a point.*

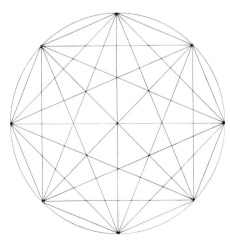

Adam and Eve driven from Paradise; Adam and Eve after the Fall (Folio 12). *In the upper scene the diagonals joining the corners of the octagonal two by two and four by four form squares and triangles in which the figures are inscribed. The angel's sword falls along the side of the octagon. Even the perspective is obedient to the diagonals. The angel's foot, where it protrudes from the frame, marks the corner of a square.*

Noah's Ark; Abraham and Isaac. (Folio 13 verso). *In the Noah's Ark, the sides of the octagon are clearly visible: at the top they end in two volutes. Abraham and Isaac follow closely the sides of the vertical triangle.*

This analysis of the *Psalter of Blanche of Castille* has uncovered for us the constant use of a geometrical design traced with the compasses—always the same one—on which the data supplied by the iconography are easily laid out. It is a most revealing fact. As I have said, this most important manuscript, representing Gothic art at its height, was a reflection of stained-glass painting, a first attempt to suggest on vellum the blazing glass paintings that were the most original contribution of the new age. And in fact the circles adorning the pages of this small book are one of the principal

Psalter of St Louis and of Blanche of Castille. *(Paris, Bibliothèque de l'Arsenal)*

The Nativity; *the* Annunciation to the Shepherds. (Folio 17 verso). *In the* Nativity *the composition emphasizes lines at right angles. In the* Annunciation to the Shepherds *the diagonals govern all the movements of the shepherds, the inclination of the tree, the direction of the angel's arm.*

The Baptism of Christ; *the* Temptation in the Wilderness. (Folio 20). *In the* Baptism *the octagon rests on one of its sides, and the composition is established on two verticals. In the* Temptation *the* Christ *and the* Devil *are built on two diagonals crossing one another like an* X.

elements in the composition of the stained-glass windows: the leads are usually arranged in circles or quatrefoils, and within these frames the scenes likewise conform to extremely simple schemes, square or polygonal. The medallions of the *Life of St Thomas à Becket* at Sens have exactly the same arrangement as those of the *Psalter*.

So, in this field also, the compasses exert the mastery, as indeed through-out the cathedral: there is not a curve, not an outline, not an ornament

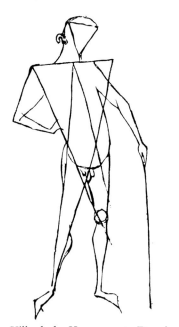

Villard de Honnecourt: Drawing Book. *Examples of the art of portraiture. By the curious triangulation he imposes on his small figures, Villard de Honnecourt seems to be trying to show how human figures can be inscribed within parts of geometrical schemes of extreme variety. Certain figures from the Psalter of Blanche of Castille are clearly established in the same way as those of Villard de Honnecourt. (Paris, Bibliothèque Nationale. Photo Giraudon)*

Psalter of Blanche of Castille: Devil.

that does not obey them. This is one of the differences that strike one, when one goes back in thought to Romanesque art: compared to its living flexibility, Gothic art, which until the fourteenth century tended towards greater nervousness, seems pure as an abstraction.

The term 'geometry', as used by Villard de Honnecourt[16], here acquires its full sense. It designates the whole collection of geometrical figures—triangles, starry polygons, rectangles or circles—to which the human figures may be bent in accordance with the demands of this or that total scheme. The examples given by Villard are simple and unpretentious models, and their triangulation is quite arbitrary; but if one compares some of these figures with others taken from the *Psalter*, they appear in a fresh light.

In short, however naïve, this was an attempt to resolve the great antinomy of Gothic art, that of an art in love with liberty, enchanted by nature and capable of rendering faithfully its many aspects, yet at the same time rigorously subject to design.

Villard de Honnecourt was an architect, architecture was the leading art of his time, and it is patently clear that the geometry which governed decorative art and 'portraiture' governed architecture as well. This takes us a little aside from our subject, but Gothic art is a whole which it is difficult to break up, and it is important to establish here that, while harmonic proportions and the search for balance and compensation belong to all periods, purely geometrical composition done with the compasses is particularly characteristic of the Gothic style.

The ground-plans of the cathedrals exist and are extremely strict (as for instance that given by Villard de Honnecourt), but we have to wait until the end of the fourteenth century to find a document on the elevation of a cathedral. When Milan Cathedral rose from the ground, several eminent men were brought together to decide on its height. Should this be established *ad quadratum* or *ad triangulum*? The opinion given by the mathematician Stornaloco, dated 1391, has been preserved[17]. It needed Italy, that country in which debates of the kind were frequent and were pompously set down[18], to leave us such a document: we might otherwise very easily have had none, for in the West, where cathedrals were growing everywhere like trees, these problems were generally settled orally, and the principle chosen—the square or triangle based on the breadth of the ground-plan—was determined by local tradition, by what the architect was accustomed to do, or, very often, by the monument taken as model.

This idea of a model is extremely important in the Middle Ages, a period wholly dominated by respect for authority. To the persistence of the

16. Villard de Honnecourt, *Album*, Paris, Bibl. Nationale, manuscrits français 19093. Facsimile edition: Bibl. Nationale, Paris, 1906. Cf. also Villard de Honnecourt, Gesamtausgabe des Bauhüttenbuches, ms. fr. 19093 der Pariser Nationalbibliothek, (edited by Hans R. Hahnloser), Vienna, 1935.

17. Stornaloco proposed an elevation *ad triangulum* (Milan Cathedral Archives). Cf. also Julius F. M. Lund, *Ad Quadratum*, London, 1921.

18. Cf. p. 103.

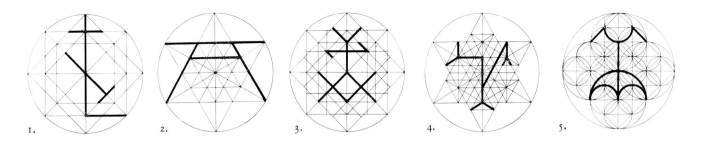

Stone-masons' Marks, Gothic period: *taken from F. von Rziha,* Studien über Steinmetz-Zeichen, *Vienna,* 1883. *1 and 2. Strasburg Cathedral. 3. Freiburg-im-Breisgau. 4. Ulm Cathedral. 5. Prague, the St Charles Bridge. 6. Church of St Barbara, Kutná Hora, Bohemia.*
These marks, engraved on the stone of certain Gothic monuments and even of some Renaissance ones, are 'signs of honour'—practically the heraldic emblems of guilds. (Cf. P. du Colombier, Les Chantiers des cathédrales, *Paris,* 1953, *p.* 98.) *They are based on geometrical figures that may be derived from the circle: certain lines chosen from this maze suffice to compose these firm signs with their pure lines. The schemes which Rziha suggests are sometimes rather complicated, but they certainly fit in with the geometrical designs that govern Gothic ornamentation and painting.*

iconography was added the persistence of certain geometrical forms bound up with it by custom. The result is a singular agreement between subject and composition, because certain themes not only imposed certain attributes and no others, but were also governed by an arrangement that was constant. Some ideas, indeed, could not be thought of in the abstract, but only in the form of an image—the symbolism of the circle, of the polygon, etc.

Caught between such strict disciplines, the personality of the artist had less free play than in later ages; but the artist was not bullied by the clerics, as has too often been asserted. He accepted these traditions, customs and consecrated correspondences quite willingly: he was naturally modest, and his aim was not to make an original work of art but a beautiful one. Authority did not crush him: he found support in it and revered it.

I have attempted to bring out the character of the geometry of the Middle Ages: I shall now show how it worked in painting (on vellum or on wood), until the coming of those great theorists who at length, in the fifteenth century in Italy, wrote down the ancient principles and gave them an entirely new philosophical cast.

One of the first masterpieces of panel painting in the West is the *Wilton Diptych*, in which the King of England, Richard II, kneels before the Virgin. Prefiguring Fouquet's famous diptych and many others (they became a fashion in the fifteenth century), it consists of two wingpieces closely connected by their subject and also by their composition, and forms a simple geometrical figure.

Here the composition on the square is not too obvious, at least in the case of the panel containing the Virgin: she, breaking through the barrier, springs from a semicircle of adorers. But this division, with the diagonal of the square forming the axis of the whole composition, is frequently found in vertical pictures and established itself as the current method in the fifteenth century[19]. In the *Wasservass Calvary*, which is a horizontal oblong panel, Christ in the centre cuts the picture into two equal parts, each of them based on the diagonals of the squares (cf. p. 42). Here we see a rather timid artist face to face with a large-scale composition which

19. Cf., among others, the 1420 *Crucifixion* and the small *Crucifixion* in the Cologne Museum.

The Wasservass Calvary. *The Christ is on the line which divides the picture in two, the thieves on lines dividing it into four. Half the breadth, if folded over on to the height, forms two squares. Oblique lines from the middle points of the four sides trace a lozenge, and with this the inclined crosses at the bottom of the picture coincide. Two other slanting lines, parallel to these and ending, on the right and on the left, at the top outer corners of the two squares, demarcate the crowd and support the central circle. (Cologne Museum)*

evidently alarms him: he therefore has recourse to the long-standing practice of the miniaturists and makes use, with a good deal of naïveté, of a quite simple but strictly applied linear scheme, upon which he supports his numerous close-ranked figures.

A good contrast to this naïve painter can be found in that great artist, Dirk Bouts. In the *Justice of the Emperor Otho III* (Brussels Museum) he uses the same scheme much more cleverly. Here also the two wings of the diptych are closely unified by an internal symmetry[20].

It is a curious fact that this division springing from a square, with the groups distributed in two triangles marked out by the square's diagonals, later became very general because it fitted in with perspective. Towards the end of the fourteenth century—to be more exact, at the moment of that extreme refinement known as the 1400 style—there arose a new conception of space which, gradually perfected, had a long run. It was a convention—in art all is convention or symbol—but it yielded a largely sufficient equivalence to reality and made it possible to represent a vast scene in a small picture.

20. In other celebrated diptychs also the composition is subtle and hidden and unites the two parts—the Virgin (principal picture) and her worshipper. The symmetry is concealed but is always there, even when the Virgin is impassive and frontal and seems to ignore her adorer (diptychs by Van der Weyden at Caen and Brussels, by Memling at Bruges, and by Fouquet at Antwerp and Berlin).

Diagram of vanishing points.

Let us again start from an example. Let us take the *Très riches Heures du duc de Berry*, that masterpiece which is in everyone's memory, thanks to splendid reproductions. Let us turn the pages: everywhere the horizon is very high up, generally coinciding with the top of the square or not far below it with the principal vanishing points at the sides, at the upper angles of the square. Thus the most obvious lines of recession follow the diagonals of the square, and the masses of human figures bunch together in the two triangles so formed, so that we have, as it were, a double distribution, in the plane of the book and in space.

This space is still not very large, but it became so in the course of the fifteenth century, as flexibility was given to the earlier formula, resulting in a tendency not towards exact realism but towards an astounding inclusiveness of detailed description that nevertheless avoids shocking the sense of the probable. In the narrative manuscripts that became common in the fifteenth century, those great French or Franco-Flemish chronicles that had not yet undergone the influence of innovators like the Van Eycks, the scene is viewed from a high imaginary hilltop or tower, but the foregrounds are shown from the side, so one may see the façades of the monuments and even, through a wide opening, what is going on inside; in this way the monotonous and useless sight of the roofs is avoided. In these works, therefore, the perspective is extremely flexible. The vanishing points are not placed on a single line, but are distributed on either side of a division marked out by the composition based on the square, or approximately so. The eye circles like a bird, rising, falling and examining at one and the same time a vast landscape as a whole and all the details that may interest it.

Much later, as I have already remarked, Veronese was to use a similar procedure, transforming the spectator into a hundred-eyed Argus. But in that great decorative artist the aim was a quite different one: not to make us, like a bird of prey, ransack a huge extent of ground, but to make us slide over an intact mural surface, while giving us a sensation of space and truth to life.

The golden number in the Middle Ages

The compositions studied up to now were based on the square, on the triangle, on the circle, or on a hexagon or octagon within the circle. But there is one regular geometrical figure we have not yet mentioned: the pentagon. Does this mean that that symbol of the platonic quintessence[21] did not have its place in the Middle Ages? On the contrary, it acquired an outstanding importance at that time. This was because its elements have a certain mutual proportion which was then looked on as divine; a strange mysticism was attached to it; the rather complicated operation

21. Luca Pacioli, whose cast of mind is still medieval, connects the construction of the dodecahedron, a body limited by twelve pentagons, with the idea of the quintessence as expressed in the *Timaeus* (*Divina proportione*, ch. V; cf. p. 76 below).

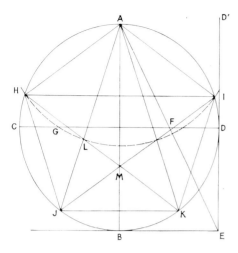

Construction of pentagon.

Construction of golden section.

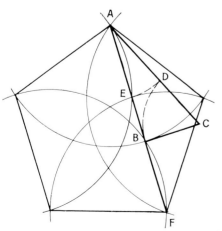

of tracing it with the compasses was one of those secrets of the art that were jealously guarded and were given an often exaggerated importance. This was natural, for the drawing of the pentagon was bound up with the famous *golden section*[22].

To construct the pentagon from the side, one must first take the golden section of this side; it is a construction that can easily be done with the compasses[23]. But it was not this that interested the medieval artists: they preferred to start from the circle, as we have seen in the case of the *Psalter of Blanche of Castille*, and to inscribe various polygons within the circle. The inscription of a pentagon within the circle by means of the compasses was one of the small secrets of the medieval guilds. It can be done in several ways, but here is the most useful one:

Let there be a given circle. Draw the diameters AB and CD perpendicular to one another and the tangents parallel to these DE and BE. Join EA. EA will intersect CD at F. Revolve FA upon FC, giving the point G; AG equals the side of the inscribed pentagon. Draw a line of this length from A, intersecting the circle at H. Draw similar lines HJ, JK, KI, IA. This establishes the pentagon. The golden section is produced by the intersection of any two diagonals of the pentagon, and is also the ratio of the side of the pentagon to its diagonal. For example, a given diagonal HK intersects the diagonal AJ at L: L is then the golden section of HK and of JA, and LK equals the side of the pentagon. LK intersects AB at M, and M is the golden section of LK. This unique proportion, constantly recurring, enchanted the Ancients and made them consider the pentagon as a perfect figure.

Now let us return to the *Très riches Heures du duc de Berry* in which, as we have already noted, the geometrical compositions coincided with a perspective based on the square. The life of Jesus opens with a representation of the *Earthly Paradise*. Paradise, clearly, is the image of perfection; and perfection, surely, must be the most beautiful of diagrams, the one based on the golden section—a proportion whose truly divine perfection was guaranteed by its very mysteriousness, for was it not incommensurable[24]? And we have the pentagon with all the purity of a diagram. The gate coincides with the line FE and the fountain with AB. But what is even more remarkable is the original, and curiously asymmetrical, way of placing the circle on the page: this is so strange as to strike the eye at the first glance. The reason for it is a 'marvellous' one: the two

22. Division of a length by mean and extreme ratio: *the two parts are related to one another as the greater of the two is to the whole.*

$$\frac{a}{b} = \frac{b}{a + b} \qquad b^2 = a(a + b)$$

23. Let the given side be AB. From B draw at right angles to AB the straight line BC equal to half AB. Describe an arc with radius CB intersecting CA at D and an arc with radius AD intersecting AB at E. This is the golden section, and makes possible the construction of the pentagon: if AB is carried to F so that BF equals AE, AF is the diagonal of the pentagon, which can be completed by repeating the lengths AB and AF with the compasses from A and from F.

24. Cf. p. 76.

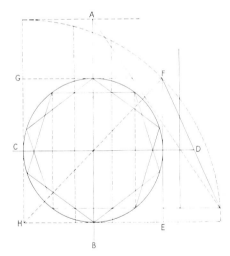

axes of Paradise, the two diameters AB and CD, place the image at precisely the golden section.

This example of a preparatory tracing that is still perfectly visible in the main lines of the composition, even taking the place of any other scheme and, in short, by itself serving as composition, is no isolated curiosity, and we shall find other examples from the last years of the fourteenth

Weltchronik des Rudolf von Ems: Nativity. *Example of golden section constructed from the mean dimension, which is here the side of the square forming the upper part of the picture. The road in the landscape runs up along the diagonal of the square, the Virgin follows the curve of the arc given by the minor dimension. (Munich, Staatsbibliothek)*

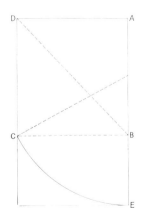

century, that period when interest in plastic relief was relatively weak, when linear grace was triumphant and the agile point of the compasses held the mastery. Let us take, in particular, a *Nativity* of which the assigned date is 1370[25].

Here it should be noted that there are two very simple ways of finding a golden section. As indicated above, it can be found by starting from the greater length, from the totality of the segment. The ratio $\frac{a}{b} = \frac{b}{a+b}$ being a continuous harmonic progression, the greater length may also be found from the mean length. Let AB be the mean length; construct the square on AB, ABCD, and join C to the middle of AB. Rotate this slanting line to the other side of B, at E. A, B and E are in the golden ratio.

It is this construction of the golden section from the mean length that constitutes the scheme of the *Nativity* just mentioned. The wheel is placed at the square, along CB, which intersects the height at the golden section, and the Virgin lies along the arc CE.

The idea that the pentagon is a perfect figure and the golden proportion a divine proportion certainly haunted the artists of the Middle Ages; the best proof is the use made of these constructions in the greatest masterpieces of the period. This applies not only to architecture. Unquestionably, at all periods, architects have had recourse (along with other geometrical proportions) to this continuous and particularly harmonious progression, making use of the golden section—in other words, of dynamic rectangles—and, less frequently, of the pentagon. Here we shall concern ourselves with painting only and shall look for our examples in the work of the greatest painters of the Middle Ages, the fifteenth-century masters. Their attitude was not the same as that of the architects: they did not spread themselves in space, but were limited by the frame, whose hold on the work, as we know, is all-powerful, and therefore they were less interested in a continuous progression than in the infinite refinements of which the pentagon and its divisions are capable. Progression had, nonetheless, its place in that complex of surfaces—almost an architectural ground-plan—constituted by a polyptych. The most celebrated of all these, the *Mystic Lamb* of the brothers Van Eyck, has unfortunately lost its predella; but its divisions lengthways correspond to the golden progression[26]:

$$\frac{b}{a} = \frac{a+b}{b} = \frac{a+2b}{a+b} = \frac{2a+3b}{a+2b} = \frac{3a+5b}{2a+3b}$$

and since the vertical composition also corresponds, it is likely that, to follow out this progression, the height of the predella was equal to the difference between the heights of the upper and the present lower parts.

25. *Weltchronik des Rudolf von Ems*, Munich, Staatsbibliothek; J. Meder, *Die Handzeichnungen*, Vienna, 1923, p. 507.

26. The golden progression is obtained by adding or subtracting, turn by turn, the successive ratios of the golden proportion; it is also obtained by means of the compasses—and this is naturally the means that was used by the artists.

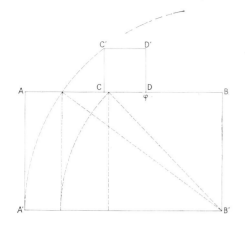

Roger van der Weyden: Descent from the Cross. *The construction of this altarpiece is based on rabatment of the diagonals of the square and rectangles and on the golden number. The height and breadth of the altarpiece are proportional, respectively, to 1 and $\sqrt{3}$.*

Altarpiece of the Mystic Lamb, and golden progression.

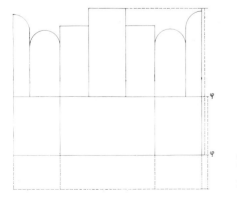

This, obviously, is only a hypothesis. In the Roger van der Weyden *Last Judgment*, already studied, the proportion between the height of the wingpanels and that of the centrepiece—a proportion so strongly emphasized by the middle point of the rainbow—can at a pinch be considered a golden proportion.

The most important example of the use of the pentagon will be found in the same artist's *Descent from the Cross* in the Prado Museum. Its frame is a strange one; it makes one think of a kind of triptych amalgamated into one block; the symmetry and the ternary composition inherited from the triptych are still there. The construction of the frame is closely bound up with that of the contents: starting from a square whose side is BB′, the rabatment of the diagonal transforms this square into a rectangle; the diagonal of this rectangle, when also rabatted, gives the total breadth of the altarpiece, A′B′; and, when raised above the rectangle, it determines the upper corner of the central part, which is constructed on the golden ratio of this same dimension:

$$\frac{AC}{CD} = \frac{AD}{AC} \qquad \frac{AD}{DB} = \frac{AB}{AD}$$

The cord of the arc A′C′ intersects the upper part of the frame at E (and on the other side the symmetrical cord gives the point F). These two points will be of particular interest. With EE′ and FF′ as diameters, circles are described which are tangential to the frame and can be inscribed in the original square. Their point of intersection O is the centre of another circle of the same radius, tangential to the upper side of the small rectangle on top and intersecting AB at G and G′. Clearly it is within these circles (with a flexibility that only a great master could attain) that the whole composition is organized. The balance is perfect, and the dramatic effect is increased by the curve of the supple bodies bent towards two poles of convergence—the Virgin and the Christ. In these circles are inscribed pentagons whose diagonals contribute a vigour, an architecture, to what would otherwise be a mere eddying. Note that the lateral corners of the central pentagon fall precisely on the points G and G′[27].

27. Cf. also the *Entombment*, also by Roger van der Weyden, in the Uffizi. This fits perfectly into a pentagon, as René Huyghe has perceived. (*Dialogue avec le visible*, Paris, 1955, p. 79, pl. 68; English translation: *Discovery of Art*, London, 1959, p. 79, pl. 68.)

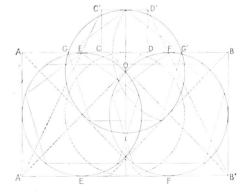

Roger van der Weyden: Descent from
the Cross. *This subtle composition based on
pentagons and on the golden number is analyzed
on the previous page. (Madrid, Prado. Photo
Anderson)*

Let us turn from this master to a Rhineland artist who perhaps owes all his science to him—Stefan Lochner. When confronted with the tremendous works of Roger van der Weyden one is seized by their dramatic feeling and does not, at first, realize that a hidden geometry governs the tragedy; but in front of the *Virgin with the Rosebush*, a simpler, more naïve work, the existence of a scheme leaps to the eye, although its working out is highly professional: the Virgin is enclosed in a double pentagon, which serves to plot the positions of the trellis and partition.

Stefan Lochner: Virgin with the Rose-bush. *A circle touching the sides encloses a double pentagon. The pentagon on its base, situated equidistant from the top and bottom of the picture, determines the position of this circle. Some of the diagonals of the pentagons, when produced, give the construction of the trellis. The low wall just behind the Virgin follows the arc used in drawing the pentagon that stands its point. on (Cologne Museum)*

69

Maître de Moulins: Coronation of the Virgin. *The small circle has its centre at the intersection of the vertical axis with the horizontal line established by the golden ratio. The distance from the lowest point of the large circle to the centre of the small one equals the diameter of the small one. (Moulins Cathedral. Archives photographiques)*

It is in France that the last fruits of this splendid Flemish tradition ripened: no painting from the second half of the fifteenth century attained the perfection of the *Virgin of Moulins*, or of the paintings of Fouquet. The *Virgin of Moulins*, a divine apparition, having no contact with the earth, is pure geometry. A perfect figure governs the obediently bent attitudes of those angels with their enchanting faces, whose Reims smiles are bathed in a strange light: Le Nain children at the fireside already. This geometrical figure is a double pentagon, which supplies the framework for the mystic circles.

Enguerrand Quarton (Charonton): Coronation of the Virgin. *The length of the sides divided at the golden ratio determines the height of the centre of the circle. This circle touches the top of the altarpiece, and its lowest point determines the height of the predella. A double pentagon is inscribed in the circle: the diagonals of the pentagons, prolonged outside the circle, establish the rhythm of the small figures at the sides. (Villeneuve-lès-Avignon. Photo Giraudon)*

The pentagon recurs in the Villeneuve-lès-Avignon *Coronation of the Virgin*, a huge, homogeneous composition owing nothing to the triptych, nor to the set altarpiece formula. It is of considerable dimensions, it exhibits a multitude of figures on very different scales (presented on very different planes of thought), it confronts us with a real landscape in a real light, and with a mystic theophany; this grandiose programme is realized by means of a total composition that is simple and clear, indeed almost naïvely symmetrical, yet with a nucleus, a hidden soul, consisting of a large circle in which are inscribed two pentagons with the same centre.

Jean Fouquet: Virgin and Child adored by Etienne Chevalier.

The Virgin: *The diagonals of a pentagon define the basic triangle. A second pentagon combines with the first to construct an interior rectangle (which rises from the chair and from the row of red angels).*

The diptych as a whole is inscribed in a semicircle with radius equal to the height of the panels.
The precise positioning of the panels is indicated by the lines of perspective. (The Virgin is in the Antwerp Museum, the Etienne Chevalier *in the Berlin Museum. Photo Bulloz)*

Let us linger slightly longer over the greatest painter of the period, Jean Fouquet, and over his masterpiece, the *Etienne Chevalier Virgin*. As in all the diptychs of this kind, the Virgin, who is presented full-face and forms a devotional picture on her own, has a self-contained composition more complex than that of the donor's wingpiece; and yet, if the two wings (now unfortunately separated) are placed together, a bond of symmetry between them emerges and makes them a single work of art.

This Virgin and Child of Fouquet's—what contrasts the entrancing picture contains! It is a portrait of a pretty woman, of grace and femininity, yet at the same time a divine image, which owes its nobility and majesty above all to its abstract design. Here again it is a pentagon, the perfect form, that imposes its design on the excessively pretty Agnès Sorel. She indeed fits into it with absolute ease, holding her cloak along the diagonals and base of the figure, of which the uppermost point is on the median axis; and this axis of symmetry, which is strongly marked, is echoed by the sides of an inscribed rectangle.

If now the two wingpieces are brought together, a new symmetry becomes evident, and the whole work inscribes itself within a semicircle. But exactly how were these two wingpieces arranged? Our attention is drawn by the lines of perspective in the wingpiece. These all converge, as the eyes do, upon a single point, which can only be the Virgin—or rather, the axis of symmetry on which she is placed. The picture was, therefore, meant to have a rather broad frame, and the composition then fits precisely into a semicircle whose radius is the height of the panels.

This line of research could be continued, by analyzing many other works of the period and finding in them the pentagon and the golden section; but this by itself would not provide us with an irrefutable proof, for it could always be objected that, to a symmetrical work with a regular composition, several different diagrams may often be satisfactorily applied. Why then necessarily find in it the golden number, if no one in the Middle Ages has mentioned it? Is it not one of the manias of our time, to look for the golden number everywhere, even in artistic circles where it was unknown or unvalued? But in fact, in the Middle Ages the golden proportion was considered as the expression of perfect beauty, and this is established by a text that reveals the thinking of long centuries of oral tradition—Luca Pacioli's treatise on Divine Proportion.

Divina proportione by Fra Luca Pacioli of Borgo San Sepolcro, a Franciscan friar, was published in Venice by Paganino Paganini of Brescia in 1509; but it really dates from 1498, as is clearly indicated in the two surviving manuscripts of it, that in the Ambrosian Library at Milan and that in the Bibliothèque Civique at Geneva. It is dedicated to Ludovico il Moro, and was finished at Milan in the midst of the circle of artists and savants which had collected round the court of the Sforzas—the circle whose most striking figure was Leonardo da Vinci. It is written in the vulgar tongue, in a fairly readable Tuscan. The best edition is that of 1956, based on the manuscript in the Ambrosiana[28].

In the first twenty-three chapters the author expounds the thirteen increasingly wondrous effects of divine proportion, which makes it possible to attain the various simple figures, above all the pentagon; from chapter XXIV onwards, he shows how it enables us to construct the five regular solids, and from these (ch. LVI ff) all the other solids. The *Compendio della divina proportione* ends there, after the seventy-first chapter; but it is followed by applications to columns and to lettering.

The work thus falls into three distinct parts: the plane figures, then the 'solids' (volumes), then the artistic applications (in the Milan manuscript the order of the two last parts is reversed). Only the first part is devoted to expounding the divine proportion.

After the dedication to Ludovico, prince and friend of the sciences, the author introduces himself and his work and sings the praises of mathematics, basis not only of all the sciences but of the arts (chs. I to III). In chapter IV he justifies his frequent references to Euclid, 'our philosopher'. Then (chs. V and VI) he defends the title of his work, 'the divine proportion'. Why divine? It is made so, as we shall see a little later, by five properties. And now (chs. VII to XXII), Pacioli analyzes in succession the thirteen different 'effects' of the divine proportion.

The first 'effect' defines it precisely (ch. VIII): it is an irrational proportion between three terms, such that if the greatest of them is 10, the mean term will be $\sqrt{125}-5$ and the smallest $15-\sqrt{125}$. This is the golden ratio with which we are familiar, $\dfrac{a}{b}=\dfrac{b}{a+b}$. The modern mathematicians who have worked it out designate it by φ and give it the precise value of: $\dfrac{1+\sqrt{5}}{2}$, or approximately 1,618... ($\varphi\, a = b$ and $\varphi\, b = a + b$). The proof is easy. If we multiply by φ Pacioli's smallest term, $15-\sqrt{125}$, we get the major, $\sqrt{125}-5$, and if we multiply this by φ we get 10, that is to say the sum of the two[29].

Next come the other twelve 'effects' which are described as 'essentiale', 'singular', 'ineffabile', 'mirabile', 'innomabile', 'inestimabile', 'excessivo',

28. Luca Pacioli, *Divina proportione*, Fontes Ambrosiani, XXXI, Milan, 1956. C. Winterberg's edition (*Quellenschriften für Kunstgeschichte*, Vienna, 1889), with a German translation, is still an excellent working edition.

'supremo', 'excellentissimo', 'quasi incomprehensibile' and 'dignissimo'. These are the main mathematical applications of the proportion. Let us note in particular the seventh 'effect'—that the sides of the hexagon and the decagon intersect in accordance with this proportion; the ninth—intersections of the diagonals of the pentagon determining the ratio of side to diagonal; and, above all, the thirteenth—'How, without this proportion, it is impossible to construct an equilateral and equiangular pentagon.' All these developments are illustrated very simply by geometrical figures in the margin. In concluding, Pacioli presents the elegant figures which will illustrate the second part of his book and thanks *Lionardo Vinci Fiorentino* for having drawn them with his skilful pencil.

Leonardo da Vinci—it is a name that lays open a wide future, and we seem to be a long way from the Middle Ages. But let there be no mistake. Up to now we conducted our search as best we could by questioning various works of art and trying to co-ordinate their replies; but now we have come upon a text, and this text holds our attention because it does not, like all the older texts from Pliny to Cennini, merely contain philosophical speculations on art or technical recipes, but reveals a secret. Though the text is a late one, the ideas which it expounds for the first time are of long standing: the real innovation consisted in writing them down, in expounding as a coherent whole a doctrine that had long been transmitted orally within the corporations. Let us follow Pacioli more closely: again and again we shall see, under the humanist, the man of the Middle Ages showing through[30]. The very title[31], that long phrase beginning with *Divina proportione* and ending with *secretissima scientia*, sets us down in a climate which we shall not leave.

Now let us turn to the five properties which earn for this marvellous ratio the epithet 'divine' (chs. V and VI):

29. Here is the first proof (the second is equally simple):

$$\sqrt{125} - 5 = (15 - \sqrt{125}) \frac{1 + \sqrt{5}}{2}$$

$$\frac{5\sqrt{5} - 5}{15 - 5\sqrt{5}} = \frac{1 + \sqrt{5}}{2}$$

$$\frac{\sqrt{5} - 1}{3 - \sqrt{5}} = \frac{1 + \sqrt{5}}{2}$$

$$2(\sqrt{5} - 1) = (3 - \sqrt{5})(1 + \sqrt{5})$$

$$2\sqrt{5} - 2 = 2\sqrt{5} - 2$$

30. This is how Sir Anthony Blunt has described the essential characteristic of Luca Pacioli's book: 'There are passages... which might almost have been written in the thirteenth century, and Pacioli's favourite authorities are not the Classics but St Augustine and Duns Scotus.' (*Artistic Theory in Italy*, 1450-1600, Oxford, 1940.)

31. *Divina Proportione Opera a tutti glingeni perspicaci e curiosi necessaria ove ciascun studioso di Philosophia, Perspectiva, Pictura, Sculptura, Architectura, Musica e altre Mathematiche suavissima sottile e admirabile doctrina contegiura e delectarassi con varie questione de secretissima scientia.*

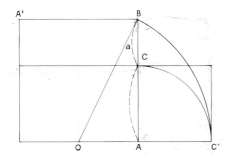

Fig. A. The Golden Proportion according to Euclid. *The point C on the line AB is obtained by rabatment of the horizontal line OB, which is a diagonal of the half of the square, then by transferring AC' to AB. The surface of the rectangle made by AB and BC (in our figure, by A'B and BC) equals the square on AC. Thus the ratio is* b² = a (a + b), *as noted by Pacioli (cf. p. 64).*

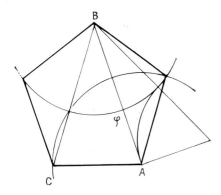

Fig. B. The Pentagon according to Euclid. *By construction as above, the point is obtained on the line AB. B equals the base of the required isosceles triangle; it will be the side, AC, of the pentagon, of which BA and BC are the diagonals.*

1. Like God, it is unique.

2. As the Holy Trinity is one substance in three persons, it is one single proportion in three terms.

3. 'As God cannot be defined in words, it cannot be expressed by any intelligible number or rational quantity, but is always occult and secret and is called by the mathematicians irrational.' The expression '*occulta e secreta*' emphasizes the mysterious, magical character of the branch of knowledge which Pacioli is revealing to us.

4. Like God, it is always similar to itself.

The fifth property is the subject of the whole second part of the book, which is devoted to the construction of the regular solids. To it too Pacioli attributes a divine element. As the celestial virtue or quintessence has made possible the creation of the four elements from which the whole of nature has arisen, so our sacred proportion makes possible the formation of the duodecahedron (that volume formed out of twelve pentagons), 'which Plato the ancient, in his *Timaeus*, calls the very expression of the quintessence. Without this proportion, therefore, it is impossible to obtain the five regular solids, of which this, the most complex, is the fifth'.

A little farther on (ch. VII), Pacioli says of his proportion that it is '*dal ciel mandata*'—heaven-sent—and once again marvels that his three terms cannot be expressed in whole numbers.

That Leonardo da Vinci drew the figures for the original manuscript must be true; Pacioli says so with such insistence (above all in chs. I and XXIII) that we must believe it. But it is interesting to note that, in spite of this collaboration, which proves that the divine proportion was no secret to him, Leonardo da Vinci shows no further interest in it. We have found so few traces of it in his mathematical work and in the geometrical figures with which his manuscripts are dotted, that it really seems as if the golden number was not of much interest to an innovating mind like his. He makes use of it in some of his works, but this proves merely the strength of a tradition: to Leonardo it was not a new and exciting idea on which his great hunger for knowledge, his creative and imaginative genius, could fasten.

Pacioli's book may therefore be considered as the equivalent, at the end of the fifteenth century and with regard to the laws of beauty, of what Diderot's *Encyclopædia* was to be, in the eighteenth century, for methods of manufacture: both books were courageous in their frankness, in revealing to everyone branches of knowledge which had been kept under a bushel and in divulging the secrets of the corporations. But perhaps this turning of a bright light upon old secrets is the annunciation of their death. In point of fact it marked the beginning of the decline. Some time had still to pass between the great *Encyclopædia* and the Industrial Revolution: in the same way, although the divine proportion had lost its magical attraction, we shall see it still intervening in the composition of works of art—in a great many cases under the influence of this book, whose late publication aroused men's curiosity.

Did Pacioli then look entirely towards the past? Certainly not. He was also a man of his time. His passion for mathematics was that of a humanist. He admires its sure progression towards the truth, so satisfying to the human spirit. Hence his devotion to Euclid, whom he always calls 'our philosopher' and to whom he constantly refers. There is a very fine portrait of Luca Pacioli in the Naples Museum: the monk is studying an enormous lump of quartz, cut with twenty facets (a combination of the tetrahedron and the hexahedron), and is leaning on a copy of Euclid. Here we have the whole man as he wanted to be seen. Pacioli's greatest concern was to take his proportion, still 'divine', still charged with confused mysticism, and make of it a clear idea of which a systematic knowledge would be possible. Euclid's construction of the pentagon, starting from the isosceles triangle[32], is not as simple or as quick as the one given above on page 64, which was certainly known in the Middle Ages and is called Ptolemy's construction; but Pacioli felt a deep need to base his work on an author as strictly logical as Euclid[33]. He says of Euclid: 'It is not his custom to introduce into his proofs later matters of which he has not made mention, but only the antecedent matters, and this order is followed in all his fifteen books.' (ch. XXII).

Pacioli has also, like all the humanists and *cortegiani*, a reverence for Plato; but the Middle Ages had already been permeated by the ideas of the *Timaeus* through the writings of the theologians—only the knowledge of these ideas was then less direct.

Finally, to Pacioli, mathematics are the foundation of perspective and of music (ch. III). This brings us to the heart of the preoccupations of the fifteenth century. Pacioli was a pupil of Piero della Francesca, that great geometer, to whom, as we shall see, he owed more than he admitted; he was a friend of Melozzo da Forlì, who like him was a pupil of Piero but in painting and was, by that time, a famous artist engaged on important works at Rome[34]; and he was friends with Leonardo, already a very famous man, whose magnificent equestrian statue, in particular, he admired and warmly praised.

Thus Pacioli stands at the turning-point between two worlds. His naïve admiration for mathematics was not yet that of a pure rationalist, but was permeated with metaphysical ideas: to him mathematics were the expression of perfection, therefore of the divine. But on the other hand, perfection is also beauty: Pacioli marvelled at the beauty of the five regular

32. 'To describe an isosceles triangle, having each of the angles at the base double of the third angle' (Euclid, bk IV, proposition 10). Let AB be a side of the triangle. 'Divide it at the point C, so that the rectangle AB, BC may be equal to the square on AC.' With A as centre and AB as radius, 'describe the circle BDE, in which place the straight line BD equal to AC,... and join DA. The triangle ABD shall be such as is required...' (Cf. *Euclid's Elements*, Everyman edition, London, pp. 122, 123.) C is at the golden section of AB, and the major (AC) is equal to the base of the triangle.

33. The frequent references to Johannes Campanus are also a homage to Euclid, on whom this thirteenth-century mathematician, highly honoured in his time, was a judicious commentator.

34. A large part of chapter LVII is devoted to him.

solids (ch. V). He said: 'Far from degrading the other proportions with which it is associated, the divine proportion magnifies them.' (ch. VII). Is that not already a theory of the beautiful? What freshness there is in a search for knowledge that is still so human, so deeply lived! Such enthusiasm in the presence of the joy of discovery is very moving: '*Gran jubilo e summa letitia che have Pictagora quando con certa scientia ebbe trovato la vera proportione de le doi linee recte che contengano l'angolo recte*' (Great joy and supreme gladness had Pythagoras when with sure science he found the true proportion of the two straight lines which contain the right angle! —ch. LIV)[35].

In short, Pacioli tries with all his strength to de-mystify the proportion which he still calls divine and to give it a solid basis, that of Euclid. Hence the complexity of this text: it reveals the split tendencies of a mind divided, like all those of his time, between the rational and the irrational.

35. Let us note, in conclusion, an observation by Luca Pacioli in his *Summa de arithmetica* (Venice, 1494, dist. VI, treatise I): 'A thing may only endure in nature if it is duly proportioned to its necessity.'

Pollaiuolo: Martyrdom of St Sebastian. *In this highly symmetrical composition the attitudes and movements of the figures are governed by the golden ratio and the network of lines derived from it. The group of archers is also inscribed in a circle touching the bottom of the picture and two of its sides. (London, National Gallery. Photo Anderson)*

IV THE MUSICAL CONSONANCES

We come now to the generation of artists who lived at Florence or in Northern Italy in the middle of the fifteenth century and are known as the artists of the early Renaissance. Their period has also been called the age of humanism: some of these artists, with minds far above the ordinary, enthusiastic and incapable of keeping their discoveries to themselves, not only showed themselves innovators in their works but also expressed their thoughts in books that had a profound effect on their contemporaries. They were pioneers, theorists: Alberti, Serlio and Palladio for architecture, and Piero della Francesca for painting.

In his excellent book *Architectural Principles in the Age of Humanism*[1], Rudolf Wittkower says with great wisdom: '...in trying to prove that a system of proportions has been deliberately applied by painter, sculptor or architect, one is easily misled into finding in a given work those ratios which one sets out to find. Compasses in the scholar's hand do not revolt. If we want to avoid the pitfall of useless speculation we must look for practical prescriptions of ratios supplied by the artists themselves. Curiously enough, that has never been done systematically.' Let us try to apply to pictorial composition this admirable method applied by Wittkower to architecture, taking our stand, in the case of Piero della Francesca, on his own works and, more generally, as regards the whole of that generation, on the work of Alberti, which is just as essential in regard to painting as it is to architecture.

What is it that we find in these books? More mathematics. The prestige of mathematics is far from having diminished. As in the Middle Ages, men still traced that science back to Pythagoras through Plato's *Timaeus* and looked to it for the secret meaning of the universe; but the knowledge of it had now become much more precise, and it was, above all, not now the same kind of mathematics. In the Middle Ages all research had been done with the compass-point. This had made possible a daily use of incommensurable quantities and, in particular, of the golden ratio— practical geometry in conformity with methods of working and studio tricks embellished by a mystical philosophy but still, after all, a labour of craftsmen. In contrast, the humanist generation plunged into books:

Raphael: School of Athens, *detail. Pythagoras explaining the musical consonances with a diagram. (Rome, Vatican. Photo Anderson)*

1. London, Tiranti, 1952, p. 110.

it studied the *Timaeus* in Ficino's commentary, of which printed editions were becoming available; it recovered direct access to Euclid, Vitruvius and Ptolemy, and looked for the distant Pythagoras in books on musical theory like that of Boethius. The result was, first, precision—clear ideas and exact numerical calculations; and in consequence less and less liking for compass-drawn figures that could not be calculated, and a growing taste for simple ratios. Wittkower[2] has shown what is the deep reason for this taste for simple, measurable relationships: it was the desire to attach the plastic arts to the major art, music, by the use of *musical relationships*.

Albertism

Any study of the period must start from Alberti: one cannot seriously try to recover the state of mind and tastes of that generation without reading his three books—the *De re aedificatoria*, published in Latin at Florence in 1485, the *De statua* and the *De pictura*. Their effect was considerable.

The latter book, though written in 1436, was not published till the sixteenth century; but it very quickly circulated in the artists' studios in manuscript copies or extracts and was certainly known to Piero della Francesca, who drew inspiration from it in his *Prospectiva pingendi*. The *De re aedificatoria*, which was also known long before it was published, had an even wider influence. It is a treatise on architecture, but some of its chapters on proportion and on ornament are of interest to all artists, and the tone of the book, the peculiarly calm and serene aesthetic that emerges from it, awakened great sympathy in the painters.

Leaving aside the first books, devoted to problems that are largely technical (ground-plans, building materials, the organization of the work, etc.), let us look at book IX, which treats of the adornment of buildings. Here the conditions of beauty are laid down in a most precise way. In chapter V Alberti explains that the musical intervals agreeable to the ear, the octave, fifth and fourth, correspond to the division of a string in 2, in 3, or in 4 ($1/2$, $2/3$, $3/4$). These proportions, known at the time as the *diapason*, *diapente* and *diatessaron*, will also serve as bases for the plastic arts, and first of all for architecture. This is then studied in detail in chapter VI[3], which treats of surfaces:

The 'short areas' will be square, or $2/3$, or $3/4$. If one of the dimensions has to be longer than the other, twice these proportions will be taken, that is to say twice $2/3$, which gives, if we start from 4 as the small side, 4, 6, 9 for the large side ($4/6 = 6/9 = 2/3$); or else twice $3/4$, which gives, if we start from 9/9, 12, 16 ($9/12 = 12/16 = 3/4$).

2. *Op. cit.*, pp. 100-103.

3. English translation by James Leoni, entitled *Ten Books on Architecture;* London, 1726, 1739 and 1755: republished by Tiranti, London, in 1955, edited by Joseph Rykwert. Bk IX, ch. VI, runs from p. 197 to p. 200 of this edition.

Or again, one may simply take the ratio 1/2, the octave or diapason, not forgetting that the octave is made up of the fifth and fourth, or of the fourth and fifth. The former combination will divide the wall like this: 4, 6, 8 (4/6 or the fifth, and 6/8 or the fourth); the latter will divide it, for instance, like this: 3, 4, 6 (3/4 or the fourth, 4/6 or the fifth).

These proportions can be doubled or combined, but without ever exceeding the number 27, the third cube, for the Ancients observed that the mathematical laws of music were valid only for the small numbers.

Finally, Alberti recommends sticking to a single ratio: if in a building the length is twice the breadth, we shall not use for the height ratios deriving from the triple proportion...[4]

This analysis will become clearer if we refer to the text of Alberti's *De re aedificatoria*, book IX. In chapter V of this book, Alberti expounds the theory of the musical relationship. Here are the salient points:

—The *Diapason, octave* or *double*: 'The Numbers answer to one another in a double Proportion, as two to one, or the Whole to the Half.' (Octave = 1/2)

—The *Diapente, fifth* or *sesquialtera*: 'The String which produced it bore the same Proportion to that to which it is compared, as one and an half does to one... The longer String must be allowed three, and the shorter, two.' (Fifth = 2/3)

—The *Diatessaron, fourth* or *sesquitertia*: '...where the longer String contains the shorter one and one third more.' (Fourth = 3/4)

—The *Diapason-Diapente* or *triple*: 'They answer as three to one, or as the Whole to one third of itself.' ($1/2 \times 2/3 = 1/3$)

—The *Tonus*, 'which was also called the *Sesquioctave*..., wherein the long String compared to shorter, exceeds it one eighth part of the shorter String.' $(1/8)$[5]

'Of all these Numbers,' Alberti comments, 'the Architects made very convenient Use, taking them sometimes two by two, as in planning out their Squares and open Areas...'

In chapter VI Alberti applies this theory to architectural ground-plans, or 'areas'. He says:

'Of these Proportions we are now to treat more particularly, and first we shall say something of those Areas where only two[6] are used.

'Of Areas, some are short, some long, and some between both. The shortest of all is the perfect Square, every Side whereof is of equal Length, all corresponding with one another at Right Angles. The nearest to this is the *Sesquialtera*, and the *Sesquitertian* also may be reckoned among the Shorter Areas.' (figs. 1 and 2)

'These three Proportions therefore, which we may also call simple, are proper for the smaller Platforms. There are likewise three others, which are proper for middling Platforms: The best of all is the Double (fig. 3),

4. 'As, for Instance, in the Elevation of a Room which is twice as long as broad, they make use, not of those Numbers which compose the Triple, but of those only which form the Duple...' (p. 199).

5. Cf. note 8 below.

6. i.e. length and breadth.

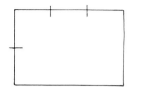

Figure 1: Sesquialtera (Diapente 2/3).

Figure 2: Sesquitertia (Diatessaron 3/4).

Figure 3: Double (Diapason 1/2).

Figure 4: Double sesquialtera (Double diapente 4/6/9).

Figure 5: Double sesquitertia (Double diatessaron 9/12/16).

and the next best is that which is formed of the *Sesquialtera* doubled (fig. 4), which is produced as follows: Having set down the least Number of the Area, as, for instance, four, lengthen it to the first *Sesquialtera*, which will make six, and then add the *Sesquialtera* of this six, which will produce nine[7]. Thus the Length will exceed the Breadth in a double Proportion, and one Tone more[8].'

'For moderate Platforms also; we may use that Proportion which arises from the *Sesquitertian* doubled in the same Manner as the former (fig. 5); where-in the Length and Breadth will be as nine and sixteen[9]. Here the longer Line contains the shorter twice, excluding one Tone[10].'

'In the longest Areas we either add the *Duple* to the *Sesquialtera*, which will produce the *Triple*[11] (fig. 6); or add the *Sesquitertia* to the *Duple*, which will make the Proportion as three to eight[12]; or lastly make the Lines correspond to each other in a *Quadruple* Proportion.'

The Renaissance artists took Alberti's text literally, preferring to base their practice on the numbers given by him as examples, and even marking them in their diagrams[13]. The 'mean areas' were particularly right for the painters, who therefore took a special interest in the ratios 4/6/9 and 9/12/16. The 'long areas' were of little use to them, since their proportions rarely corresponded to those of a picture.

We are here a long way from Pacioli's book, in which a certain proportion, called 'divine', was held up to admiration precisely because it was incommensurable. Here, on the contrary, beauty resides in the relations between the first whole numbers, simple relationships easily read at a glance and always measurable. Not just any relationships, it is true, but only those that are found in the musical scale: the resulting aesthetic is different from that of Pacioli, but the intellectual attitude is not really so far from his; it is still permeated by that great metaphysical quest which was the glory of the Middle Ages. Alberti is merely taking his stand in a more considered way on the exalting spiritual doctrine of Plato.

It is very moving to contemplate the wonder of the Ancients when they found in the outside world a confirmation—in the form of simple ratios of length—of consonances evident to the ear, such as the octave or the fifth. Their joy arose from a need for reassurance. The complexity of the creation frightens us. We do not find outside us that aspiration to unity, to logic and to clarity which is a need of our spirit and seems to us a reflec-

7. As is plain, Alberti has his own way of deriving his ratios. He always starts from the smallest measure. In this case it is 4, which is two-thirds of 6; then the length 6 is two-thirds of 9.

8. 9 is twice 4 plus 1, which is a *tone* (1/8) of 8.

9. Here again Alberti starts from the shortest measure, 9, which is three-quarters of 12, as 12 is of 16.

10. 18 (the double of 9) exceeds 16 by 2. The tone (1/8) of 16 is 2.

11. $1/2 \times 2/3 = 2/6$, or $1/3$.

12. $1/2 \times 3/4 = 3/8$. According to the method already used, 1/2 is taken and then 3/4, starting from 3: this yields 3, 6, 8.

13. Cf. below, p. 98.

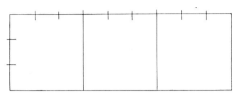

Figure 6: Diapason diapente 1/3 (3/6/9).

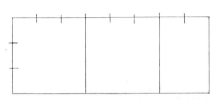

Figure 7: Diapason diatessaron 3/8 (3/6/8).

tion of the divine. Therefore any coincidence between the forms of our mind and the outside world enchants us. Is not the fact that to stop a string at its middle, or 2/3 of the way along, yields intervals so satisfying to the ear a proof of the existence of God? '*Certissimum est naturam in omnibus sui esse persimilen*.'[14] 'Certain it is that nature is in all things similar to itself.'

A similar confirmation was looked for in the proportions of the human body; but these are very imprecise, all men being different, whereas music demands perfect mathematical ratios: if you stray in the slightest degree from the proportion 2/3, your fifth will be out of tune and will sound so to any good ear. Sir Kenneth Clark[15] quotes a letter of Alberti's about the construction of a building of which he had made the plans and drawings: he forbids Matteo dei Pasti to make any change, because if any detail is altered '*si discorda tutta quella musica*'.

The way in which this music is realized, the grace and purity with which it emerges from the monuments built by Alberti and from the masterpieces of the architects, painters and sculptors who were filled with his ideas, is miraculous. For Alberti did not remain in the field of speculation. He was an artist, and thought in terms of action. In his treatise on painting his aesthetic is laid down with precision: composition is the harmonious arrangement of the various surfaces in their right places (bk II). There must be no rough or sharp surfaces like old women's faces, but beautiful, smooth, calm surfaces. Never fear emptiness, nakedness or even poverty; fear rather an excess of abundance and agitation. This is what Focillon[16] has well named the '*loi des vides*' ('an image needs a solitude') and the '*loi de la lenteur*' (which is made up of balance and moderation). And Focillon defines Albertism by the word *concinnitas*: the intellectual harmony born of a right ratio of numbers.

Now let us look for a few typical examples of Albertism in painting. From among that great flowering of the early Renaissance it is difficult to make a choice. Also there is great confusion, past and future are mixed up; the persistence of the Christian iconographic themes brought with it a persistence of the old conceptions of form, whose prestige was enhanced by the splendour of the Franco-Flemish masterpieces.

Yet simplification took place: there was a return to a wholly naïve symmetry, to a child's geometry. One has only to compare an *Adoration of the Magi* by Lippi, Ghirlandaio or Botticelli with a similar scene by Roger van der Weyden to see that all that complex refinement of polygons was no longer of interest to the Florentines. But we shall find the Alberti style, with its marvellous *concinnitas*, much more purely realized in the complete freedom afforded by the new mythological and allegorical subjects which the platonism of the Courts of Love brought to the fore.

14. Alberti, bk IX, ch. 5. He goes on: 'From whence I conclude that the same Numbers, by means of which the Agreement of Sounds affects our Ears with Delight, are the very same which please our Eyes and our Mind.' Translation James Leoni, *op. cit.*
15. *Piero della Francesca*, London, 1951, p. 18.
16. Henri Focillon, *Piero della Francesca*, Paris, 1952, p. 111.

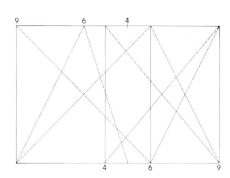

Let us take first the most typical painting and freshest flower of the Florentine Renaissance, Botticelli's *Primavera*. So much has been written about the *Primavera* and there is still plenty to say: its symbolism, its composition—every aspect of so deliberate a work deserves close study[17]. Let us confine ourselves to a general observation, one that is indeed so obvious that no one seems to have thought of making it: the design is apparently symmetrical, but not really; the principal figure, Venus, stands under a niche of foliage and is not really in the centre. On one side there are four people, on the other three. That this garden of the spirit did suggest a kind of platonic Paradise, and that these exquisite goddesses

17. Cf., for instance, A. Chastel, *Art et humanisme à Florence au temps de Laurent le Magnifique*, Paris, Presses Universitaires, 1959, pp. 173 ff, on the relationship of this painting to the ideology of the platonic circle of the Accademia di Careggi, in particular the references to Marsilio Ficino. (Cf. also Edgar Wind, *Pagan Mysteries in the Renaissance*, London, Faber, 1958; in particular p. 18, p. 41 and pp. 100-110.)

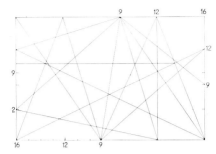

Botticelli: Birth of Venus. *Here Botticelli chooses the second of Alberti's characteristic ratios, the double diatessaron, 9/12/16. Venus stands on the sloping line between the caesuras 9 taken, on the top side, from left to right and, on the bottom side, from right to left. The lines that support the Winds and the Nymph form the sides of the triangle whose apex is the top of this sloping axis of Venus. The tilted position of this triangle accentuates the translatory movement. (Florence, Uffizi. Photo Anderson)*

Botticelli: Primavera. *Like all the painters of his generation, Botticelli was attracted by Alberti's doctrine of the division of surfaces and tried to use the very ratios chosen by Alberti as examples. Spring pastimes in the presence of a great lady were a theme well fitted to a design based on musical harmony. Botticelli chose the double diapente, 4/6/9, and adapted his composition to it so well that each section of the picture comprises as many figures as units. (Florence, Uffizi. Photo Alinari)*

should be dancing to the sound of the music of numbers, ought not to astonish us. In fact, the picture is constructed on the double diapente (4/6/9). The niche is inscribed on the two caesuras 4 and 6. On one side four units and four people; on the other side three units and three people (the little Cupid hovering above the musing lady who presides over this play reminds us that in the middle there are two units). This curious symmetry with the slightly displaced axis recurs in the *Birth of Venus*, a picture that is equally representative of its time and has similar proportions. In so balanced and so simple a work the sideways shift of that fine classical statue of Venus which forms the axis is surprising. The composition is large, calm and stark, like a wall by Alberti or Palladio; it is governed by the double diatessaron, and Venus stands where the music dictates, in the ratio 9/16.

When Mantegna did the allegorical pictures for the 'grotta' of Isabella d'Este, the minute particularity of the instructions he received—a detailed precision that exasperated Giovanni Bellini and discouraged Perugino— must have weighed on him also; but the atmosphere of humanism surrounding that great lady certainly corresponded to his tastes as an artist. In the *Triumph of Virtue* he was hampered by a detailed and absurd programme and could only indicate the caesura 4/6/9. But in the *Parnassus*, the subject of which visibly delighted him, the austere master unbent. He made this hymn to the dance a hymn to music and, adding subtleties of his own to those ordered by the exigent princess, he amused himself by giving the dancers a rhythm based on the double diatessaron, putting into his picture nine Muses, sixteen figures in all—the double diatessaron being a ratio of 9/16 units. The divisions by 9/12/16 are very strongly

Mantegna: Parnassus. *In this complete expression of humanism the use of the Platonic musical ratios was essential. Here Mantegna obeys the demands of the double diatessaron, 9/12/16. The caesura 9 from the right gives the axis of the picture, determining the position of Mars and Venus at the top, and at the bottom the movement of the legs of the Muses. The same ratio is repeated from the left and makes possible the establishment of sloping lines. Mantegna carries the symbolism a long way: he already has nine Muses, but he also sees that there are sixteen figures in all. (Paris, Louvre. Photo Giraudon)*

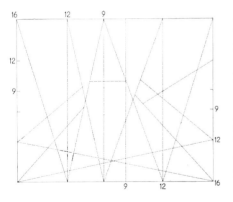

marked, starting from the right: main axis of the composition at 9, accentuated by the almond formed by Mars and Venus close together; secondary axis at 12, violently stressed by a precipitous cliff.

The other artists of that generation used the same musical sections. It was one of the fashionable novelties, along with the mythological subject matter; but they were introduced also into the religious pictures.

In Ghirlandaio's fresco of the *Birth of the Virgin* in Santa Maria Novella, the 'area' of which, as Alberti would say, is 2 by 3, the edge of the pilaster on the left is 2/3 of the way across the picture's breadth, so railing off a square on the right. This is the 2/3 division or diapente. In the other scenes of this set, the architecture is often symmetrical, but the musical division of the panel establishes the place of the principal figure. The portrait of a great Florentine lady paying a visit is recognizable and the work was criticized at the time for its profanity. In contrast, in the frescoee of Masaccio[18], which are so profoundly religious, the figure in the placs of honour, so to speak, in the place marked by the caesura, is again

18. Masaccio, like Uccello, was a companion of Alberti in his youth, and he was scanning the figures of his frescoes to musical ratios some thirty years before the *De re aedificatoria* was compiled.

Ghirlandaio: Birth of the Virgin. (*Florence, Santa Maria Novella. Photo Anderson*)

the principal one. Thus in the *St Peter and the Tribute Money* the majestic figure of Christ is situated 4/9 of the way across.

We have already mentioned the symmetry that is dominant in Benozzo Gozzoli's frescoes in the Palazzo Riccardi: this is indeed obvious, with its division in the centre and its arrangement of the horsemen at equal distances from this axis. But this cannot be pushed much further: the subdivision of the right half is not repeated to the left. Here is a good example of the octave's division into fifth and fourth—2/3/4 (2/3, 3/4); also we find four units in the breadth and three in the height (3/4).

The division of the sides into four or into three is, as we have already seen, supplied by the armature of the rectangle itself (cf. p. 43, above). Alberti's musical theories do not, therefore, introduce into painting any great revolution in practice with the ratios 2/3 or 3/4—the division of the sides of a rectangle into two, three or four equal parts was already well known. But the new method did bring out a rather subtle refinement —a displacement in the symmetry and, with it, the harmonic reason for this displacement. Underneath the many possibilities of asymmetry thus offered, there lies the taste for simplicity, for that marvellous simplicity in the arrangement of the parts which takes its stand against the attraction of crowded compositions and of complicated patterns, and which agrees so well with the architecture of Alberti himself and of Palladio. This simplicity and limpid clarity, as we shall now see, triumphed in the work of Piero della Francesca and of Raphael.

Masaccio: St Peter and the Tribute Money. *Painters who wished to stress the musical proportions had a choice of two solutions: first, to place the principal figure at the caesura; secondly, to use the caesuras to form an imaginary frame enclosing the figures. In this picture Masaccio uses both: the first caesura falls upon the Christ, and the second, at the corner of the buildings, shuts off the scene of the tribute. (Florence, Santa Maria del Carmine. Photo Anderson)*

Piero della Francesca

Piero della Francesca was certainly the most original man of the Quattro-cento. He expressed the aesthetic of Alberti in all its purity, adding to it the fruit of his own meditations, and in the Arezzo frescoes he has left us an astonishing series: calm, built up of great empty spaces, and full of a radiant serenity. Although the aim of this book is to study the various attitudes to the problem of composition rather than the various artists in their chronological order, I propose to turn aside for a moment from the subject of the harmonic intervals and to deal with the work of this exceptional artist as a whole, for in him painter and theorist cannot be dissociated.

Twenty years before his death and in spite of his well-attested success, this singular man is said to have given up all artistic activity and devoted himself to mathematics. Was this a change of direction caused by disap-pointment? Surely not. The Duke of Urbino treated Piero with respect; his frescoes were famous; and great painters like Signorelli and Melozzo da Forlì counted it an honour to be his pupils. But let us not forget that Luca Pacioli also recognized him as his master and Luca was a pure mathe-matician. The truth is that Piero was obsessed by two passions and carried on simultaneously two activities which, in him, in the end coincided and were integrated into each other—painting and mathematics, or rather geometry. For, like his pupil Pacioli, that fervent admirer of Euclid, Piero was a geometer, and it was as a geometer that he approached painting, which he saw as an application to the problems of perspective and of the expression of volumes. And all this would still be of no value if he had not also possessed the wonderful gift for light.

Vasari[19], whose biography of Piero reveals a special sympathy for him, presents him as a great mathematician, devoted to mathematics and geometry from his youth, even though his books on these subjects were written only at an advanced age. He tells us also that Piero went blind when he was about sixty, which explains why we have no paintings dating from his last twenty years. No doubt the truth is that his sight went gradually, and he was certainly quite blind during the last two years of his life; but how comes it that his three books on mathematics—even the last one, which he is said to have written 'in his extreme old age'—are completed with admirably drawn diagrams from his own hand? It seems likely that Piero carried on his studies of perspective and of volumes in space throughout his life, in parallel with painting, and that, when he grew very old, all he had to do was to put his notes in order with the help of a disciple—perhaps of Luca Pacioli. These books remained unpub-lished, and Vasari covers Fra Luca with opprobrium for having plagia-rized his master instead of piously publishing his work. We shall see how far this indignation was justified.

19. Vasari, G. *Le vite...*, published by Ragghianti, Milan-Rome, 1945, pp. 681 ff. (English translation: A.B. Hinds, Everyman's Library, London, 1949; I, pp. 331-336.)

Benozzo Gozzoli: Procession of the Magi.
The musical ratio is obvious: 2/3/4. *Division
of the octave* (1/2) *into fifth and fourth*
(2/3 *and* 3/4). B *falls at* 2/3 *of* AC, *and*
C *at* 3/4 *of* AD. *This plastic music is
scanned by the great trees.* (*Florence, Palazzo
Riccardi. Photo Anderson*)

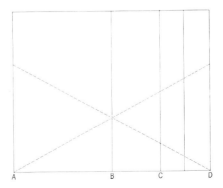

A　　　　　B　　　C　　D

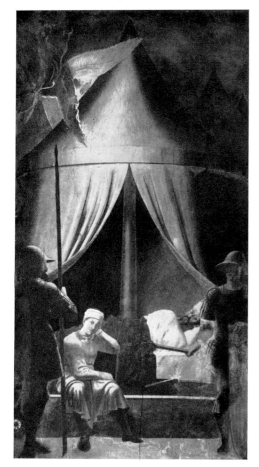

Piero della Francesca: Dream of Constantine. *The arrangement of the figures in the lower part is governed by a circle which touches the sides of the picture and the half-way point of the upper third.* (*Arezzo. Photo Anderson*)

The *De prospectiva pingendi*[20] is Piero's first manuscript; it is dedicated to Duke Federigo, who died in 1482, and was therefore written before that date. It is a treatise on perspective, and we shall not deal with it in detail here, but it is addressed to painters and opens with an idea borrowed from Alberti. The art of painting, said Alberti in book II of his *De pictura*, comprehends three parts: *circumscription, composition* and *distribution of light*. For these words Piero della Francesca substitutes *design, measures* and *colour*. The nuance is interesting: Piero is thinking as a painter; he uses the more precise word, *design*, and, reflecting with penetration upon the text of his source, discovers something that the modern painters did not understand until Cézanne—that the distribution of light is a problem of colour. Generations of painters, before and after him, superimposed colour upon monochrome; he alone, set upon this path by the intuitions of his master Domenico Veneziano, understood the principle of the synthesis of light and colour; and this, surely, is the secret of the radiance and freshness of his light. Passing on to the second of the three 'parts' of painting, let us note that Piero insists, even more than Alberti, on the predominance of numbers. We may fairly say that he is more Albertian than Alberti when he replaces the word *composition*—arrangement of surfaces—by the word *commensuratio*.

The second manuscript is a short work on arithmetic and geometry, entitled *De abaco*. We come now to the third, the *De quinque corporibus regularibus*[21], which was offered by him to Duke Guidobaldo for his father's library. The title of the book reminds us that Luca Pacioli's study, after twenty-three chapters devoted to the divine proportion, begins in its twenty-fourth a fresh treatise linked to the other by this tenuous transition: 'As the said effects [of the divine proportion] aid in the consideration of the five regular solids...'; then, down to chapter LII, Pacioli explains how to draw the complicated figures representing the five solids—the *tetrahedron* with its four triangular facets, the *hexahedron* or cube, the *octahedron* with its eight triangular facets (a double pyramid with a square cross section), the *icosahedron* with twenty triangular facets (a double pyramid with decagonal cross section), and lastly the *dodecahedron*, which he stresses for his own special reasons, the fifth and, to him, the noblest of the solids, being formed of twelve pentagons. Apart from this last one, the regular solids owe little to the divine proportion which, expounded at such length in his first twenty-three chapters, is of hardly any help towards an understanding of the next part. The truth is, no doubt, that what confronts us is a fusion into a single book of two distinct treatises[22]: the *Divine Proportion*, which is Luca Pacioli's own original contribution,

20. There are editions by C. Winterberg (Strasburg, 1899) and G. Nicco Fasola (Florence, 1942), based on two manuscripts at Parma and Milan.

21. Edition by C. Winterberg, *Repert. für Kunstwiss.*, IV, 1882, pp. 33 ff.

22. Cf. Jordan, *Jahrbuch der Kgl. Preuss. Kunstsammlungen*, I, 1880, p. 112. The author compares in parallel columns the text of Piero della Francesca with that of Luca Pacioli. The latter's text is more concise: there are close resemblances, but not an absolute identity.

and the *Five Pythagorean Solids*, a work shamelessly borrowed from his master and here unacknowledged.

The dishonesty of our friend the monk—with whose cunning face we are familiar from the Naples portrait already mentioned and from the one so candidly placed behind the Virgin in the *Pala Brera* by his good master—is here apparent. Pacioli quotes Piero and praises him in the dedication of his *Arithmetic*, which seems to be his own work, yet where he is copying Piero almost with servility he does not even name him. In short, Pacioli was a popularizer: old ideas or new ones, ideas guarded among the traditions of the corporations or buried in the manuscripts in libraries—all was grist to his mill.

To conclude: it is clear that the *Divine Proportion* is not by Piero della Francesca, or in any case does not figure in the manuscripts left by him; Luca Pacioli was his pupil, and the ideas revealed by him in his book, ideas that went back a long way, were well known to Piero, but not a major preoccupation of his. Piero was opposed to complication, and what he did was to carry out the synthesis between the old elements of medieval geometry and the new ideas of the theorists of his own time, giving his preference definitely to the simplest divisions of the surface.

We shall find confirmation of this when we analyze his works. Let us first look at the admirable series adorning the square choir of San Francesco at Arezzo. Two walls facing each other on the west and on the east, to right and to left of the window, bear three bands of frescoes. These two walls are cut from top to bottom by a light-coloured vertical stripe, which is sometimes discreetly indicated by a void but can always be felt: it marks out the middle of the wall and serves as an axis to the panels as a whole. On the west wall, this vertical axis follows the outline of the tree in the *Death of Adam* and is then frankly stressed by the left edge of the column of Solomon's palace and by the lowered muzzle of Constantine's horse. On the east wall, it is a naked strip between the Cross and the tree, between the two groups of people face to face, a sort of band of void that continues in the *Finding of the True Cross*, where it runs along the wall of the church—that astonishing Albertian façade—and then, in the mêlée of the *Battle of Heraclius*, follows the pole of a standard.

To find in this great geometer-painter the strictest observation of the monumental laws is not surprising. The scale of the figures is well chosen, the monumental perspective extremely strict: the upper scenes are silhouetted against open sky, the middle bands have a very low vanishing point, level with the knees of the figures, and the battle pictures at the bottom (though this can only be seen clearly in that of Constantine, on the west wall, since the other is too crowded) have a higher ground level which puts the horizon almost halfway up the scene[23].

A respect for the architecture of the church is also evident in the composition: it is the reason for the vertical axis, which falls from the top of the lunette.

23. Cf. p. 25 above.

Piero della Francesca: Virgin and Child with Saints. *This picture, divided into two in both its height and its breadth, is also a composition on the ratio 2/3; and its vertical, motionless figures are inscribed in a circle. It is the architecture that immediately reveals these peculiarities: the dark band comes at two-thirds of the height; the two circles given by the vault cut another circle with its centre at the lower third of the height, and in this are inscribed two hexagons. If the sides of one of the hexagons are prolonged till they meet and form a triangle, its apex determines the height of the vault. And so, in spite of an apparent recession in space, the composition is as monolithic as a Pythagorean solid. (Milan, Brera. Photo Anderson)*

But consider now in more detail the two scenes situated halfway up the walls: their arrangement turns out to be one of the simplest—they are each divided into two halves, as we have seen, and these two halves are in turn divided into two, but more discreetly. The cut in the middle is stressed by the central vanishing point and the gravity of the architecture: both the cornice of Solomon's palace, on the right, and that of the church, on the left, fall vertically upon the axis. But it is curious to note that the two frescoes have been designed on the same architectural scheme. The light-coloured column in the middle on the right corresponds to the void space that runs along the church in the left-hand fresco; the ceiling beams of Solomon's palace, at first in perspective and separated by two columns, then forming two horizontal strips, recur at exactly the same place in the other fresco—except that the beams are replaced by the slant of the roofs and the two horizontal lines of the church, and the columns by the luminous vertical lines of the houses.

The *Annunciation* (on the window wall) is also divided into two equal parts by a column, exactly divided by a horizontal beam barring the bay of the storey above the Virgin. The whole scene is an assemblage of squares and semicircles and has a diagrammatic strictness.

Its pendant, the *Dream of Constantine*, is composed upon a circle touching the sides and resting on the line that would divide the height into three. A division of the lower and upper thirds into two parts establishes the bottom of the bed and the top of the circle. Many painters have used geometrical diagrams: in the work of some of them the result has been a monotonous symmetry, but others have striven to hide the guiding points under an appearance of anecdotal spontaneity. There is not one whose whole work is as deeply permeated by a geometrical conception of beauty. The figures—simple solids forming harmonious masses—are not submitting as though with reluctance to the exigencies of a scheme, but they express it and embody it. Here the circle and the simplest divisions of the surface are one with the bed, the tent, the impassive watchers.

Piero della Francesca remained always faithful to the system of division by the small numbers, by 2/3/4, in accordance with Alberti's principle. We shall see, nonetheless, that his last work is a more complex composition, based on the hexagon.

The *Baptism of Christ* (National Gallery, London) is constructed upon the number three. Its breadth is divided into three, with axes falling upon the right edge of the tree and the left side of St John (which stretches upwards along the vertical). Its height is divided also into three, or, more exactly, into two if we merely consider the rectangular part, which has a ratio 2/3. The semicircle on top of it, forming its third part, is in reality a complete circle which we can follow along the left arm of St John and the upper curve of the loin cloth of the Christ. The dove, perfectly horizontal, shows us the exact position of the top of the rectangle and the centre of the circle. This composition is so simple that it recalls those of the miniatures of the early Middle Ages[24].

24. Cf. p. 54.

Piero della Francesca: Baptism of Christ.
Following Alberti's example the composition is built on a low ratio grid. The tree trunk divides the total width in the ratio 2/3 and the dove is placed in the same ratio to the height. Notice how the circle continues in the line of St John's arms. The diagonals of the lower rectangle are also important. (London, National Gallery. Photo Anderson)

The Borgo San Sepolcro *Resurrection* is constructed upon exactly the same scheme: division of the height and of the breadth into three, with a clearly marked median axis. The slanting lines start from the base of this axis.

Let us give slightly more time to the Urbino *Flagellation*. Its architecture recalls that of the *Queen of Sheba*, but the general impression is very different. Here there is something singular about the composition, in contrast to the other's squareness and restfulness. Sir Kenneth Clark has felt this, and has looked for an explanation which is highly complicated[25]. In point of fact it is the iconography that is strange—three secondary personages being placed in the foreground, while Christ, much farther away, is only pointed at, so to speak, by the slanting lines of the perspective. As for the composition, it recalls very closely that of the Ghirlandaio frescoes in Santa Maria Novella, an architectural feature cutting across it in the same way, not in the centre but near it. One may expect, therefore, to find a musical division here, too, and in fact the picture is divided in accordance with the double diapente: 4/6/9. As we have seen in other examples, this division stresses the principal person: a line 4/9 of the way from the right coincides with the column and the edge of the man's cloak, and a line 6/9 of the way from the right falls upon the Christ, who is thus designated for our attention by the harmony of numbers.

The *Pala Brera*, which he executed for the Convent of San Bernardino near Urbino and which is now in the Brera at Milan, is the last known picture by Piero della Francesca. The colouring is dull; perhaps the artist's sight had grown weak; he did indeed seek assistance for the painting of the hands. But the picture is certainly his, conceived and thought out by him alone, and it may be considered as his last will and testament in painting. It is a composition based on the 'regular solids' and on the small numbers, 2 and 3. Its breadth to its height is as 2 to 3, a ratio discreetly recalled in the vault, which has 6 coffers in one direction and 9 in the other (6/9 = 2/3). The vertical median axis is stressed by the mysterious thread on which there hangs an egg: it is the axis of the Virgin, upon whose head converge the lines of the perspective. The whole picture is organized by means of two intersecting circles—a large one below, in which are inscribed two hexagons, and a small one above, defined by the niche. Their radii are also in the ratio 2 to 3. The apothem of the hexagon is equal to the staff carried by the figure on the left.

The consonances in the sixteenth century

Thus Piero della Francesca, being both painter and geometer, realized a wonderful fusion between his two visions of the world, different as they were. His world, purified by geometry, is as solid and luminous as a crystal.

25. *Op. cit.*, p. 20.

Piero della Francesca: The Flagellation. *An example of two schemes superimposed. The architecture and the perspective are established by folding the short sides over: the positioning of the pavement stones, of the columns in the foreground, of the height of the room and of the bands of the ceiling—all are derived from this scheme. But the figures are distributed according to the musical ratio 4/6/9, starting from the right: 4 falls at the limit of the three men standing in the foreground, 6 falls upon the Christ. These divisions add to the strictness of geometry a more subtle harmony. It can be seen, for instance, that the diagonal of the square on the left, which follows the beam of the ceiling and the edge of the white strip of pavement, is broken by the man wearing a* mazzocchio *on his head: by a curious optical illusion this sends the perspective askew. (Urbino, Palazzo Ducale. Photo Anderson)*

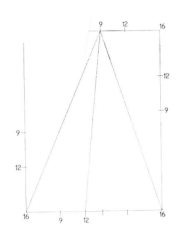

Raphael: Portrait of Joan of Aragon.
The refined arabesque and the long negligent hand with its Michelangelesque influence make this picture a forerunner of early Mannerism. The figure is placed on a slightly sloping axis which answers to the caesuras 9 of the musical ratio 9/12/16, taken on the right at the top and on the left at the bottom. (Paris, Louvre. Archives photographiques)

Raphael, on the contrary, was nothing but an artist: he refused to encumber himself with anything that might complicate his art, which blossomed like some splendid plant. With his open disposition, welcoming novelty yet remaining balanced, Raphael was aware of all the ideas of his time, appreciated them, yet kept his freedom and varied his type of composition according to circumstances. In consequence we cannot study him *en bloc* like Piero della Francesca, but must keep coming back to him. For the moment let us look at the use he managed to make of the musical proportions.

The striking proof that he was aware of them and understood their application is the eminent place he gave them in that representation of philosophical doctrines face to face known as the *School of Athens*. In the left corner Pythagoras is writing in a large book; by his side two other philosophers are gazing with excited attention at a panel which a boy is holding up before the master. On this panel there appears, precisely, the diagram of the musical consonances with, in Greek, the indications 'tone', 'diatessaron', 'diapente', 'diapason', illustrated in the clearest possible way by the following ratios: diatessaron, 6/8 and 9/12; diapente, 6/9 and 8/12; diapason or octave, 6/12. Below them is the number ten, which is obtained by adding together the first four whole numbers[26].

Is it not significant that we should find the diagram of the musical proportions in a painting—it is the only case, to my knowledge—and that the painter who exhibits it should be Raphael? In this marvellous fresco Harmony is on the left, Geometry on the right (in the form of a figure traced on the ground), and in the centre Plato, with the *Timaeus* in his hand, represents the philosophical synthesis of beauty.

The fresco itself is composed upon the diatessaron—upon the ratio 3/4. This is the division dominant in all the huge frescoes of the Vatican *Stanze*. It is particularly clear in the *Fire in the Borgo*, but can be found also in the *Disputà*, in the *Heliodorus*, etc. It is an extremely simple division: the breadth is cut into four, the height into three. By re-establishing the rectangle with its inscribed semicircle, one finds, here again, the armature of the frame in one of its most natural applications. Raphael, while aware of all the musical relationships, as the diagram just mentioned proves, employs only simple relationships in his great compositions: he finds the divisions 2/3 or 3/4 very often useful. See, for example, the cartoons for tapestries and some of his Madonnas (the *Orléans Madonna*, the *Belvedere Madonna*). In his portraits, however, he uses the divisions 4/6/9 or 9/12/16, whose subtly displaced accents have more charm; it is here that composition is really musical and no longer in servitude to the frame (cf. the *Baldassare Castiglione* in the Louvre, the *Giuliano de' Medici* at Berlin, the portrait of an *Unknown Man* at Cracow and the *Joan of Aragon* in the Louvre).

Leonardo da Vinci is the most secret and most scientific artist we have yet approached. He had a passion for music and speaks with great subtlety

26. Wittkower, *op. cit.*, p. 109.

Raphael: School of Athens, *detail. The musical ratios, which by tradition go back to Pythagoras, are here offered by one of his young pupils to the philosophers for their approval. At the top of the tablet is written the word* ΕΠΟΓΛΟΩΝ, *standing certainly for* ΝΕΠΟΓΔΩΝ, *the word used in the* Timaeus *for a whole augmented by an eighth of itself—that is to say, the interval of a tone, as measured on the string. (Cf. Alberti, Chapter V, as summarized on p. 83 above).*

Below it come the words ΔΙΑΤΕΣΣΑΡΩΝ (diatessaron), ΔΙΑΠΕΝΤΕ *(diapente) and* ΔΙΑΠΑΕΩΝ *(diapason), so arranged that the diatessaron (ratio 3/4) binds 6 to 8 and 9 to 12, the diapente (ratio 2/3) binds 6 to 9 and 8 to 12, and the diapason (octave 1/2) binds 6 to 12. At the bottom the triangle of the four first whole numbers, whose total is ten, recalls the preference of Alberti's followers for these small numbers. (Rome, Vatican. Photo Anderson)*

of its relations with painting, but his way of looking at those relationships is certainly a peculiar one[27]. His meditations on all subjects were too profound and too hidden for us to pretend to reconstruct them. Nonetheless the *Last Supper*, the only monumental composition of his to have come down to us, follows a simple arrangement. It is a figure of the diapason, the double square; but, since the composition is centred on the Christ, the diagram includes a central square between two half squares. In the central square is inscribed a small square of which the top corresponds to the height of the lateral panels of the room: this is limited to right and left by the windows and at the bottom by the edge of the table. If the circle indicated above the central bay is continued, it forms a wide halo about the head of the Christ. The diagonals of the rectangle give the perspective of the top line of the room's lateral panels, and this perspective converges on the body of Jesus.

But it is no good trying to relate Leonardo da Vinci to his contemporaries. Leonardo was, above all, a lone wolf. He imitated no model, he was unwilling to look to any master or to anyone else's work, but only to nature itself,—and then not to copy it, definitely not, but to wrest from it its secrets. In his famous *Treatise on Painting*, in the chapter about colour, he is singularly in advance of his time—as he was in everything he touched. Some of his remarks might have been signed 'Delacroix', others 'Cézanne' or 'Gauguin'[28]. All the problems of painting in our own time are studied

27. Leonardo tells the story of King Mathias who on his birthday, when a poet presented to him a poem in his honour and a painter a portrait of his beloved, preferred the painting, and said to the poet: 'Do you not see that, in your science, there is no proportion created at a[given] instant, but one part is born from the other successively and the next is not born unless the former dies? For this reason I judge your work of art to be distinctly inferior to the painter's, simply because no harmonic proportion is composed by yours.' (Cf. *Paragone*, Oxford, 1949; p. 68.)

28. 'Of several colours, all equally white, that will look whitest which is against the darkest background. And black will look most intense against the whitest background. And red will look most vivid against the yellowest background, and the same is the case with all colours when surrounded by the strongest contrasts.' (*Literary Works*, ed. J.P. Richter; Oxford, 1938, vol. I, p. 227.) 'The light which illuminates the blue [object], having a yellow tinge, produces the same effect as mixing together blue and yellow, which compose a beautiful green.' (*Treatise on Painting*, codex urbinas; translated by A. Philip McMahon; Princeton, 1956, vol. I, p. 87.)

there, and the solution given by Leonardo is valid. What is curious is that no trace of all this remains visible in his painting. Similarly he makes no use of his highly scientific perspective except in certain of his drawings, and he reserves for the backgrounds of his pictures those delicate gradations of shading and line which he himself called 'aerial perspective'.

Leonardo da Vinci: The Last Supper. *The central square, flanked by two half squares, is divided by the play of its diagonals into six in both directions. In this way two fresh squares, inscribed in each other, are formed. In the centre the small square encloses the Christ, its limits being the sides of the windows and the edge of the table. About this, the intermediate square sets the limits of the walls at the far end of the room. The height of the lateral panels is given by the diagonals of the rectangle. (Milan, Santa Maria delle Grazie. Photo Anderson)*

In his many wonderful drawings he allowed his imagination a much freer flight. He loved arcs and circles, and delighted in inserting his forms into their rings. In certain pen or pencil studies the many curves with which he enlaces the figures transform them into whorls. Tintoretto, taking up this kind of drawing, carried it on into his paintings and drew from it lyrical power, whereas Leonardo in his concealed all this work under a close, refined brushwork and made it into a mystery.

The studies and researches of the Quattrocento humanists were given a widespread influence by the printing of their books. So it came about that Alberti's *De re aedificatoria* had a more direct effect than his *De pictura*, which remained unpublished. In the same way Luca Pacioli reached a large public, while the works of his master, Piero della Francesca, were familiar only to a few privileged persons. But oral tradition, so active during the whole of the Middle Ages, had not yet lost its effectiveness.

There is a striking proof of this in a passage from one of Dürer's letters. In 1506, when he had been in Venice for a year and was thinking of going home, Dürer wrote to his friend Pirkheimer that he intended first to travel to Bologna 'for the sake of the art [of painting] in secret perspective, which someone is willing to teach me[29].' It was still, then, worth while in 1506 to make a journey in order to see and listen to a man for whose spoken words there was no substitute. The terms used here by Dürer are curious. Who was this man? Dürer does not tell us. And what does he mean by 'secret perspective'?

It has been supposed, and even asserted without proof, that what was meant was the golden number and that the man was Luca Pacioli. His book was not yet published but had been on paper for a long time. Also it is known that Pacioli had been teaching in the University of Bologna in 1501-1502. But this by no means proves that that great vagabond, who taught mathematics in so many cities of Italy, was still there in 1506. What is more, Dürer, brought up in the corporations like all the artists of the North, knew the golden number as well as Pacioli did. Indeed one has only to study his works a little to notice that he used the golden section very frequently at every period of his life, and especially in his youth. The *Apocalypse* wood engravings, which date from 1498, are composed upon this division, as are many of the paintings. The golden section could clearly be called 'secret' because it was not divulged outside the studios, but for Dürer it had not the attraction of a novelty, and he would surely not have made a long journey on horseback to hear someone talk about 'the divine proportion'. What he wanted to know was, on the contrary, one of the secrets of the Italian artists of the new school. He had already tried to discover one of these secrets by questioning Jacopo dei Barbari about the perfect proportions of the human body. If it is legitimate to take the word *perspective* in a sense that goes beyond the usually accepted one, it may at a pinch signify 'geometry applied to art': in this case, could not the mathematical proportions explored by the architects who came after Alberti be meant? Who then would the Bologna master be? Bramante has been suggested[30]: he stopped there for a short time in that year, in the course of a journey on which he accompanied Pope Julius II... It is possible, although it would make the meeting a very hurried one. To me it seems more likely that Dürer went there to question Sebastiano Serlio. Born at Bologna in 1475, that great theorist hardly left his native town before 1511, the date at which he is mentioned as painting 'perspectives' at Pesaro. Serlio, a fervent disciple of Alberti, had not yet published anything, he was young and little known, and might well have consented to teach a foreigner.

29. '*Ich bin in noch 10 Tagen hier fertig; darnach würde ich nach Bologna reiten um der Kunst in geheimer Perspective willen, die mich einer lehren will.*' Venice 13 Oct. 1506. (*Letters of Dürer*, published by M. Thausing, *Quellenschriften*... Vienna, 1872, pp. 21-22.) Cf. also: A. Dürer, *Records of the Journey to Venice and the Low Countries*, Boston, 1913.

30. W. Stechow, *Dürers Bologneser Lehrer. Kunstchronik, Neue Folge*, XXXIII (1922), pp. 251-252.

The authors of the books on Dürer have noted that the Italian influence on him is particularly marked after that journey. A first stay in Venice, when he was very young, had hardly modified his style at all: he remained a German of the Middle Ages. After his 1506 journey, on the contrary, there is a visible change in him. But this change is not the simple effect of Venetian painting, and perhaps no one has yet brought out its real profundity: it amounts to an initiation, which marked Dürer for the rest of his life. Up to then, like many other German artists, he went in for tormented forms; his engravings were dense and had no empty spaces. All of a sudden the forms blossom freely in an airy space, balance one another without stiffness, and the purposeless picturesque disappears. From that time on, Dürer's works produce an impression of simplicity and calm which is a quite new thing in German art. His handling of the pencil or the graving tool remains the same: the change is in the spirit, not in the execution. It was his thought, his conception of art, that had matured in Italy and had taken a more philosophical turn. He had had revealed to him those proportions which, transferred from music to the other arts, supply the unity of the Beautiful.

It is very interesting to compare the engravings done before and after this journey. In the *Apocalypse* and in the *Life of the Virgin* nearly all the scenes dating from before 1506 are based on the golden number. In contrast, those two strange engravings, the *Penitence of David* and the *Beheading of John the Baptist*, which date from 1510, are divided according to the musical ratio 4/6/9. With their bare, almost abstract architecture, made up of wall expanses without doors or windows, they look like studies in pure composition: the calm of their large planes reminds us of the *loi des vides* and the *loi de la lenteur* of Florentine Albertism with their striking opposition to the Gothic accumulation of detail.

It was, then, a secret that Dürer brought back from Venice, and it is tempting to think that that was what he meant when he wrote to Pirkheimer. Serlio could have taught it to him (in book I of his *Architecture* Alberti's theory of areas is resumed), but Dürer could also have learnt it without leaving Venice, from one of the assistants of Carpaccio, Giorgione or Titian. If this was the case, then the 'secret perspective' of which the famous letter of 1506 speaks might simply be the theory of perspective, which he could have studied in Piero della Francesca's unpublished books, then circulating in manuscript copies[31]. As we shall see, this Italian perspective was not exactly the same as that of the Northern artists.

In any case Dürer is one of the most striking examples of conversion to the new theory. He became a pure humanist. His greed for knowledge and the powerful originality of his thinking enabled him to assimilate the ideas acquired in Italy. In a circle in which the Renaissance was still, on the whole, a bookish thing, he alone saw them clearly and felt them as an artist. Lastly, he grasped the contradiction between the new know-

31. Erwin Panofsky, *The Life and Art of Albrecht Dürer*, Princeton, 1955, p. 252.

ledge and that of the past, and in this he stands as a symbol of the divided mind of his time (*Melencolia I*).

Dürer has brought us to the Venetian artists, among whom he sought so eagerly for the secrets of the new art. It was to Venice, indeed, that the centre of humanism moved, towards the end of the fifteenth century, when Florence was recovering with difficulty from the shock caused by Savonarola and was also losing many of its painters to Rome. The great Venetian printers, those fervent humanists, preserved at Venice that spirit of the Renaissance which, in the cities where it had first blossomed, was now coming into conflict with other tendencies. Venetian publishing was a wonderful instrument which had suddenly, in the 1480s, reached a state of complete readiness for full-scale productivity, yet was short of nourishment. What was it to publish, other than the works of the past and certain books of popularization, resuming and rendering assimilable the already long-standing values of humanism? It gave those values a second crop of topical interest and delayed the onset of the lassitude and of the search for new emotions already visible at Florence. In addition, the presence in Venice of many foreign artists, contact with whom was to enrich the Venetian school, created a fresh reading public, naïve and full of enthusiasm.

So it came about, however paradoxically, that in Venice printing had on the whole a conservative effect, and that a city open to novelties was the last one that remained faithful to the spirit of the Quattrocento. Which, indeed, are the finest books printed by Jenson, the Gregorii brothers, Aldus Manutius and the others? Those of the ancient Greek and Latin authors, Petrarch, the *Hypnerotomachia*. This last, written to the glory of the ancient monuments in the enthusiastic yet austere spirit of Mantegna, maintained for a time at Venice—its French edition also, later on, had a far-reaching success—a taste that was already old-fashioned in the rest of Italy.

In 1525 Bernardo Vidali published in Venice the *De harmonia mundi totius* by the monk Francesco Giorgio, a book in which the whole of the musical philosophy was once again given expression. Wittkower very pertinently reminds us that in 1534 the same Giorgio commented on a project of the architect Sansovino in a memorandum in which he insisted on the rigorous application of the ratios of consonance[32]. What is particularly interesting is that Titian, called in along with two others to give his opinion on this memorandum, found nothing singular or arbitrary about it. This proves that the ideas which Dürer had come upon in Venice were still considered there as current and perfectly natural in the full tide of the sixteenth century.

32. *Op. cit.*, pp. 90 ff.

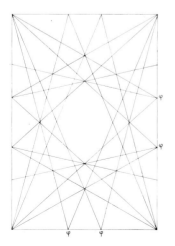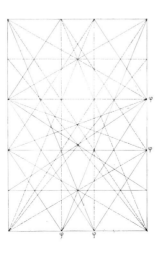

Dürer: The Apocalypse. *The Opening of the Sixth Seal.*

Dürer: Life of the Virgin, the Assumption.

Heir to a long line of artists trained in the guilds, Dürer used the golden ratio in almost all the wood engravings of the Apocalypse, which date from 1498, and in other works of this period. He never altogether abandoned this ratio. (Photos Giraudon)

Dürer: Beheading of St John the Baptist.

Dürer: Penitence of David.

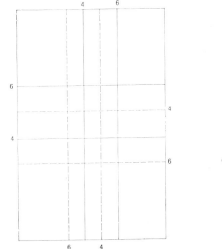
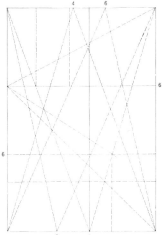

These two wood engravings were done after the Italian journey. The Gothic spirit still dominant in the Apocalypse has vanished: it has given place to a purely Albertian conception. Is it not strange to find that certain points of the underlying framework of these engravings are based on the musical ratio? (Photos Giraudon)

Titian: Presentation of the Virgin in the Temple. *A great rectangle subjected to division in accordance with the diapason-diapente, a proportion reserved by Alberti for 'large areas' in the precise form of 3/6/9. The 1/9 sections give the architecture its rhythm; the vanishing point of the perspective comes at the third vertical division on the left; and the child Virgin stands at the place where the sixth vertical division crosses the sixth horizontal one. (Venice, Accademia. Photo Anderson)*

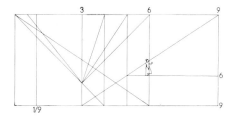

It was roughly at the time of this memorandum that Titian composed his *Presentation of the Virgin in the Temple* (Venice, Accademia), a work in which the musical proportions are applied with notable assurance; the architecture, the perspective and the position of the child Virgin on the steps are established by the diapason-diapente ratio, 3/6/9, and this gives to the whole work that simple and restful nobility which, as much as strictness of ratio, is music according to Alberti.

These same ratios are to be found in other pictures by Titian, especially in those that are most calm, most classical, least affected by the modern '*furia*' which was to draw the splendid works of his ripe age on towards a whole new conception of art. His youthful pictures of *Bacchanals* (in the Prado and in London) have their grouping and movement governed very precisely by lines drawn to the points 4/6/9 on the sides of the rectangle; and the figures in them, as though plotted by a ballet master, dance in their exact places and are careful, in their whirling, not to disturb the ratios. His *Resurrection*, which owes so much to Piero della Francesca, is composed like a work of the Quattrocento: the divisions here are at 9/12/16 (the double diatessaron). But his renderings of *Venus* are still more interesting, because in them one finds an extremely subtle alliance of the musical relationships and the circle. The *Venus with the Organ Player*, in the Prado, is constructed on the 4/6/9 ratio, which is one of the most common in Titian, and the arc of the circle on which Venus softly reclines as in a hammock has its centre upon one of the musical divisions—4 from the right. All these pictures of Venus derive from that of Giorgione in the Dresden Museum, an inimitable prototype although so often imitated; and this is composed in the same way: the arc on which Venus reposes is

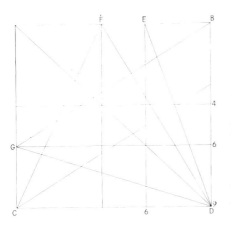

centred upon the division 9 or the ratio 9/12/16, a division which, in the other direction, gives the horizon line of the landscape.

Meanwhile, in Florence and in Lombardy, it was the heyday of what has come to be called Mannerism—a rather too simple label, which does not fit the traditional artists or the independent ones, though it characterizes the fashionable style rather well. In 1584 Lomazzo published at Milan his *Trattato dell'arte della pittura*, which is the codification of the new school. We shall see later, when we come to study dynamic and sinuous compositions, that Lomazzo's position is as far removed as it could well be from Alberti's aesthetic; nonetheless, Lomazzo mentions the musical consonances and quotes that great theorist of the past[33]. What is more, he uses, without feeling any need to explain them, expressions of the musical terminology derived from the *Timaeus*, which Alberti had made current.

33. Bk I, ch. iii, p. 33. The references are to the original edition (Milan, 1584), but there is another good edition (Milan, 1844). Reference is also made to the English edition of 1598 where possible; this, however, comprises only the first five books.

Titian: Bacchus and Ariadne. *Ratio 4/6/9. Bacchus is on the caesura 4, taken from the left. The same caesura, taken from the top, establishes the stature of the figures. The vertical caesura 6 determines the positioning of the tree trunk; the sloping line ED, drawn from this caesura 6 on the top side to the bottom right-hand corner of the rectangle, gives the thyrsus held by the figure on the right. The sloping line FC, drawn from the top of the caesura 4 to the bottom left-hand corner, governs Ariadne's leg and her movement in walking. The sloping line BG, from the top right-hand corner to caesura 6 down the left-hand side, gives the line of Bacchus's flight towards Ariadne and Ariadne's movement of fear. (London, National Gallery. Photo Anderson)*

It is true that these expressions are already to be found in Vitruvius, of whom excellent editions with good commentaries were circulating everywhere in the sixteenth century; but in him they have a very restricted meaning and are applied only to the proportions of the human body and of columns. It was in this sense, indeed, that Lomazzo wrote:

'*Proportion is a correspondencie [consonanza] and agreement of the measures of the partes betweene themselves, and with the whole, in every worke.* This correspondencie is by *Vitruvius* called *Commodulation*' (I, iv, p. 35; p. 27; English version, 1598). But it is more on Alberti, who generalized the use of the consonances, and on Alberti's followers like Serlio, that Lomazzo bases his thought when he writes that in the proportions of a church the architect finds the diapason consonance; and he mentions Peruzzi's drawings for Serlio's book V (I, xxviii, p. 97). Again, Lomazzo has painting constantly, indeed chiefly, in mind:

'Such is the importance and vertue of *Proportion*, that nothing can any way satifie the eie, without the helpe thereof' (I, iii, p. 32; English, p. 25). And 'I speke of such who not knowing the vertue of proportion, affect nothing else but the vaine surface of garish colours, wrought after their owne humor, who proove onely dawbers of Images and walles throughout the whole worlde; mooving the beholders partly to smile at their follies, and partly to greive that the arte should be thus disgraced by such absurde Idiotes...' (I, iv, p. 35; English, p. 28).

This explosion of anger shows the importance Lomazzo attaches to the science of proportions, the respect he has for 'those who are familiar with it'—and at the same time the vagueness, the extreme imprecision of his teaching. In it there is more the remembrance of a science than any real science: the decadence of Albertism is beginning.

Titian: Venus with the Organ Player. *The double diapente both from the right (4/6/9) and from the bottom (4'/6'/9'). Caesura 4 gives the axis for the fountain, and its intersection with a sloping line AB, which joins caesura 4' to the top right-hand corner, fixes the centre of the circle on whose arc Venus is lying. The radius of this circle is not a matter of indifference: it is established by the distance to the centre from point X, the point of intersection of caesura 6 with the sloping line DE which joins the bottom left-hand corner to caesura 6' on the right. This sloping line is also the chord of the arc within which Venus lies. (Madrid, Prado. Photo Anderson)*

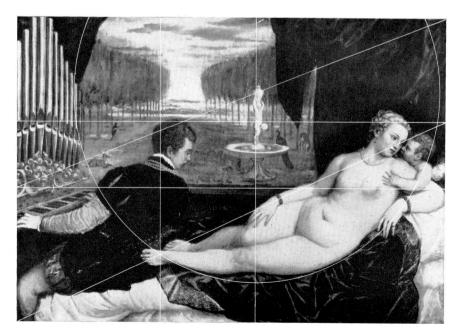

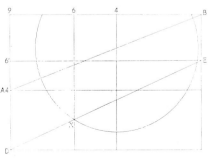

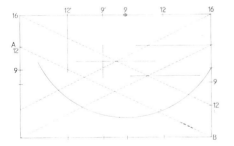

Giorgione: Venus. *This picture had a considerable influence on the Venetian school. It is remarkable for its strictness and simplicity. In it the ratio 9/12/16 is taken in both directions on each side of the canvas, as in Mantegna's* Parnassus, *giving four caesuras on each side. The sloping line from* A *on the left to the bottom right-hand corner* B *forms the chord of the arc determining the body of Venus. (Dresden Museum. Photo Alinari)*

The Academies and music

In the great artists of the second half of the sixteenth and of the early seventeenth centuries, awareness of the musical proportions remained more or less clear, but the use of them became occasional, and what then survived was the method alone, detached from the style of which it had been an emanation and an essential aspect.

Tintoretto, in his *Presentation of the Virgin in the Temple*, takes up again Titian's moving idea, the child all alone on the steps, and, like him, places the little girl in accordance with the musical proportions (at the 12 of the 9/12/16 ratio of the breadth, and at a height between 9 and 12 of the same ratio). But how different the two works are: what a breath of modernism, in the later one, sets the perspective swaying, accentuates the slanting lines and casts theatrical shadows! Titian's picture was still Albertian; this no longer is.

Tintoretto uses this same ratio several times: for instance in the *Christ in Limbo* (Venice, San Cassiano) and in the *Brazen Serpent* (Venice, San

Rocco). Veronese preferred the ratio 4/6/9 (the *Supper at Emmaus* in the Louvre); though less bold than Tintoretto in his compositions, he nonetheless juggles with the various linear systems and mingles them gaily in one and the same picture. This is already eclecticism; and in fact, at the Academy of Bologna, where eclecticism was the rule, we shall find a complete awareness of all the methods of composition in use at that time: thus Annibale Carracci's *S. Rocco Distributing Alms* at Dresden, a considerable composition with a great many figures, is arranged at the same time on the armature of the rectangle and on the ratio 9/12/16.

Poussin was a thinker, or rather a markedly reflective painter. But his thought was still somewhat imprecise, as Sir Anthony Blunt[34] has shown clearly, and from the considerations to be found here and there in his correspondence it is difficult to extract a new theory of art.

Poussin uses the musical ratios infrequently, and then in a way that is entirely his own. He seems to have taken a formula which he regarded as too complicated and transformed it to his own use, reducing it to two terms: those he prefers are the ratios 9/16 starting from the left and 4/9 from the right, ratios that come very close to each other. One habit of which he is fond is that of making a whole bundle of lines converge towards a single point in the picture, often designated by the perspective. In the *Philistines struck by the Plague* (Louvre) the vanishing point, situated on the rabatment of the shorter sides of the rectangle, divides the whole composition into convergent sectors. Often this point is designated by the musical ratio: this is so in the *Rape of the Sabines* (Louvre) in which the point from which the lines radiate comes at the 9/16 ratio in both dimensions. This point, which is slightly to the left in the Louvre pictures, is placed according to the same ratio but to the right in the Richmond *Rape of the Sabines*[35] and in both these pictures the figures, as we shall see, respond to a different rhythm.

Poussin's awareness of the musical consonances can, I think, be deduced from his painting, but he himself never mentions music except to praise (in this he follows Zarlino) the ancient modes[36]. We have also an indirect proof of it in the reports of the conferences of the Académie royale de Peinture et de Sculpture.

In 1669 Félibien published an account of the lectures of 1667[37]; and in the preface, taking Poussin as his authority, he ventures a comparison between painting and music:

34. *Bulletin de la Société d'Histoire de l'art français*, 1933, p. 125.
35. Now in New York, Metropolitan Museum.
36. Letter to Chantelou, 24 November 1647.
37. *Conférences de l'Académie royale de peinture et de sculpture pendant l'année 1667* (by Félibien), Paris, 1669.

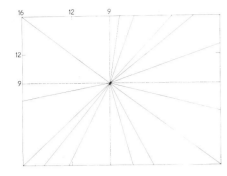

Poussin: Rape of the Sabines. *Poussin seems to have been fond of confirming the importance of a point by making it the vanishing point of the perspective. Sometimes this point will be established by the golden ratio, sometimes by some other measure; in this case, by the ratio 9/16 in both directions. (Paris, Louvre. Photo Giraudon)*

'The soul that loves proportion and equality takes more pleasure in the sounds of instruments and in the accents of voices in which the numbers are whole, and in which there is less dissonance. So also painting of which the whole beauty consists in symmetry and fine proportion... '

Consonances, equality, sounds in which the numbers are whole, proportion—these are words that to us have a quite precise meaning, but it is rather unlikely that Félibien wholly understood it.

The idea was taken up again in the following year by Le Brun (in the *Relation de Guillet de Saint-Georges*[38]), and this time we find an even more vague reflection of the master's ideas:

'M. Le Brun also reminded the Académie of an observation he had made some time before on all the works of M. Poussin... He said that M. Poussin, conforming to the harmonic proportion which musicians observe in their compositions, desired that in his pictures all things should contain reciprocal harmonies and should conspire to the same end...'

38. Paris, Ecole des Beaux-Arts, manuscript 138; and Fontaine, *Conférences inédites de l'Académie royale de peinture et de sculpture*, Paris, no date, p. 117.

Le Brun adds his own reflections on Poussin's application of the theory of modes (taken from the famous letter to Chantelou) in his pictures of *Rebecca* and of the *Philistines*. He insists that he was the author of the comments in question, and with some bitterness reproaches Félibien with having 'dragged this observation into his preface to the conferences printed in 1669 without specifying from what source it came, as if he had been afraid to quote an obscure name that would be unworthy of the preface'.

In reality, apart from the considerations on the modes, it seems rather to have been Le Brun who was borrowing from Félibien: Félibien had known Poussin well and was engaged in writing his moving *Life* of the great painter, which he published in 1685[39]. 'It is as if I can still see him,' he was to write; and, a little farther on: 'I was still in Rome when the idea [of the *Rebecca*] came to him'—that is to say, in 1648.

Fifty years later Coypel, in his *Discours*[40], again speaks of music, and not without taste. He makes acute observations on the part played by dissonances[41], but here the comparison with painting is already on a quite different plane: Coypel is no longer dealing with proportion, that basis common to the two arts, but contents himself with an entirely literary image, which is like the use of the words 'brilliant colouring' or 'subdued shades', etc. to describe the execution of a piece of music[42].

Here the part played by the musical consonances in painting is practically at an end. In architecture they were to prolong their influence, or at least their prestige, for some time. The great controversy between Blondel and Perrault was concerned, precisely, with their value and whether or not they should be taught. A late and final echo of that controversy, which had produced so much emotion in the Académie, is to be found in the curious *Traité du Beau essentiel* by Briseux[43], a fanatical partisan of Blondel, who resumes the whole history of the consonances from Vitruvius and Alberti onwards. Perrault, on the contrary, said that 'the proportions are not a natural thing, but have merely been established by a surrender on the part of those architects who have imitated the works of various others... These proportions can be replaced by others; all depends on taste, experience and intelligence.'[44]

39. Félibien, *Entretiens sur les vies et sur les ouvrages des plus excellens peintres...* Paris, 1666-1685, 4th part, pp. 318 and 342.

40. Antoine Coypel, 1661-1722, *Discours prononcés dans les conférences de l'Académie royale de peinture et de sculpture*, Paris, 1721.

41. *Op. cit.*, p. 10: 'The perfect harmonies in music must be rendered in a picture by a perfect sympathy of colours; and the great painter must, just as much as the musician, make a proper use of dissonances, which are strong oppositions of chiaroscuro and of colours, and, in order to wake up his picture from time to time, fill it with an agreeable variety that ravishes, astonishes and takes the spectator unawares.'

42. 'Has not the painter, just like the musician, his treble, alto, tenor and bass, sometimes produced by the gradations of his lights and of his browns, and at other times by the shadings of the colours?' *(op. cit.)*

43. C.-E. Briseux, *Traité du Beau essentiel dans les arts...*, Paris, 1752.

44. Quoted by Briseux, *op. cit.*, in his preface.

These words have a distinctly modern ring, or perhaps, more simply, a breath of common sense. The musical consonances were an idea of the humanist Renaissance, which saw in them a means of unifying and rationalizing the arts; they now became no more than a doctrine imposed by authority, accepted blindly, and without value to the really thoughtful.

V GEOMETRY AFTER THE MIDDLE AGES

When we turned aside to follow the new invention of the Florentine humanists down to its final stages, the various aspects of geometry and the application to painting of diagrams drawn with rulers or compasses were left by us at the point they had reached at the climax of the Middle Ages. But it would be wrong to forget them: even the painters who had adopted the ideas of Alberti with enthusiasm, even those most under the spell of the asymmetrical rhythm and equilibrium created by the musical ratios, continued for the most part to use the simple, regular and perfect elements made available to them by geometry.

Perspective as geometry

One discipline connected with painting makes constant use of the data of geometry: this is perspective. We have already come across it, and now must devote a little time to it. So-called 'rational' perspective, here opposed to those types of perspective that are simply expressive, had perhaps been known in Antiquity[1], but had been lost; it was rediscovered simultaneously in the North and in the South between 1415 and 1430—in the North empirically, with the Van Eycks, in the South mathematically, in Florence.

The fantastic and charming perspective of the *Très riches Heures*, with the multiple vanishing points, gave place to the perfect perspective of the *Turin Book of Hours*. In Van Eyck's *Virgin* in the Louvre and in the London double portrait (1426-1434) the vanishing point is at the level of the heads, but the ground still rises too much—that is to say, the space is too great and is seen as though in a convex mirror. The miniature-painting of the period had produced a taste for the picture as microcosm, and exact perspective had had to compete with imaginative perspectives that were more supple and held a wealth of infinite possibilities (cf. p. 63).

Van Eyck was a marvellous eye: in Florence, on the contrary, they were intellectualists. Diagrams of perspective were laid down, based on Euclid's *Optics* and on the work of the medieval mathematicians such as Grosseteste

Jacopo Bellini: Page from book of drawings. *The horizontal tie-rod bisects the drawing. The intersection of the diagonals of the lower rectangle is the vanishing point of the whole of the architecture. (Paris, Louvre, Cabinet des Dessins)*

1. Euclid, who sometimes takes up again branches of knowledge dating from well before his time, speaks of the visual pyramid and the optical angles; but these conceptions had hardly found their way into the world of painting.

Woodcut, Lombard, 15th century.
(*Paris, Ecole des Beaux-Arts. Photo Seuil*)

and Bacon which it would never have occurred to the Northern artists to use. Brunelleschi was the first to teach mathematical perspective: he transmitted it to Masaccio (who died in 1427) and to Donatello (the Siena bas-reliefs, 1428); and by about 1435, after Ghiberti, they were all using it, even Fra Angelico, and it was then that its first codification appeared—Alberti's *De pictura*. Perspective occupies only one chapter of that book; but after the profound studies of it by Paolo Uccello and Piero della Francesca, it was to be the sole subject of the latter's manuscript, *De prospectiva pingendi*.

It happens that perspective is not only an effort to construct space: it can also create an illusion, or even take the place of geometrical composition. It is often a source of illusion in the work of the Northern painters, who avail themselves of its almost magical powers of evocation.

The perspective 'of the Italian type', on the contrary, is more linear and abstract, and encloses the forms of a picture in a network of straight lines converging at a point, like a spider's web. The artists were certainly struck by the decorative power of this network (there is no need to insist on the use they made of pavements with their multitude of lozenges); it may well have suggested to them a thousand curious combinations; and artists of our time being more superficial would not have failed to avail themselves of this strange net and to extract from it original effects. But the artists of the fifteenth century were serious, they would have despised what seems to us 'curious' or 'amusing', and in their hands the serried lines of the perspective were made to contribute to the composition rather than to decoration.

In the British Museum and Louvre drawing books of Jacopo Bellini, whose date cannot be put later than 1450, the vanishing point is central and the lines of recession coincide with the diagonals, openly giving the whole composition its axes. Much more virtuosity is to be found in Leonardo da Vinci. Perspective fascinated him, as did everything that appealed to the intelligence; and his drawing for an *Adoration of the Shepherds* in the Uffizi is furrowed with converging lines which construct the perspective of the site in which the figures are grouped: it is obvious that these lines influenced the composition and that Leonardo could not detach his mind from them. In Florence, the home of new learning, examples abound. In the paintings of Paolo Uccello the vanishing point is still at the centre, and the perspective coincides with the geometrical composition (as in the *St George and the Dragon* and the three pictures of the *Battle of San Romano*). As we have seen, much the same is true of Piero della Francesca: the vanishing point falls on the main division of the composition, and the perspective accentuates, confirms, the artist's abstract intentions.

I shall conclude these observations by recalling the charming *tondo* by Botticini (cf. p. 39), which pins down the vanishing point at the centre of the circle, as though on the hub of a wheel.

Thus perspective became, through its many applications, synonymous with geometry; and if this is what Dürer went to Bologna in search of, his curiosity is amply explained: the study of this science, bringing the study of geometry along with it, opened a whole world to the artist.

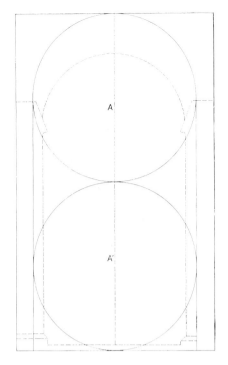

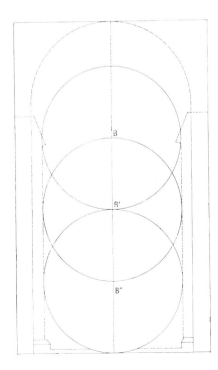

Pinturicchio: Life of Aeneas Silvius.
*All these compositions are based both on two
series of circles and on the rectangle. In the
following analyses let A and A' be the large
circles drawn within the outer arch, and B,
B' and B" the circles drawn in the inner arch.
(Siena Cathedral Library. Photo Giraudon)*

In the Middle Ages the 'geometry' of a work of art, whether picture, bas-relief or page of manuscript, consisted chiefly in the use of the regular polygons as an armature, as an interior framework, figures that were sometimes quite complicated, with five, six or eight sides, not forgetting the double figures formed by the star pentagons and hexagons. The ingenious play of these fitted in perfectly with Gothic taste, and it is not surprising to see them abandoned in favour of simpler schemes at the period of the Renaissance.

The circle is one of the figures most favoured by the architects of the Quattrocento. Its purity, its simplicity and also the symbolism that can be attached to it—all these helped to make it the favourite design for the ground-plans of churches, for the ornamentation of façades, and so on.

Pinturicchio's frescoes in the Library of Siena Cathedral, devoted to the *Life of Aeneas Silvius* (who became Pope Pius II), provide us with the example of a great series composed throughout on circles, although this does not exclude a constant use of the armature of the rectangle also. The painted vault framing each scene gives the dimensions of two series of circles according as to whether the outer or inner arch is taken as measure. Using the larger arch two equal circles may be drawn, touching at exactly the vanishing point of the perspective; using the smaller arch, two smaller circles, together with a third, of the same radius, centred at the point where they touch. The curvature of these circles or their points of intersection establish in the most striking way the architecture and the grouping of each scene.

It should be observed that Pinturicchio, though his designs are simpler, composed in exactly the same manner as the medieval artists. Just as the Master of the *Psalter of Blanche of Castille* had contrived to compose thirty-two different scenes on the same scheme (an octagon inscribed in a circle), and this without its seeming to worry him in the least, so Pinturicchio composed his ten frescoes upon the same scheme of circles, and if he had had to do thirty it would certainly not have worried him. In spite of its strictness, geometry as understood in the Middle Ages was no hindrance to the imagination. Pinturicchio was an artist of the past: the science of his period was not unknown to him, his perspective is current and his figures firmly planted, but his aesthetic was that of a different age. He submitted much more strictly than his contemporaries to that discipline which sat so lightly on the Middle Ages: it was to become more and more difficult to endure, and artists tended constantly to free themselves from it.

Raphael, who knew these frescoes well and may have taken part in the painting of them, must have made a long study of their composition. He loved simplicity, his limpid spirit did not seek mystery: it is therefore not surprising that he should have had a predilection for the simplest and most perfect geometrical figure. Apart from the *tondo*, that old form which he took up again with a rare felicity, he made a point of inscribing a circle (or even several circles) in the rectangular space of his Madonnas, who follow out its pure contour; and other subjects are treated by him according

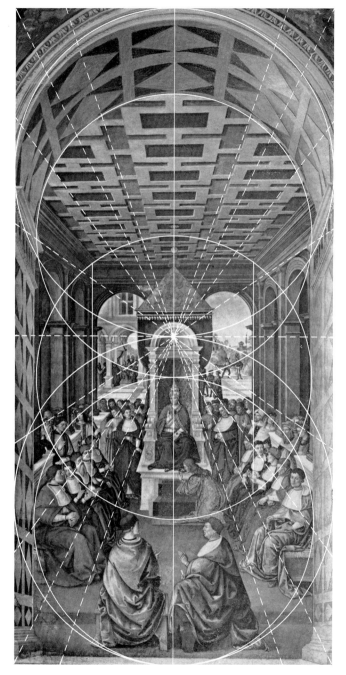

3rd Scene: Aeneas Silvius before the Emperor. *The sheaves of diagonals and other oblique lines distribute the figures of the foreground into triangular groups. The top of circle B' gives the base of the monument. The centre of circle A is at the apex of the architecture, whose lines are traced upon the armature of the rectangle.*

4th Scene: Aeneas Silvius before Pope Eugenio. *Same circles, same perspective. The rows of cardinals mirror the perspective of the ceiling beams. The lower part of the picture is governed by circles B' and B", and the bay at the back by the rectangle.*

5th Scene: The Marriage of the Emperor. *The figures are circumscribed by circle* B". *In the area where circles* B' *and* B" *overlap there is a small circle with half their radius, and the socle of the column is at the centre of this small circle. The trees are constructed on the rectangle.*

8th Scene: The Diet of Mantua. *Here a small circle is traced within the overlap of circles* A *and* B', *and this small circle determines the furthermost arch. The baldachino, the curtain and the breadth of the bay are constructed on the rectangle.*

to the same scheme. The *Bridgewater Madonna* is arranged in a single circle, as is the Rome *Entombment*. Two equal circles intersecting each other serve as interior framework to the *Virgin with St John the Baptist and St Nicholas* (London), as also to the *Marriage of the Virgin* (Milan), to the London *Crucifixion* and to the *Triumph of Galatea*. Or again, we find two concentric circles (the *Virgin with the Goldfinch)* or three *(La Belle Jardinière* in the Louvre, or the Foligno *Madonna*). The great fresco of the *Disputà* is governed by arcs whose centre is very high up, outside the limits of the picture—a somewhat exceptional arrangement which makes the whole composition soar into the sky.

The *Transfiguration*, in the Vatican, seems, in spite of its symmetry, a more complex picture; and yet a close examination reveals that all its details are established by a strict construction upon circles. The relative duality of its subject has surprised some commentators, but the profound unity of the picture is confirmed, precisely, by this scheme of composition, in which three circles are closely engaged with one another[2].

2. There is in the British Museum a drawing which corresponds to the upper part of this composition and shows its design clearly. This was long attributed to Raphael, but is now given to Vasari.

Raphael: Disputà. *Composition on the diatessaron (ratio of shorter side to larger: 3/4). The intersection of the vertical axis and the two horizontals gives, in the lower part, the vanishing point of the perspective, and in the upper part the centre of the circle behind the Christ. If a fourth horizontal is imagined at the same distance above the top of the picture, its point of intersection with the central axis will give the centre of all the circles governing the upper part of the fresco. (Rome, Vatican. Photo Anderson)*

Raphael: Transfiguration. *Composition on the circles. Within a large circle touching the bottom and sides of the picture, two squares are inscribed, forming an octagon, whose diagonals distribute the figures of the lower zone. Higher up there are two small circles, whose diameter is equal to the side of these inscribed squares. The upper of these small circles touches the top of the picture, and the second has its centre on the top side of the 'horizontal' square. Each one of the figures, for all the ease of their attitudes, takes position with perfect strictness within this geometry. (Rome, Vatican. Photo Anderson)*

Raphael: Virgin, Child and St John. *Not all Raphael's Madonnas are constructed on circles: this one is based on the rabatment of the squares, with the use of some of the possibilities to which this scheme gives rise. For instance, horizontal lines drawn through the corners of the small square determine, by their intersection with the diagonals of the squares obtained by rabatment, the placing of the architectural elements behind the Virgin. (London, National Gallery. Photo Anderson)*

The circle was never again used so faithfully as it had been by Pinturicchio or Raphael. But it does recur very frequently in those compositions that have a semicircular top: it is rare for this semicircle not to be carried on into the picture and not to be repeated once or even twice. This happens, in particular, in Titian's *Assumption of the Virgin*, in the Frari, and in the same painter's *Pentecost* in the Salute; compare also Veronese's *Martyrdom of St Justina*. Examples could be multiplied; and, quite apart from this particular form of frame which makes the circle almost inevitable, there are some circles to be found in pictures of all periods.

Sometimes, too, the painters would choose an open arc, or perhaps other simple figures like the triangle and the square. This is the place in which to quote a very curious passage from Lomazzo:

'That which is chiefly fitting is to indicate the point whence derive all the lines which come from their places on the circumference, as they do in the triangle, in the square, in the circle, and in all other forms... In the triangle which has three sides the figures placed upon each of these sides must look likewise at the point, and so in the square,... so, finally, in the circle, as many figures as it is desired to make about it must all gaze at the point, as at the principal cause and principal subject whence all the other parts derive[3].'

Sometimes, again, the painter would use lozenges, or a play of slanting lines starting from divisions of the sides into six or into nine—divisions that recall, surprisingly, the musical divisions. We shall find this in an isolated and archaizing painter who may, nonetheless, have been affected, more than is thought, by certain influences from Italy: this is the Elder Bruegel.

Here it is perhaps necessary to repeat that in the present book each work of art is studied without any preconceived idea, without any attempt to find in it this or that principle of composition which fits into a pre-established plan, but relying for guidance on documents or writings of the period, when these are available. In the case of Bruegel I shall give the result of my research without claiming to establish, by any forced logic, a connection between his practice and other similar methods.

In several pictures by Bruegel I have noticed vertical and horizontal divisions into nine parts—in the *Children's Games*, the *Dulle Griet (Mad Meg)*, the *Hunters in the Snow*, the *Massacre of the Innocents*, the *Parable of the Blind*, etc. These nine parts are, of course, not always clearly marked: some pictures will be found to have six divisions, others five or four; but these always coincide with some of the divisions into nine, whether going across or up and down. As his pictures often tend to constitute a microcosm and are packed very close, Bruegel gives them rhythm by means of slanting lines that start from the nine divisions on the four sides. To be more exact, he makes a choice from among these nine points, and chooses also the angle at which the lines shall slant; but once this choice

3. *Op. cit.*, bk VI, ch. 2, p. 283.

is made, he seems to stick to it throughout the picture. Lastly, he uses perspective as well. The *Children's Games* (Vienna) is entirely constructed by means of the divisions into nine and of the perspective.

Bruegel uses semicircles also: in the *Fall of the Rebel Angels* (Brussels), the Paradise is simply indicated by a semicircle, and then four others give rhythm to the battle. In the *Christ Carrying the Cross* (Vienna) two semicircles, one of them high up on the third division from the left and the other low down on the same division from the right, balance the composition, while another, larger one embraces the crowd, with the Christ at its centre.

Thus Bruegel's pictures present a rather exceptional system of composition; the vertical and horizontal divisions and the diagonals that form the armature of the rectangle would provide only four, six or twelve divisions, never nine. We know that Bruegel went to Italy (in 1553?) and brought back some admirable drawings of the Alps. Is the division into nine parts, for which he seems to have a preference, a memory or an interpretation of the musical ratios?

Bruegel: Parable of the Blind. *In Bruegel's pictures the rhythm is always extremely tense. There is a set of parallel oblique lines which join some of the points dividing the sides of the picture into nine equal parts; other oblique lines, each at a constant angle to the first ones, form another network; it is these angles that give to each of his pictures its peculiar rhythm. (Naples Museum. Photo Anderson)*

Bruegel: Children's Games. *The miniatures had created the taste for cramming into a picture a bird's-eye view of a microcosm. A perspective receding practically to the top of the page made available to the artist a relatively large surface, in which he was able to inscribe a great number of objects. Here the picture surface is divided into nine in both directions: this establishes the verticals and horizontals of the architecture; and the same divisions into nine are the starting points of a whole network of straight lines upon which is built the perspective. (Vienna, Kunsthistorisches Museum)*

The armature of the rectangle

The lines that cross within a picture, starting from the corners and from the simple divisions of the sides, have been called in this book the 'armature' of the geometrical figure formed in and by the picture. The word can suggest any kind of supporting framework, as for instance the leading of stained-glass windows. But, falling in with the taste of the painters for musical analogies, I am recalling another sense which the word 'armature' has in French, that of a key signature—an idea which illuminates what I have in mind by stressing the impersonal, objective necessity of that inner framework which emerges from the form itself and not from the artist's choice. He may, in accordance with his idea of art, arrange his picture upon the musical consonances or the golden proportion, or inscribe open or closed curves within the area—in all this he is free; the armature, on the contrary, is given him: he will make more or less use of it, but will never be able to do without it entirely.

We have already considered one example from the art of the Middle Ages (p. 40 above) and have shown how in the Beaune altarpiece the armature of the great rectangle which encloses its nine parts and the squares inscribed in that rectangle supply a valid and extremely simple explanation of that complex whole, in which people have thought to find so many subtle intentions. We could take other examples from every period; and it should be observed that those artists who are most independent of theories are precisely the ones who return most faithfully to these exigencies of the shape of the picture itself.

Of those independents the best example is Titian, who, though thoroughly familiar, as we know, with the musical consonances, was so free that he completely mastered the principles and fashions of his time. Some of his most beautiful pictures are composed simply on the armature of the rectangle. Already Giorgione's *Concert champêtre* was organized upon the divisions of the sides into six and upon the diagonals: Titian's *Sacred and Profane Love*, that perfect and utterly simple picture, is composed upon the divisions into two and into three. Other pictures to compare with this are the *Virgin with the Rabbit*, the *Entombment*, the *Christ with the Crown of Thorns* (all in the Louvre) and, finally, the *Urbino Venus* (in the Uffizi), in which a play of exquisite curves is added to this architecture of strict and sober lines.

And now let us devote some time to certain very significant drawings, which give us the key to the method under discussion—those drawings by Claude Lorrain upon which the essential lines and armature of the rectangle are marked.

There are about ten of these drawings in public collections[4]; the lines drawn across them have intrigued the experts, many of whom describe

Titian: Sacred and Profane Love. *This picture is constructed on the armature of the rectangle, which is reduced to divisions into two and three in both dimensions. But a second rhythm is superimposed on this: its principle is the division of the breadth of the picture into five, which Titian obtains by the rotation of the height (2/5). This latter division gives the attitudes of the figures the chance to escape from symmetry. (Rome, Borghese Gallery. Photo Anderson)*

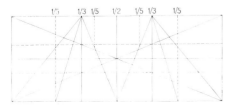

them as a means of enlargement, a particular variant of 'squaring'. But in the drawings I have been able to examine directly the lines marked

4. 1. British Museum 1952 - 1-21-47 (Cavendish Album). - 2. British Museum Hind 223. - 3. British Museum Hind 256. - 4. British Museum Hind 257. - 5. British Museum Hind 295. - 6. Frankfurt, Städelsches Kunstinstitut. - 7. New York, Pierpont Morgan Library. - 8. Paris, Ecole des Beaux-Arts, no. 939.

with black or red chalk are clearly underneath the drawing itself[5]. The same point was noted by Meder in the case of the Frankfurt[6] drawing and it seems likely that it would prove true of many others, although the distinction is sometimes difficult to make when the lines are in ink. Before sketching out his composition, therefore, Claude Lorrain noted down on his sheet of paper the main lines of the armature of the rectangle, their purpose being to help him in the placing of the groups of trees, the hills, the buildings and the ships.

The most complete of these diagrammatic markings occurs in the *Sea Port* in the British Museum. Upon the points of intersection of the diagonals the vertical divisions into four parts are traced. For the most part Claude was content to indicate the essential lines, and he confined himself to a few strokes which would serve him as reminders. He used, nonetheless, many other divisions of the rectangle; but he knew them well enough to find them without effort, to lay hold of them almost instinctively, starting from the diagonals which he marked as his guiding lines. Let

5. All Parisians have recently had the chance to see this for themselves, in the case of the *Sermon on the Mount* from the Pierpont Morgan Collection, New York (no. 7 above), which was no. 20 in the exhibition at the Orangerie in 1958/59. The lines are drawn in red chalk when the sketch underneath the drawing is in red chalk (cf no. 8 above). They are drawn with a ruler and a very sharp pencil, and are sometimes traced again heavily in ink, as in the drawing studied below (cf no. 1 above).

6. Meder, in his classic book *Die Handzeichnungen* (Vienna, 1923), observes that horizontal and vertical lines, triangles, circles, etc., have always been used, and that 'these Claude drawings contain that old division of the plane into regular areas by means of the cross and diagonals, in order to make easier the symmetrical establishment of the masses in foreground and background' (p. 304). This in reference to no. 6 above.

Claude Lorrain: Landscape; drawing. *The diagonals and the perpendiculars to the middle of the sides, traced before the drawing was done, govern the distribution of the masses of the landscape. (Frankfurt, Städelsches Kunstinstitut)*

Claude Lorrain: Port with a Sailing-ship; drawing. *The quarters of the rectangle and their diagonals are strongly marked. Claude also makes use of the thirds and sixths of the surface. (London, British Museum)*

us take, as an example, the *Port with a Sailing-ship* in the British Museum (no. 1 on our list). The quarters of the whole surface and the diagonals of those quarters are alone marked, though with a somewhat exceptional insistence: they serve to determine the positions of the tower in the middle, of the buildings, of the ship's prow and sail; but the divisions of each half into three are also fully present to the mind of the draftsman. He uses them vertically to give the edge of the house on the left and the line of an extremely slender mast, and horizontally in the bands of shade in the sky and foreground. The line of the ground, continued by the sea, is at a distance of 1/3 from the bottom, and the quayside starts along the diagonal of the lower horizontal half.

These compositional drawings by Claude are of extreme interest. Similar evidence is to be found from time to time in the enormous mass of drawings by other masters: I shall later refer to one by Girodet, and Meder has drawn attention to one by Fyt[7]... but they are rather rare, and their very

7. *Op. cit.*, p. 300; and see the Girodet drawing on p. 197 below.

Claude Lorrain: Landscape; drawing. *On the reverse of this drawing there is a preparatory sketch, showing a tower on the left and on the right a weighty mass of trees: the initial idea for the Frankfurt drawing. In this one we see the constructional scheme in its final form: everything—the distribution of the various elements, the striving for equilibrium in the arrangement of lighter and darker patches and the strict attention to planes— fits in with the classic conception of the* paysage composé. *(Paris, École des Beaux-Arts. Photo Giraudon)*

rarity is a fact that needs to be stressed. It seems that, for the most part, painters did not define the composition strictly till they reached the picture; while the paintings themselves are governed by a scheme that can usually be rediscovered, the drawings that are studies for it—even those in which the whole subject is drawn—are uncertain, are capricious. In them the work on the groups is done from the centre outwards, and the artist's research grows like a plant: the frame, as we have seen, is established afterwards (cf. p. 46). Once the idea has been brought to the stretcher, the forms are subjected to a kind of verification and are corrected in accordance with certain principles of distribution—an aesthetic refinement added by the artist at the stage of definitive execution[8].

Claude Lorrain's practice is, of course, not peculiar to him. He was applying the principles of the *paysage composé*, which continued down to the end of the nineteenth century. Claude Lorrain certainly started the movement in France (where it ended in Corot) and perhaps even in England (Wilson and, in certain aspects, Turner); but it would be true to say that the *paysage composé*—its laws and even its choice of subjects —comes from Italy.

8. Cf. the analysis of the *Raft of the Medusa*, p. 199 below.

It is not surprising to find in Poussin the same taste for very simple compositions that take their basic lines from the armature of the rectangle. This quest for calm and stability answered to a need of his spirit, but resulted also from a conscious and stubborn reaction against a whole tendency of art then triumphant at Rome. The successful painters who received the most attractive commissions were Lanfranco, Pietro di Cortona and their school: their art was in fashion and was multiplying with profusion—indeed vulgarizing—that dynamic stress, that vital urge, to which Rubens was elsewhere giving higher expression. Poussin's reaction—for classicism is a reaction—looked back to the academy of the Carracci and Domenichino; but (and this is what makes him great) it kept a firm control over the desire to please, characteristic of the Carracci, and over Domenichino's somewhat heavy interpretation, going back directly, on the one hand, to the Titian of the *Bacchanals* and of the landscapes, and, on the other hand, to the glorious works of the Greeks and Romans which Poussin had before his eyes.

As I studied Poussin, painting by painting and drawing by drawing, I noticed in him a characteristic trait, in addition to the converging lines already mentioned and to those diagonals and those divisions at the points of intersection of diagonals which govern nearly all his pictures: a marked taste for horizontal and vertical bands—the much discussed parallels with the frame, which later aroused such disapproval in the eighteenth-century academies—and for buildings presented frontally and at right angles to the picture plane.

Poussin's way of grouping his figures in rectangular friezes is, without any doubt, derived from sarcophagi. It is impossible to overstress the deep study he made of the relief carvings of Antiquity—many drawings bear witness to it—and, particularly, the use he made of this study in his pictures. Even apart from the *Hunt of Meleager* in the Prado and the *Offering to Hymen* (Richmond)[9], which are frankly friezes (the former seems to go back via certain Roman triumphs to the Parthenon frieze of horsemen), and apart from the *Parnassus*, also in the Prado, in which the frieze is again clearly admitted, many other pictures of his show horizontal bands of figures with their heads all at the same height: *St John the Baptist preaching*, *Eliezer and Rebecca*, the onlookers in the *Judgment of Salomon* in the Louvre, and the London *Bacchanal*. Moreover, Poussin's plastic erudition, no doubt allied with his striving for perfection, led him to employ two rhythmic networks simultaneously in a single picture. In many of his paintings (in the Prado *Parnassus*, the Chantilly *Massacre of the Innocents*, the Louvre *Bacchanal*, the Louvre and New York *Rape of the Sabines*, and yet others) he uses, though more cunningly, the old practice of the medieval illuminators: the diagonals of the two squares inscribed within the rectangle and partly overlapping, with all the resulting harmonics. But there are always verticals and horizontals to calm the picture down, and this quality is still further accentuated by the emphatic frontality of the buildings. These are derived from Titian and Campagnola, and

9. Now in the Sâo Paulo Museum.

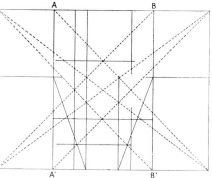

Poussin: Parnassus. *Here Poussin uses
the rotation of the shorter sides upon the
larger. The lines AA' and BB', which limit
the inner squares, divide the picture into three
parts: in the middle Apollo and the Muses,
to right and left the poets. The upper and
lower corners of the small central square
standing on a point establish, by horizontals
drawn through them to the sides of the rectangle, the dimensions of the figures in the
second plane. The intersection of the diagonals
of the squares and those of the rectangle
determines the height of the poets. There are
also oblique lines from the bottom of the middle
section, which give their direction to the Cupids
in the foreground. (Madrid, Prado. Photo
Anderson)*

Poussin: Philistines struck by the Plague.
*Composition on the rotation of the shorter sides
of the rectangle. The vanishing point of the
perspective is also the central point of the
composition: it lies where a vertical drawn
from one corner of the small central square
intersects a horizontal drawn from the point
of intersection of the diagonals of the squares
and of the rectangle. (Paris, Louvre. Photo
Roger Viollet)*

to compare them with those of these masters is most revealing. The great Venetians were already in the habit of transforming humble houses into admirable blocks with simple, single surfaces gloriously receptive of the sunshine; but they often showed corners, at which the light and the shade met in opposition. In Domenichino the buildings sometimes become as cold and abstract as in an architect's elevation. Poussin put them back into the living light, but without making them lose their abstract quality (see the *Taking of Jerusalem*, in the Vienna Museum, the *Pyrrhus saved*, in the Louvre, the *Sabines*, etc.). The most striking ones are those in the *Funeral of Phocion*, in the Louvre, where all the temples are fully frontal and set against horizontal walls, and in the *Ashes of Phocion* (Lord Derby), where instead of the walls there are straight strips of ground prolonged by rectilinear terraces with strongly lit perpendiculars cutting them at right angles.

The older he grew, the more Poussin broadened his style of composition[10]. His classicism seems to be constantly purified, his reaction against the Baroque strengthened. All his life he used the lines of the rectangle, which by their regularity served as the loom on which his supple and balanced symmetry was woven. And Poussin's predilection for horizontals and verticals came in the end to dominate the taste for curves and sinuous forms. This is the impression that comes out at us from the *Summer* in the Louvre, and again from that moving drawing (also in the Louvre) for the last, unfinished picture, *Apollo and Daphne*, in which the clearly separated planes and groups obey a composition founded on straight lines.

The golden number after the 'divine proportion'

The publication of Pacioli's book in Venice in 1509 gave a new topical interest to the *divine proportion*, although it was now no more than a memory of the past. Chiefly in Venice, but also in the rest of Italy, these traditional conceptions, till then transmitted orally, were considered with fresh attention, simply because they were presented in book form, the only form then thought worthy of respect. From that time on, the golden number, like the musical ratios, was available to artists in theoretical treatises of which they could make use, and in which they would delve with increasing eclecticism. But it would be a grave error to look for a close connection between such sixteenth- and seventeenth-century compositions as employ the golden number and the medieval compositions.

In the Middle Ages, composition was generally based on one of the Pythagorean figures: it followed out the complex design of this figure even to its minutest requirements, though often concealing it from profane eyes. The golden proportion was arrived at, nearly always, with the help of the pentagon, which contains it in all its parts. As the construction

10. Cf. the *Orpheus and Eurydice* and *Winter*, in the Louvre.

Diagram showing the harmonics of the
Golden Section.

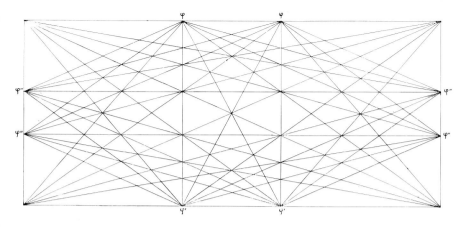

Peter Halt: Perspectivische Reiss Kunst,
Augsburg, 1525. These studies, contempo-
raneous with Dürer's, reveal the same passion-
ate interest in geometry. (Photo Seuil)

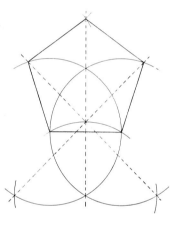

Dürer's Diagram.

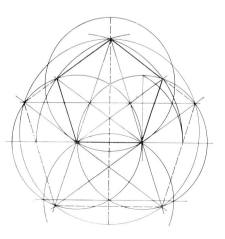

Diagram of Hippocrates.

Peter Halt: Perspectivische Reiss Kunst,
Augsburg, 1525.

of this is rather difficult, the first thing that occurred was an attempt
to simplify it. Dürer, in his 'Course in the Art of Measurement with
Compasses and Ruler'[11], attempts, like the medieval artists, to construct
the various geometrical figures easily, with the compass point. He was
perfectly familiar with the classic way of constructing a pentagon (the
one given on p. 64 above), but he proposes another, done with a single
angle of the compasses; it is a good approximation: Panofsky[12] thinks it
must have come from the practice of the cabinet-makers. It should be noted
that this ingenious method is a simplification of Hippocrates's diagram.
It was evidently much appreciated, since it was published separately
(*Modo di formare un pentagono... descritto da Alberto Durero*, Bologna, 1570).

But to artists these polygons, these scientific constructions, came to
seem more and more irksome, and soon all they retained of the golden
section was a manner of distributing lines and surfaces in harmonic relationships without troubling to follow out a geometrical figure. This
is the whole difference between a medieval composition and, for instance,
one of Vermeer's.

Some part in this fundamental transformation of the way in which the
golden section was used must be attributed to the discovery of ancient
frescoes in the Roman villas and baths, that discovery which had so
great an influence on Raphael, on his pupils and on the whole style of
decoration for several centuries. What was known at that time? It is
hard to be sure in detail, but certainly more than the decorative elements
that were called 'grotesques': it included several composed scenes (like
those later found at Pompeii), which follow a conception of the golden
number very different from that of the Middle Ages, and, be it said, much
more modern; the ratio is taken directly on the sides of the frame and
from there it governs the figures, the wall surfaces and the architecture.

To conclude: as the faith of the painters in a proportion no longer
'divine' grew less and their weariness increased, the golden section came
to be no more than a habit of dividing compositions at a certain distance
from the frame—a division that became, so to speak, instinctive.

Veronese and Tintoretto liked to use it, in conjunction with other
schemes. Veronese, for instance, often constructed his portraits upon
the golden number: for example the portrait of *Francesco Franceschini*
(Holford sale, London, 1927), the *Daniele Barbaro* (Florence, Pitti Palace),
the *Count Porto and his Son* (Rome), the London and Budapest portraits
of *A Nobleman*, etc. In other portraits Veronese uses the musical ratio:
the *Lady with her Son* in Paris and *La Belle Nani* in the Louvre are based
on the 9/12/16 ratio. Or again, he used simply the armature of the rectangle,
as in the *Pace Guariente* (Verona), the *Portrait of a Man* in Dresden and
the one in the Colonna Gallery in Rome. I am not, of course, claiming
to show the existence of scientific and elaborate schemes in these cases:

11. *Underweysung der Messung mit dem Zirckel und Richtscheyt*, 1525 (revised edition
1538).

12. *Op. cit.*, p. 256.

Veronese: Feast in the House of Levi. *The architecture is governed by the golden ratio with its range of harmonic recessions. The points of intersection of the lines which join the ratios φ, φ', φ'', φ''' to one another and to the angles of the rectangle are the harmonic points enabling the painter to place all the columns correctly. The diagonals of the rectangle are strongly marked by the stairway balustrades. (Venice, Accademia. Photo Anderson)*

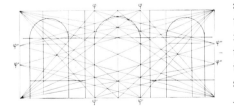

the scheme, in my opinion, determines the position of the head, and in a portrait, where what is interesting is the sitter and the quality of the brushwork, this is sufficient.

Among the paintings by Veronese based on the golden ratio, mention must be made of the *Christ and the Centurion* in Dresden, the *Christ and the Doctors* in Madrid and the *Annunciation* and the *Raising of Lazarus* in the Uffizi. In the London *Family of Darius before Alexander* the architecture is governed by the golden number and the figures by the armature of the rectangle. In the Venice *Feast in the House of Levi* the architecture, consisting of three arcades enclosing the loggia on which the meal is taking place, is based on the golden ratio, with harmonic regression of the same ratio. The two diagonals of the rectangle give the slope of the double stairway in the foreground. On the other hand the Milan *Feast in the House of Simon the Pharisee* is based without the slightest ambiguity on the musical ratio 9/12/16, as also is the Dresden *Adoration of the Magi*. This shows Veronese's eclecticism.

In the Louvre *Marriage at Cana* Veronese seems, on the one hand, to have made use of the simplest of schemes based on the golden number, while, on the other hand, the diapente appears to have inspired the general proportions.

In the works of Tintoretto also we come across the golden number quite frequently, as for instance in the *Miracle of St Mark* and the *Finding of the Body of St Mark* in Venice and in the Florence *Leda*. The Florentines, too, returned to it with their usual insistence on following a linear scheme right through its minutest requirements.

Tintoretto: Resurrection. *Tintoretto establishes his figures and his zones of light and shade upon the sloping lines created by the golden proportion when this is marked out twice in alternation on the four sides of the picture.* Note: *In the course of such studies as this, we may be confronted by a picture whose original dimensions have been somewhat altered. This is a source of error only if the alterations have been considerable. In the present case the upper part of the picture may have been cut down: perhaps by some 30 or 40 centimetres as against the 5.25 metres of the actual height. If so, the constructional scheme here proposed would be drawn out in length, but the change in the angles of the lines would be extremely small and would not affect the spirit of the composition. (Venice, Scuola di San Rocco. Photo Anderson)*

It is not surprising to find in the Netherlands a persistent faithfulness to the golden proportion, as to other habits of the past. In that part of the world, with its solid traditions of painting, the transformations of thought and taste that had arisen in Italy did not penetrate except in weakened forms and, in any case, did not destroy a continuity due, above all, to the way in which teaching was organized. The guilds died hard: in them the pupils, just as in the Middle Ages, followed the practical guidance of a master; and the great desiccating breath of the Academies, which did so much to intellectualize art but at the same time cut it off from its past, did not reach them.

In Flanders the influence of Rubens was preponderant: it introduced a new way of composing pictures, which will be studied later in this book. But Holland, for political and religious reasons, escaped the Baroque movement. Italianism did not become prominent except in the Utrecht school and in certain belated Mannerists, and the ancestral taste for intimate pictures executed with a familiar realism did not suffer encroachment.

To enumerate the Dutch masters who liked using the golden number would be wearisome. It is enough to say that Rembrandt uses it, for instance, in his *Syndics of the Clothmakers' Guild*, and that Vermeer's use of it is particularly frequent. He may almost be said to have preferred it to the other methods, though he was perfectly familiar with these. (For instance: the *Woman Seated at the Virginals* (London, National Gallery), the *Music Lesson* (Buckingham Palace), the *Woman Writing* (New York, Frick Collection), the *Artist in his Studio* (Vienna).

But even in Holland, a country slightly off the beaten track, following its own straight path in art and not suffering any violent invasion of new ideas, the geometrical designs were gradually simplified and lost much of their importance. It would not be true to say that they changed: it was the artist's attitude to them that was no longer the same. Though he used them, his interest was elsewhere—in the construction of space (to which we shall have occasion to return), or in the poetic effect of light. The Dutch were contemplative, not eloquent. They were not, like the Italians, enamoured of story-telling, but they were the first to observe nature and to make landscapes that are merely landscapes, drawings from the life, done in the open air. So it was that they grew accustomed to the refinements of lighting and became atmospheric painters—which makes them the real precursors of the painting of the late nineteenth century.

The Académie royale and the French eighteenth century

Florentine Mannerism penetrated into France like a hurricane, sweeping away many habits but not settling there as firmly as in Italy or Germany nor preparing the way for the Baroque. The French national temperament was too rational; also, the spirit of the Counter-Reformation met with little appreciation. And so a great void began to be felt, and it is strange to observe the preponderant influence exercised by an absentee, Nicolas

Vermeer: The Artist in his Studio. *Vermeer constructs his space with tables, chairs, an easel and hangings—in fact, with lines, planes, angles and perspective. These lines, if reduced to the surface of the picture, turn out to be inscribed in a network of lines at right angles and oblique lines, all governed by the golden section. But there is more in it than this:* *Vermeer was trying to restore accurate perception of things by means of the play of colour, light and depth; and to this he brought a cleaner, more luminous palette, free from broken tones, and an unerring analysis of the colour of the objects and people at first so deliberately organized. (Vienna, Kunsthistorisches Museum. Photo Bulloz)*

Poussin. Having lost faith in their genius, the French clung proudly to the great Frenchman in Rome, whose classicism they loved; and through him they joined hands with the eclecticism of the Carracci and of the Academies. Of these there were, by then, many in Italy (at Bologna, Rome, Florence and Milan), and the very principle of an academy of art enchanted the French mind.

The Académie royale de Peinture et de Sculpture, founded by Colbert in 1648 and the first in Europe that was not simply a private association, was the greatest effort yet made to raise the fine arts to the level of the other disciplines studied in the *collèges* and to turn their teaching into dogma. The men of the period of Alberti and Leonardo had struggled to get painting accepted as one of the liberal arts: now it was raised to the rank of the humanities. Although the results of this teaching were not always brilliant and the system was open to criticism, honour is due to the Académie for having offered young painters courses in geometry, perspective, anatomy and history—for having, in short, tried to make them into cultivated men or, in the phrase then current, *honnêtes hommes*. The art of the century of Louis XIV is a court art, it is true, but the painters were no longer domestic servants; they had acquired a new dignity.

The teaching was rounded off, from 1667 onwards, by public lectures, in which the Academicians expounded the essential principles of painting by analyzing works of the masters. Here was painting being taught in the light of day and *ex cathedra*; here were traditions being replaced by ideas, workshop recipes by the expounding of principles of art. Unfortunately, one's impression is that the poor young people must have left those lectures still hungry, and returned, disappointed, to their master, who could at least teach them technique. For what, in fact, did those fine speakers say? Some very vague phrases; and on composition, very little. At last there was an opportunity to expound the theory of it, but teachers whose knowledge of it was only vestigial—vestiges that had become tricks whose origin had been forgotten—were not anxious to draw attention to it during the course of these essentially rational dissertations.

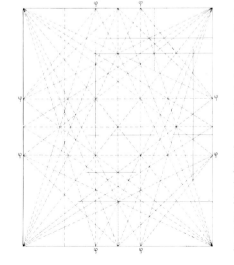

So composition became desiccated and impoverished. The painters obeyed the forms suggested by the rectangle with a monotonous insistence. The extra-pictorial striving for dramatic expression, brought into fashion by Le Brun, but luckily counterbalanced by the demands of mural decoration, occupied the minds of artists until the great king grew old. Then, in a return of Mannerism, which was given new life by Rubens, but also tempered by the healthy influence of the sheer joy of living, the inimitable style of the French eighteenth century flowered. Even then the play of the linear frameworks no longer aroused interest: to innovate in that field requires deep thought. Watteau alone—that exceptional genius who pursued his own way, independent of period—tried to introduce an extreme refinement into the basic lines, and even so without any real innovation.

Claude Lorrain died in 1682, Watteau was born in 1684. Watteau took the poetic feeling of Claude Lorrain and gave it more actuality. Claude takes us into mythological landscapes, shows us harbours of Antiquity bathed in a dreaming light. Watteau's fairyland is close to his, yet there is a world between. The comedies of Molière had brought real life nearer to art, and the people in Watteau's pictures are his contemporaries; what is more, they are not used, like those of Claude, to animate a landscape, but have a life of their own, like those of Rembrandt. They seem, in the midst of their diversions, to have other thoughts, and often those thoughts are sad. Compare them with the peasants of Rubens, in his *Kermess:* these are gay lads, absorbed in the pleasure of the moment; between them and Watteau's elegant people has stepped the doubt of the libertines, their 'what is the good of it all?' *The Indifferent* is only a dancer, but the name suits him well; he and his companions make one think of actors sad at leaving the world of illusion—the illusion of life.

When Watteau set out to paint a picture, he chose from among the mass of his admirable drawings, with their movingly restrained strokes, the elements he needed, and then arranged them with a combination of ease and strictness. Like Claude Lorrain, he began by taking as his basis simply the armature of the rectangle *(Embarkation to Cythera)*. But very soon he came to prefer the refinements that can be obtained from the intersection of the rectangle's diagonals with those of the squares. This method was not new: Poussin had already used it, though more soberly; and the nineteenth-century artists were to show a predilection for it;

Watteau: Embarkation to Cythera. *The slow procession follows an extremely simple basic scheme: the armature of the rectangle. It could be one used by Claude Lorrain. But the next illustration will show to what masterly subtlety Watteau sometimes carried the science of composition. (Paris, Louvre. Archives photographiques)*

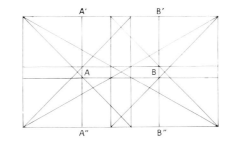
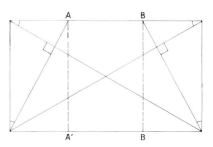

Watteau: Gersaint's Signboard. *This is a masterpiece both of painting and of composition. Watteau has contrived to get the maximum subtleties out of the rotation of the shorter sides of the rectangle. Everything is derived from the two lines A'A" and B'B" (in the small diagram), of which Watteau makes the far corners of the shop. A'A" and B'B" are drawn from the intersections A and B of the diagonals of the squares and the secondary horizontals, these horizontals being established by the intersections of the diagonals of the rectangle and the sides of the squares. From these two points A and B, everything is developed with the strictness of a theorem. Great sheaves of radiating lines sweep across the scene and give their rhythm to the figures, which are inscribed exactly within the acute-angled triangles. Note that the lines A'A" and B'B" can also be obtained by constructing the reciprocals of the rectangle—by dropping from its four corners the lines perpendicular to its diagonals. But as Watteau uses the rotation of the shorter sides in many other pictures of his, it seemed to me that this was the sounder method for us to follow. (Berlin-Dahlem, Staatliches Museum. Photo Bulloz)*

Watteau: Gilles. *Without the explanation furnished by the diagram, the composition of* Gilles *seems baffling. The rotation of the shorter sides of the rectangle on to the longer was a scheme which Watteau was fond of using, and it is the only one capable of accounting very simply for the position of* Gilles *on the canvas: his axis is given by the points of intersection, to the left, of the diagonals of the rectangle and the diagonals of the squares.* (Paris, Louvre. Archives photographiques)

to David and his pupils it was to become an obsessive practice, to Delacroix a convenient and discreet device. But we must go as far as Seurat before we find, in a very different interpretation, subtleties comparable to those of Watteau (in the *Charms of Life, Gersaint's Signboard*, etc.). Let us pay special attention to *Gilles*, that simple yet astonishing figure: why is he not in the centre of the picture? The diagonals of the squares on the shorter sides supply the key to this eccentricity—and determine the figure's position with a striking directness.

Pater and Lancret, less refined artists, simply take up once more the constituent lines of the rectangle.

Other artists of the period—whether like Boucher, they went in, for decorative painting or, like Chardin, Greuze and Fragonard, for genre pictures—followed the same rudimentary geometrical methods. The simplicity of this practice made it a lasting one: it could be applied easily to all cases, even to that of the Rococo frame, which can always be resolved into a square or a rectangle; and whether one is analyzing one of Boucher's gallant or mythological scenes, which he rendered with such virtuosity, or one of those jewels of pure painting produced by Chardin or Oudry, one is almost certain to find in it the same basic lines. I give, by way of illustration, two of Chardin's pictures, examples of his very personal way of adapting the armature. There is only one comment I would make, that will show how constantly Chardin was preoccupied with establishing his composition properly in the rectangle. As is well known, he often painted the same picture several times: when, for some reason, he decided to alter the proportions of the picture, he did not put the subject back unchanged into a wider or narrower frame, but articulated it along the lines given by the new rectangle. His *Women drawing Water*, for example, was painted a dozen times. Let me draw attention to three of these repetitions, which have different shapes. One is almost square (Wildenstein's

Greuze: Bird-Catcher. *Here again the circle is drawn in the square of the shorter side. The diagonals of the lower and upper squares give, by their intersection, the small square standing on a point, and the lines drawn from this to right and left establish, where they cross the diagonals of the squares, the verticals which fix the positions of the feet of the table on the left and of the bench on the right. The diagonals of the squares also combine with those of the rectangle to determine the man's position. (Warsaw Museum)*

Fragonard: Bathers. *Construction on the armature of the rectangle: two circles whose diameter equals the shorter side of the rectangle, and whose circumferences touch the sides of the rectangle at three points each, give the composition its life. (Paris, Louvre. Archives photographiques)*

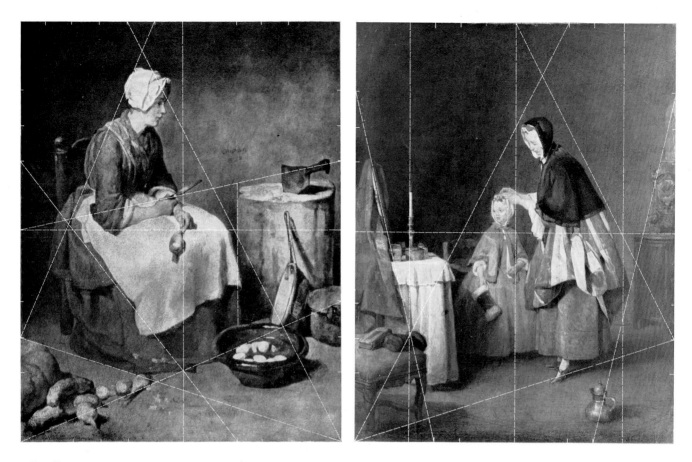

Chardin: The Cook. (*Vienna, Kunst-historisches Museum. Photo Giraudon*)

Chardin: Morning Toilet. (*Stockholm Museum*)

In some of his pictures Chardin uses the armature of the rectangle to determine six points on each side, not counting the halves and the corners. This was the preparatory work. Later a recessional triangulation was obtained by means of three oblique lines starting from some of these points.

catalogue, no. 24), one is broader than it is high (no. 26), one higher than it is broad (no. 27). In each of these pictures, the door on the right is inscribed upon the quarter of the breadth, the broom adheres to one of the slanting lines, and the handle of the pan follows the diagonal of the rectangle, the result being a variation, from picture to picture, of as much as 15°.

Since the case of Chardin's still-life paintings has arisen, this is perhaps the right place for a rapid glance at this branch of the art of painting. It was not until the sixteenth century, indeed almost the seventeenth, that the still-life became an independent genre, occupying the whole picture instead of being one element in it. And it did so, at first, modestly. In the fifteenth century the Italians had merely assigned it a *trompe-l'œil* function, and from this it was to retain an exceptional obedience to the lines of scale. It would not occur to anyone to criticize the dimensions given to a tree in a landscape painting; but to paint an apple the size of a nut or the size of a melon would be unimaginable. Hence the great variety in the size of the pictures themselves, from Snyders's luxuriant displays to Adrien Coorte's three medlars—a diversity that brought with it a relatively complex use of the laws of composition. Meanwhile in Flanders the still-life was made to bear the load of symbolism—either religious

Sanchez Cotan: Still-Life. *The strictness of this still-life is particularly marked. It was not for the sake of picturesqueness that the painter hung the wedge and the cabbage on a string in the way we see, but in order to place them exactly upon an arc of the circle which governs the composition. (San Diego, California, Fine Arts Gallery. Photo Bulloz)*

Oudry: Basset Hound. *While Chardin selected a certain number of points from the armature of the rectangle, Oudry used this armature in a still more simple way: he took a few lines and transformed them into the gun, the bird, the corner of the wall, etc. (Stockholm Museum)*

('vanities') or allegorical (the 'five senses', the 'seasons' and the 'elements'). And when finally painters confined themselves to the representation of motionless things—say, the delights of the table, or *objets de valeur*—,to the Academy the still-life remained an extremely humble genre: a still-life painter would never be admitted there as a teacher of the main art, nor even of his own speciality.

Nonetheless, as soon as it attained its freedom, still-life painting imposed its own discipline. The exigences of composition acted on it as on the other 'subjects'. Within limits, however: in this genre, more than elsewhere, it is hard for the painter to free himself from his model, and the arrangement of the objects, that actual, concrete grouping, tended to prevail over thought-out compositions.

The strictest still-life paintings are formed of objects with very pure lines, such as musical instruments, and these steer the painter towards a geometrical conception of grouping (Baschenis, Oudry, etc.). In other cases still-lifes are merely pretexts for studies that are almost abstract, as in the work of Sanchez Cotan: here the diagram rules, the curve is mistress, and the objects are obedient. Lastly, in the complicated decorative arrangements, of which the models cannot easily be brought together in the studio (as in the case of Snyders or, in France, of Monnoyer), the constructional lines once more take first place (compare the Jan Fyt drawing for a composition, mentioned on p. 127 above).

In France, in the case of Chardin, still-life painting seems to be keeping to its humble place; but with him, as later with Cézanne, it is the occasion for highly original painterly studies in the relation of colour to light, materials and volumes. Chardin is close to the Dutch painters, whose unemphatic intimacy appealed so strongly to French taste at that time. But he went further than they and, linking up with the popular and grave spirit of the Le Nains, made each of his pictures into a poetic, deeply meditated grouping, in which a very few well-chosen and carefully lit objects suggest the charm of a simple, dignified life. In such conditions, what part has geometry to play? Once the position of the objects has been decided, it is chiefly a matter of placing the frame (as we have seen in the case of certain drawings); then only there intervenes the influence of the frame and of its armature—division into three horizontal and vertical bands creating preferential zones for the objects.

The remarkable stability of the framework of pictures is one of the constants in French painting of the seventeenth and eighteenth centuries. The painters sometimes refined upon the data of the frame, but never tried to shake free from them. This exquisite art lived a somewhat enclosed life: though it had broken off connection with the Middle Ages, it still had nothing to do with the novelties that were being worked out elsewhere—with those strange impulses of violence whose genesis we shall be studying later. Nonetheless, the expansive force of French art was considerable at a time when the dynamic energy of the Baroque was exhausting itself, and when those two poles of painting, Paris and Venice, were being drawn together by a shared simplicity of taste.

Goya: Majas on a Balcony. *The height of the balcony is strictly determined by the upper square. A triangle formed by the diagonals of this square encloses the busts of the two women. (New York, Metropolitan Museum)*

But the greatest artists of that time came to maturity apart from them both. Goya's originality is so powerful that his work, which makes him the forerunner of the romantics and the visionaries, if not one of them, compels our attention. We are in for a surprise: this bitter, cruel painter, sometimes on the verge of sadism or of madness, used, nonetheless, the language—the forms—of his period.

His first works, cartoons for tapestry with a marked Venetian character, obey the armature of the rectangle with placid obviousness. His admirable portraits firmly set down a figure upon the axis, or sometimes upon a diagonal when the person is seated. I give here an analysis of two of his large compositions, the *Third of May* and the *Majas on a Balcony*, both of which later served as models for Manet.

Goya, who witnessed the horrors that ravished his country, left a violent and passionate document of accusation in the *Disasters of War*, a series of etchings done between 1808 and 1813. One is seized irresistibly by their nightmare images, which he seems to have flung on to the copper plate in a feverish rage. Yet none of his figures of martyrs or executioners is placed at random: almost all the compositions are inscribed in a pre-established scheme, and this is often the same one, in spite of the extreme diversity of the scenes. Excepting one slight variant (a taste for parallel slanting lines), Goya's method of composition is classical and its formulae are familiar ones.

Goya: 3 May 1808. *Rabatment of the shorter sides. Artists did not use in their pictures the full length of the lines of the construction, as traced by us: as long as these contributed their specific harmony to the picture, it was enough. In this canvas, for instance, the edge of the lantern is precisely in line with the tower: all that survives of the vertical on which they stand is these two small sections. It will be noted, also, that in this picture the distribution of the tone values themselves is nearly symmetrical. (Madrid, Prado. Photo Anderson)*

Geometry had not said its last word, and we shall come across it again in the nineteenth century. But it is now time to turn to other conceptions of the framework of a picture—those that nourished the Baroque *verve*, chiefly outside France, to which country they eventually returned, much later, in the work of Delacroix.

Goya: Disasters of War; etchings. *The scheme here set out is valid for many of the etchings of the Disasters: what distinguishes it is its recourse to certain possibilities of the rabatment device which are rarely used. This device, as we know, gives rise to a small square in the centre, on the median axis of the rectangle. Horizontal lines drawn through the top and bottom corners of this central square cut the shorter sides of the rectangle at four points, to which Goya leads slanting lines from the top and bottom of the vertical axis, parallel therefore to the four sides of the small square. In the larger square formed by these slanting lines four squares are inscribed, each touching with a corner a corner of the small central square. Lines produced from these yield further developments of the scheme. (Paris, Bibliothèque Nationale)*

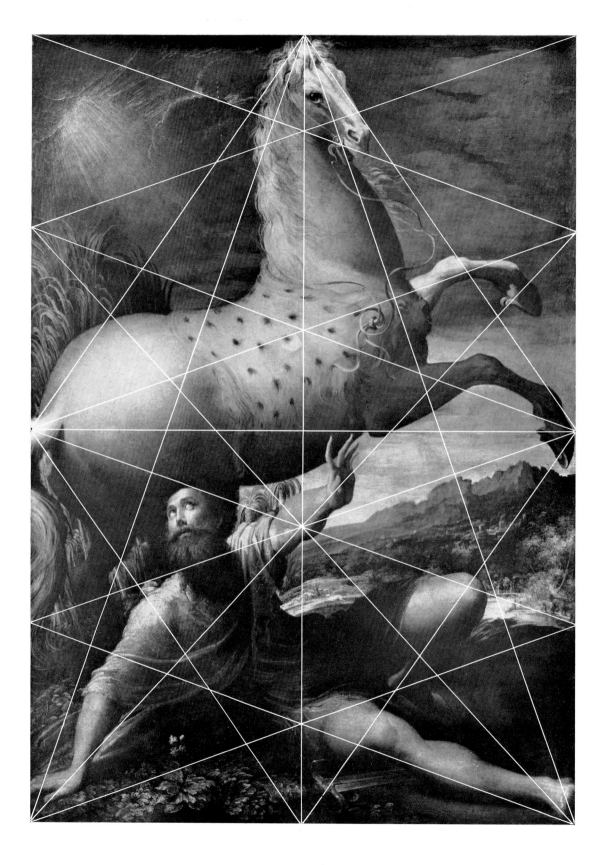

VI DYNAMIC COMPOSITIONS

Lomazzo

More than once I have quoted or referred to Lomazzo in passing, but have not yet attempted to show with any fullness the essential contribution which his books made. Published in 1584, the *Trattato* is an expression of tendencies older than that: its author, a pupil of Michelangelo, had been blind for thirteen years. In it are to be found the ideas of the Florentine Academies (which were both many and strange) and those of the Milan group of which Lomazzo, president of the Accademia della Valle di Bregno, was an important member. This *Trattato dell'arte della pittura*—followed six years later by a sort of *résumé*, the *Idea del tempio della pittura*—is the codification of the Mannerist idea of art, and it is a striking and evocative one. Though encumbered by prolixity, by digressions and by charming quotations from poetry, it is a book that expresses vividly and with many apt images the style of this period. To some extent Lomazzo is to the Cinquecento what Alberti was to the Quattrocento; for, although he now and then recalls Alberti's theory of proportions, Lomazzo is opposed to the great humanist in his essential ideas. As Sir Anthony Blunt has convincingly shown[1], he is closely akin to his Roman contemporary, Federigo Zuccaro, in his conception of beauty. Both men were anti-rationalist and mystical: beauty, they held, comes from God—it is in the spirit of the artist and not in things.

'We must not wholly observe the naturall, but we must regard the grace of the figure; And that proportion which is most decent to the eye must bee followed...[2]'

Clearly, then, this new aesthetic is as abstract as those based on the proportions, the musical consonances, or the geometrical figures. Though it professes to despise mathematics and to trust the eye[3] and instinct, it nonetheless asserts that beauty resides not in nature but in the quality

Niccolo dell'Abbate: Conversion of St Paul. *Armature of the rectangle. The artist imposes on the horse strange distortions derived from the scheme.* (*Vienna, Kunsthistorisches Museum*)

1. *Artistic Theory in Italy*, 1450-1600, Oxford, 1940.

2. Giovanni Paolo Lomazzo (1538-1600), *Trattato*, bk V, ch. i, p. 251. English translation of the first five books only; *A Tracte containing the Artes of curious Paintynge Carvynge and Buildinge*; by R[ichard] H[aydocke]; Oxford, 1598; p. 184.

3. 'For (in a word) the *eie* and the *understanding* together being directed by the Prospective arte, ought to be a guide, measure and judge of Painting and Carving' (bk V, ch. i, p. 247; English version, p. 181).

of the lines by which the artist expresses it, and this quality is *grace*. But that is not definite enough: an image is needed, and this image is *fire*.

'It is reported that *Michael Angelo* upon a time gave this observation to the Painter *Marcus de Sciena* his scholler; *that he should alwaies make a figure Pyramidall, Serpentlike, and multiplied by one two and three*. In which precept (in mine opinion) the whole mysterie of the arte consisteth. For the greatest grace and life that a picture can have, is, that it expresse *Motion:* which the Painters call the *spirite* of a picture. Nowe there is no forme so fitte to expresse this motion, as that of the flame of fire. Which according to *Aristotle* and the other Philosophers, is an elemente most active of all others; because the forme of the flame thereof is most apt for motion: for it hath a *Conus* or sharpe pointe wherewith it seemeth to divide the aire, that so it may ascende to his proper sphere. So that a picture having this forme will bee most beautifull[4].'

I have quoted this famous passage in full, because it is often the subject of imprecise references.

The *serpentine line* was the first expression of the new ideal. Lomazzo repeats the phrase several times, and always, when he does so, attributes the whole doctrine to Michelangelo.

'But because there are two kinds of pyramid, one straight (*retta*)... and the others in the form of a flame of fire, and this Michelangelo calls *serpentinata*, the painter should accompany this pyramidal form with the serpentine form..., which is the form proper to the flame of fire that waves. Which means that the figure must represent the form of the letter S upright or reversed, because then it will have its beauty[5].'

And further on:

'All movements ought to be so represented that the body have the form of the serpent, to which thing nature is easily disposed[6]'.

Lomazzo adds that if the right arm projects forwards, the left will be lost in the background and the left leg, on the contrary, will be to the fore: this is the *contrapposto*,—the principle of balanced counterpoise, clearly implied by the serpentine line.

Fire, as we all know, suggests not only curves, but life and movement. This is the essential idea of the text just quoted from Book I, chapter i. In his Book II Lomazzo adds this:

'...of *Motion* it selfe, namely with what arte the Painter ought to give *motions* best fitting his pictures... herein consisteth the whole *spirite* and *life* of the Arte; which the Painters call sometimes the *Fury*, sometimes the *Grace*, & sometimes the *Excellency* of the arte[7].'

As we shall see, a whole future lay in this last idea, and conceptions of art too often treated as opposites by modern criticism—Mannerism and Baroque—are both of them contained in Lomazzo's treatise.

4. Bk I, ch. i, p. 22; English version, p. 17.
5. Bk I, ch. i, p. 23. (Incomplete in the 1518 English version.)
6. Bk VI, ch. iv, p. 296.
7. Bk II, ch. ii, p. 108; English version, p. 4.

What concerns us here is the incidence of these new theories upon composition. It is clearly perceptible, even in the Mannerist period, though that was a period of hesitancy and refinement rather than of real creation.

One consequence of Lomazzo's purely formal ideal, on which I must now insist, is the malleability of human or animal bodies—their aptness for distortion. 'And that proportion which is most decent to the eye must bee followed,' he had said in Book V; but let us follow his idea as it continues:

'As *Raphael* and all other good workemen used in all their workes, wherein we shall find feete in pictures something too little, and legges longer than the life. In a word we shall find other particulars in their workes, which adde a wonderful grace and beauty to their pictures: for the eye delighteth to see certaine parts of the body slender, others fleshie and tender, and others keeping their naturall proportion[8].'

Thus the forms no longer set up a resistance, but may lend themselves readily to any decorative curves or designs the artist may wish to make them follow. We have met with the same phenomenon already, in the Romanesque period: it was exploited then with a much stricter logic, and pushed to its extreme consequences. Mannerism was at least a reawakening of this adaptability of forms, of this obedience of the object to the abstract intention.

The long legs of which Lomazzo speaks do not, it is true, curl about as freely as the sirens' tails around the corners of the capitals, but they do willingly follow a decorative course, and so, on occasion, marry up with the directions imposed by the frame. In this way, in Vasari's frescoes in the Chancellery in Rome (cf. p. 174), the astonishing figures in the foreground extend their vast legs like long plant stems; and in the same way Bronzino's Venus and Cupids in his *Allegory of Love* (cf. p. 42 above) fold and unfold like ribbons in docile obedience to the sides of the picture and to its diagonal.

A particularly racy example of distortion is the *Conversion of St Paul* attributed to Niccolo dell'Abbate in the Vienna Museum. An extraordinary horse, almost like a giraffe, stretches out its neck in order to place its small triangular head exactly in the armature of the rectangle. St Paul himself seems to be holding his arms out more in order to show us the direction of the diagonal than to express his emotion.

Since the calm simplicity taught by Alberti was a thing of the past and the weighty realism that had restrained all the extravagances of abstract composition was now disdained, an almost excessive fidelity to basic design led to an abuse of diagonals. And—to return to the great masters—it is instructive to compare the pictures of Tintoretto with those of Veronese: one is surprised to see how often Tintoretto's figures sway over towards the side, while those of Veronese are stable and firmly planted. This phenomenon is particularly striking in those of Tintoretto's pictures

8. Bk V, ch. i, p. 251.

Jacopino del Conte: Descent from the Cross; drawing. *(Paris, Louvre, Cabinet des Dessins)*

Jacopino del Conte: Descent from the Cross; finished picture. *(Rome, San Giovanni. Photo Anderson)*

Symmetry about the vertical axis, together with composition on the circle. This symmetry is strict, yet has the suppleness of a decorative pattern, which is here the double S: it is even more strongly asserted in the final picture than in the drawing.

that contain few figures, such as the Uffizi *Leda*, the Lyons *Danaë*, the London *Origin of the Milky Way* and his *Three Graces* and *Mercury* in the Doge's Palace[9].

But the serpentine form is not merely well adapted to follow the directions imposed on it; wavy and sinuous, it lends itself, as we have seen, to decorative curves. Here we have the final development of Mannerist composition: decoration becomes design and takes the place of the circles, triangles and diagonals. As in the Romanesque period, though with less constancy and less variety, the forms follow the regular decorative design made up of curves. The revival of a taste for a certain kind of symmetry helped to lead artists in this direction. In the passage quoted above (p. 122), Lomazzo insists on the importance of the central point: the figures should be arranged about it and should look towards it. The pattern of curves about an axis or centred on a point—that type of pattern which is derived from doubling—has here appeared anew.

9. It should not, however, be forgotten that many canvases now exhibited in museums were originally intended to fulfil an architectural function (as ceiling paintings, paintings above doors, etc.). It is clear that, in these cases, monumental perspective played a great part in the way they were worked out.

Among the frescoes by Jacopino del Conte in the Church of San Giovanni at Rome (painted in about 1540), a *Descent from the Cross* will hold our attention on account of its astonishing symmetry. As in many pictures with a semicircular top, this semicircle is continued through the bodies of the two thieves; but there is something else: the S curves and the figures forming the semicircle are reproduced so exactly on either side of the middle that all one sees is a kind of large flower, the Florentine lily. In a drawing for this picture, which survives in the Louvre, the composition is still indecisive, still being sought, but the felicitous lines which the artist has invented matter more to him than what they represent: the curve of the tree in the drawing is retained in the picture, but the tree is replaced by a piece of drapery.

Mannerism, though in Italy it was soon stifled by the flood of new forces, was to produce its finest flowers elsewhere—sometimes in very distant places; and its genius, El Greco, came late. He was an isolated genius—too personal, it has been said, to have imitators; but it would be more true to say that he was the representative of an aesthetic that belonged to the past and of an art no longer current. Mannerism, which has been so much decried, was scarcely more than an empty form, because the artists who adopted it saw in it merely a vocabulary. But El Greco put into those supple and obedient lines all his mysticism; and he showed that the artistic conception of the flame, dear to Lomazzo, can express the most sublime

El Greco: Christ on the Mount of Olives. *The inspiration of this symbolic composition is Byzantine, but the forms no longer have any contact with concrete reality; they express abstract ideas only. Certain elements, such as the sleeping Apostles, seem charged with some Freudian revelation. (London, National Gallery)*

El Greco: Feast in the House of Simon the Pharisee. *The symmetry is slightly to one side but very strongly marked. By fusing the details together it creates a decorative pattern which dies out at the top of the steeple, and its strictness is broken only by the architecture of the room. We have here an instance of the opposed 'S's of which Lomazzo was so fond. (Chicago Art Institute)*

aspiration. It should not then surprise us to find in his work the main Mannerist principles of composition, and especially decorative composition, in their most perfect and living form.

Many of El Greco's pictures strike us by their strict symmetry. The Prado *Ascension* is the most perfect example. In it there is nothing that is not a flame: of these flames the wildest is the Christ, upright in the axis; the other figures are incurved regularly about him. The *Baptism* in the Corsini Gallery at Rome is even more decorative: about the central axis its symmetry draws a series of mystic almond shapes. In the *Feast in the House of Simon the Pharisee* (Chicago Art Institute) the decorative design burgeons from the lower centre, follows the legs to the knees where they almost meet, curls about the figures till it comes together and fades out upon the church spire in the background, forming, as it were, a goblet or ciborium. But now let us turn to the *Burial of Count Orgaz*, the master's most astonishing composition. With its upper part rounded in a semicircle, this grandiose picture is composed like a Romanesque tympanum. The upper part, which constitutes the tympanum itself, is invaded by a huge symmetrical decorative design like a trefoil, reminding us of the arrangement of the figures in the Moissac tympanum. The lower part is a lintel: this is emphasized by the row of heads, which is horizontal as in almost all the medieval church doors and is centred upon a tear-shaped motif; into the middle of this motif is thrown a hand like a flower, in its calyx of lace. This motif has its axis governed by the upper part; and if they are joined together, there appears a huge palmette covering the whole area of the picture. It should be observed that the general axis of this highly symmetrical picture is slanted towards the lower left-hand corner. It could be argued that this is due to a defect of vision, for a similar slant appears rather frequently in El Greco's paintings; but the explanation is hardly satisfactory, since in some of them the axis is strictly vertical and central, as it is in those mentioned above. In the *Coronation of the Virgin* at Talavera la Vieja, El Greco takes up again the composition of the *Burial*, with its lower band stressed by the heads and surmounted by a huge palmette; here too the axis is placed slightly to the left, but this time it does not slant.

El Greco carries abstraction much further in the London *Christ on the Mount of Olives*. Here the forms are no longer organized about a decorative scheme, a harmonious curve, but, as in the work of Chagall, about an idea: the bare rock behind the Christ, which reminds one of the escarped crags in miniatures of the thirteenth and fourteenth centuries[10], is merely a curtain, a *mandorla*, isolating him in his suffering; and the sleep of the Apostles is represented in a vivid but purely intellectual way, by the shell in which they are enclosed.

10. Cf. El Greco's *Mount Sinai* formerly in a Hungarian collection.

El Greco: Burial of Count Orgaz. *In the medieval tympana, which El Greco seems to have had in mind, the numerous figures are already bound together by a kind of unanimity, an obedience to the central theme, as well as by the single scheme that closes them in. In this picture, the figures are bound together even more closely—an interdependence that was to become still more marked in Baroque art. The Mannerist agitation running through them, tying them in knots and untying them, conceals the rigorous Romanesque pattern. (Toledo, Church of S. Tomé)*

Tintoretto: Origin of the Milky Way. *Composition on the armature of the rectangle. Tintoretto is careful to inscribe the figures of this cosmographical allegory in a whole system of curves and circles suggesting the mechanics of the spheres. (London, National Gallery. Photo Anderson)*

The logical conclusion of Mannerism is a decorative, abstract art. But abstract art lacks roots in the people; it is the art of a minority, and if it is not supported it goes out. The Church, which at that time was seeking closer contact with the people, encouraged more accessible, more stimulating forms of art, and gave its support to Baroque dynamism.

Dynamism: from the Baroque to Delacroix

The taste for diagonals was already undermining the symmetry dear to the Mannerists: soon symmetry was no longer pleasing, and then it was found repugnant. What did please was the *barroco*, irregular like Portuguese pearls—in short, the asymmetrical. Besides, the diagonals help the expression of movement: it is in vain that those swaying forms obey the armature of the rectangle—they are no longer stable. The figures appear to be falling, or taking off, into space. A movement is set going, which does not stop at the frame but projects its continuing lines beyond. This is dynamism. One cannot help thinking of Wölfflin and his striking image of *open* as against *closed* compositions, of *dynamic* compositions that burst their frame[11]. Modifying his image slightly, one might say that the frame is still there and still makes its mark, but is no longer an impassable frontier; it has become, as it were, permeable, an openwork trellis, and the movements started inside it pierce through it and escape from it.

11. H. Wölfflin, *Kunstgeschichtliche Grundbegriffe*, 1915 (English translation: *Principles of Art History*, 1932.)

The flexibility of the forms also makes them well adapted to express movement, as Lomazzo had seen quite clearly. Now all the figures become agitated. Some sorcerer has touched with his wand the saints and the gods who, for several centuries, were motionless: they awaken, dance and whirl about in a continual movement. Piero della Francesca, had he seen this ballet, would have been stupefied; so even would Raphael. Baroque art has come into being, and has put into the hands of artists an easily moulded paste with which to express the upsurge of faith of the Counter-Reformation. But the abandonment of the old constraints brings with it a certain mediocrity, and only two great masters stand out from the multitude: Tintoretto, the precursor of the Baroque, and Rubens, its great genius.

Tintoretto worked, like theatre designers, with a stunning rapidity, and on the whole avoided complicated diagrammatic designs, difficult to establish firmly. Most of his paintings are quite simply composed upon the armature of the rectangle; others on the diagonal of the square obtained by pivoting the shorter side till it falls on the longer; others on the diagonals of the two squares obtained by this method (see the *Venus and Vulcan* at Munich). Often these few lines are completed by a circle (the *Three Graces* and *Bacchus and Ariadne*, in the Doge's Palace). This latter composition, for all its unforgettable perfection, is extremely simple; the three hands join at the centre, which is the point of intersection of the diagonals. In the London *Origin of the Milky Way* the armature of the rectangle is combined with several circles, perhaps meant to suggest celestial spheres.

Tintoretto: Venus and Vulcan. *The two long oblique lines from the top on the left to the bottom on the right are the diagonals of the squares: the figures take up their position obediently on them. Lines drawn to the sides from the points where the diagonals of the squares intersect those of the rectangle give the starting point (on the left and at the top) for secondary oblique lines enclosing the scene. (Munich, Pinakothek)*

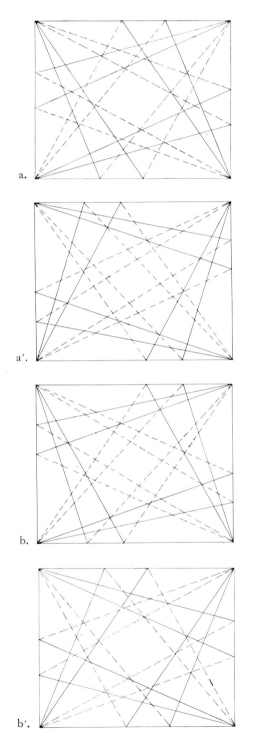

a.

a′.

b.

b′.

Tintoretto's predilection for following the diagonals given him by the frame is bound up with his constant avoidance of symmetry. This is the characteristic of all his compositions: it separates him, like Jacopo Bassano, not only from Veronese but from so pure a Mannerist as El Greco. It is true that the armature of the rectangle is, as a whole, symmetrical; but Tintoretto always takes from it one single direction, makes that the line of force of his picture, the contrary directions being recalled only by fragmentary elements. As we have seen, he uses the golden number also; and in fact this offers a line of division which is neither in the centre nor at the third, and certain ways of using it do away with symmetry. The musical ratios have the same advantage, and Tintoretto knew them well.

This asymmetry, these slanting forms launched into space and not arrested in their movement by the frame, make Tintoretto a painter who points to the future, even though he remains a Mannerist when, with the tip of a light and extraordinarily clever brush, he elongates his serpentine figures and stripes his splendid nudes with the glows of a conflagration. But what did he care for theories? His original vision was fed on the present as well as on the past, and it leads us at last definitely into Baroque dynamism.

Tintoretto is perhaps the first painter in whose work we find a particularly dynamic use of the customary frameworks: these in his hands become the means of expression for a new art. Among the great Gonzaga battle pieces now in the Munich Pinakothek, there is one—the *Battle of Pavia*—in which the foreground is a criss-cross of sloping lines delimiting zones of shade. This violent, irregular triangulation accentuates the rush of the battle, but it seems to have escaped every form of static diagram: in fact it operates a recession of musical dividing lines, which the figures accompanying our text attempt to explain. The figures a, a′, b, b′ show oblique lines shifting round in one direction or the other along the sides of the picture-area; they suggest a swaying movement, though at the same time they are firmly attached to a simple division of the rectangle. Each

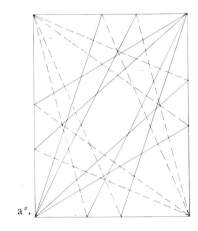

a″.

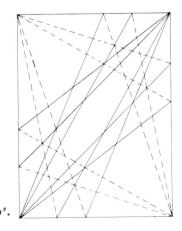

b″.

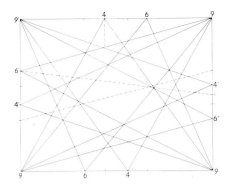

of them has its own character: the 9/12/16 framework, pivoted on the point 1/4 of the side, outlines a large central parallelogram; the 4/6/9 proportion used here by Tintoretto with its pivoting at 1/3 of the side, gives more strongly accentuated oblique bars and a small central parallelogram. Figures a″ and b″ replace the turning rhythm by a concentration of the lines of the framework upon the obliques, which they feed with their more or less open fan of lines.

Tintoretto: Battle of Pavia. *In Botticelli's Birth of Venus, as we have already seen, the movement was created by the inversion of a ratio: this method offered considerable resources* to artists with a passion for movement and dramatic expression, and in this picture Tintoretto makes authoritative use of it. (Munich, Pinakothek)*

This is a vivid example of the effort made by the Baroque artists to give suppleness to the traditional methods and to extract from them new schemes capable of sustaining the exuberance of their ideas.

Rubens lived in Italy from 1600 to 1608—that is to say from when he was twenty-three to when he was thirty-one. There he learnt his trade: he learnt, in fact, all that could be learnt there at that time. He assimilated Italian practice more or less as it was understood at the Academy of the Carracci: the force of Michelangelo, Raphael's art of composition, the colour and fire of the Venetians. He knew the musical ratios, the golden number and the possibilities of the rectangle. From Raphael he took the practice of setting a bright area in symmetry with its answering dark; from Michelangelo the powerful play of muscles, of which he remained fond till the end of his life; from the Mannerists, Michelangelo's pupils, he retained principally the theory of the *contrapposto*. A brightly lit figure, for instance, will be seen from behind, while the figure in shade will be facing us—but in a far more subtle way than this suggests. The result is that the figures seem to be dancing a ballet: in the *Story of Maria de' Medici* in the Louvre, the figures of France and Spain seem to be moving round the two princesses whom they are welcoming. In the Munich *Lion Hunt* the dance takes place around the lion. In this picture the *contrapposto* is, very precisely, a reversed symmetry; the axis of the central group (which is not in the middle of the picture, and we shall see why) divides this group into two hooks which are more or less symmetrical by reference to a certain point, but one of them is turned towards the top and left (the head of the horse) and the other towards the bottom and right (the head of the man who has fallen). The figures on the ground correspond to one another in the same way.

The dynamic outlines here reproduced on p. 156 were used by Rubens at every period of his life, but especially after his return from Italy. It is difficult to know who invented them, but the idea was certainly Italian. Such outlines are evidence of a tenacious taste for proportion, and the subtlety of these combinations of lines could only arise in the country of the great artist-geometers and theorists. The two triptychs in Antwerp Cathedral, the *Raising of the Cross* and the *Descent from the Cross*, have their axes placed with almost excessive insistence upon the diagonal; and there is a symmetrical movement of the wingpieces, with the one on the left reproducing the movement in the central panel and the one on the right reversing it. But these obvious facts do not suffice to account for the composition; they do not explain the crossing of the lines of light

Rubens: The Exchange of the Princesses. *Lomazzo, quoting the authority of Michelangelo, advised painters to present the movements of the human body in such a way as to suggest a serpentine shape. If the right arm is advanced, the left must be withdrawn, and so on. This is* contrapposto. *Rubens, in this picture, develops it not in each figure* separately but in the composition as a whole: France and Spain (wearing helmets) and the young princesses set before us a strange revolving movement of faces, backs and profiles. Note also the two 'S's of the composition, running from the curtains at the top to the Tritons at the bottom. (Paris, Louvre. Archives photographiques)

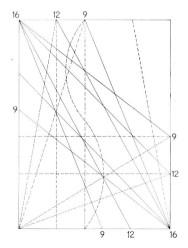

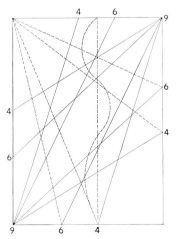

Rubens: Raising of the Cross. *To accentuate the violence of the movement and postures, Rubens groups his chosen ratios at two opposite corners of the picture: he thus obtains a composition with an enhanced dynamism. On one vertical, drawn through a point dividing a side at 9, the 'S' is entwined. (Antwerp Cathedral)*

Rubens: Descent from the Cross. *As in the Raising of the Cross, Rubens groups the ratios at the corners; but since the subject is a less brutal one, he has adopted a less close ratio. (Antwerp Cathedral)*

over the axis just mentioned. A glance back at figures a″ and b″, and all becomes clear: the *Raising of the Cross* follows the proportions 9/12/16 arranged as in figure b″, and in the *Descent* the proportion is 4/6/9 as in figure a″, a broader arrangement which spreads a wider band down the diagonal. Rubens took up these dynamic compositions again several times. He was still a young man—he was just forty when he painted the *Lion Hunt* mentioned above. In this the 4/6/9 ratios of figure a″ are used, starting from all four sides of the canvas. The vast sloping and flowing fall of the unseated horseman is clearly circumscribed, the three lances strictly positioned, the long, low oblique lines near the bottom definitely delimited. The *Battle of the Amazons*, which is perhaps slightly earlier, is governed by a design like that in figure a, and the turning diagram, which seems to sway towards the right and downwards, expresses perfectly the whirling movement of the cavalcade from left to right on the bridge, and then from right to left in the river. Rubens used a similar outline or diagram in the Berlin *Conversion of St Paul* (cf. fig. b′) and in the Antwerp *Adoration of the Magi* (figs. a and a′).

Delacroix, who had meditated on his art more consistently than many of his fellow artists, spoke of 'the immense influence that the principal lines have upon a composition...[12]' These principal lines are sometimes few. The artist takes them as his basis and founds his building on them, so that it may then develop freely. To Claude Lorrain, as we have seen, a few quite simple diagonals had been sufficient, and the outlines which, I have suggested above, were the axes and 'principal lines' of some of Rubens's compositions are likewise reduced to the bare essential—two points judiciously chosen on each side of the rectangle were enough. But Rubens soon ceased to feel the need for any dynamic outline to help him to unite his figures fierily in a single lyrical movement: more and more sure of himself, he came, like Tintoretto, to the point where he could express the most violent movement by those extremely simple means, the armature of the rectangle and the circle.

Rubens's use of the armature of the rectangle is a highly individual one. By making the oblique lines start not from the corners but from the ends of the middle lines, he opened out wide fans of directive lines which are visible with particular clearness in the *Apotheosis of Henri IV*, in the *Kermess* (both pictures in the Louvre), and in great landscapes like the *Sunset* (London, National Gallery), the *Landscape with a Shepherd* (Lord Carlisle) and the *Summer* (Windsor).

But it was the circle and the many possible combinations of circles that enabled him to produce his most varied and original compositions. In

12. *Journal*, 25 January 1847; English translation by Lucy Norton, London, Phaidon, 1951, p. 57.

Rubens: Rape of the Daughters of Leucippus. *Composition on the rectangle and on circles and arcs, combined, as nearly always in the work of Rubens, with contrapposto. The judicious use of curves and countercurves gives the whole scene a kind of amorous gentleness, in spite of the violence of the subject. (Munich, Pinakothek. Photo Giraudon)*

Rubens: Lion Hunt. *Composition on the dynamic musical ratio. The weapons, the horses' hooves and the bodies move frantically along the slanting lines which start from the points established by the ratio. In addition, the groups are balanced with a scrupulous care for* contrapposto *both in depth and in the plane, where the Mannerist 'S's produce a secret symmetry. (Munich, Pinakothek)*

the *Apotheosis of Henri IV* he places two circles upon the armature of the rectangle, one to the right and the other to the left, symmetrically. The centre of one is Henri IV, the centre of the other Marie. Around these two circles there are two larger ones. In the *Queen's Government* the circle on the left is placed higher, because there was to have been a door underneath (it is visible in the sketch); and so Rubens gives recession to his composition. To the left and high up there are the gods of Olympus, and in the

Rubens: Apotheosis of Henri IV. *Constructed on the armature of the rectangle. The king and the queen are placed symmetrically within small circles whose centres are at the points where the diagonals of the upper horizontal half intersect those of the vertical halves (starting from the bottom of the median line). Two larger circles, to the right and left, touch three sides of the rectangle: one of them encloses the lords accompanying the queen, the other the Virtues accompanying Henri IV. These circles, by their intersection, form a volute which binds the two scenes together. (Paris, Louvre. Archives photographiques)*

circle lower down to the right the elements of discord. The *Rape of the Daughters of Leucippus* (Munich), which is perhaps Rubens's most harmonious picture, is a whole formed of regular curves based on the rectangle and the circles. Rubens brings the circle into landscape painting too: the *Rainbow* and the *Wagon Sunk in the Mud* (both pictures at the Hermitage) and the Berlin *Shipwreck of Aeneas* (based on the 4/6/9 ratio with two semicircles placed asymmetrically) are examples. Circles occur again, in the Italian manner, in those of his pictures that have rounded tops: for instance, the *Last Communion of St Francis* at Antwerp (two circles touching) and the *Crucifixion of St Peter* at Cologne (two intersecting circles). Lastly, the circle sometimes whirls around like a catherine-wheel, hurling its light in all directions, as in the Louvre *Virgin with Angels*.

Rubens: The Queen's Government. *Same principle of composition as in the preceding illustration; but here the centres of the circles are inversely symmetrical, one being on the diagonal of the upper horizontal half, the other on that of the lower half. This produces harmonious curves which run through the whole composition and accompany the figure of Apollo chasing the plagues away. (Paris, Louvre. Archives photographiques)*

The circle, which in the work of Raphael had been an element of calm, of motionless perfection, in Rubens's work turns like a wheel, drawing us with it in its giddy motion.

Rubens is the virtuoso of composition. He knew all the devices used before him, whether simple or complicated, clearly discernible or subtle, and used them as he wished, making them his own by his lyricism, which seems to come flooding out, free and untrammelled. But he always retained his predilection for the reversed symmetry which Delacroix was later to adopt as his favourite method of composition.

It may seem odd to introduce Delacroix at this point. But the great romantic painter[13] was much more a pupil of Rubens than of Guérin. His personality was not the product of the studio but of the *lycée*; he hardly did any drawing until he was eighteen; and, starting when he was much more mature and more cultivated than his fellow students of art, he reacted at once against the teaching at the Guérin studio and went off to the Louvre, which he already knew well, in search of masters after his own heart. He attached himself to Rubens, studying him with passion. Of his contemporaries, his only models were his fellow student Géricault and Gros, who was older than he, but even so he kept quite distinct from them. He has the qualities and the defects of a self-taught artist: his style is slightly uncertain and groping, but is recreated constantly by meditation.

He was also a great writer who expressed with precision and in a very pure style the clearest and most sensitive ideas on art. There are few artists whose writings show such a constant concern for composition[14]. For instance:

'With a good drawing to settle the main lines of the composition and placing of the figures the sketch can be done away with...' (15 February 1847). 'I can distinguish poets and prose writers amongst painters. The rhyme, the restraints imposed by the metre, the form that is indispensable to poetry and gives it so much vigour are like the inner symmetry in a picture, the studied, yet inspired rhythm that governs the junction or separation of lines and spaces, the echoing notes of colour, etc.' (19 September 1847).

'If it were only a question of arranging lines and colours to create a visual effect an arabesque would do as well, but when you add to a composition already interesting on account of its subject an arrangement of lines that heightens the impression, a *chiaroscuro* that grips the imagination, and a colour scheme suited to the characters, you have solved a very difficult problem and, moreover, you are moving on a higher plane. Like a musician, you are adapting to a simple melody a wealth of harmony and its mutations.' (19 May 1853).

13. Delacroix did not accept this epithet, although it fits him rather well. It should, however, be noted that 'romantic' is chiefly a literary term.

14. *Journal d'Eugène Delacroix*, Paris, Plon, 1932. (Translator's note: The extracts quoted here, except the undated one, are from the selection translated into English by Lucy Norton, London, Phaidon, 1951.)

'...independently of idea, the visible sign, the eloquent hieroglyph itself which has no value for the mind in the work of an author, becomes in the painter's hands a source of the most intense pleasure...' (20 October 1853).

'In every object the first thing to take hold of, in order to render it by the art of design, is the contrast of the principal lines.' (Vol. III, p. 426).

This concern for composition is, indeed, essentially based on instinct:

'A kind of instinct teaches the superior artist to find where the chief interest of the composition should be.' (25 January 1857).

But this instinct is made up of visual memory: unable to see all the famous pictures, Delacroix studied also a great many prints and in the end, though still ignorant of the somewhat pedantic Renaissance laws of composition and equally uninfluenced by the studio tricks derived from them,

Delacroix: Bark of Dante. *In this early work, rabatment of the sides is used. The scheme is a symmetrical one, with a few radiating diagonals. It is easy to see, already, which master Delacroix has chosen. (Paris, Louvre. Archives photographiques)*

Delacroix: Lion Hunt. *Rabatment of the shorter sides. The horizontal and vertical lines drawn through the corners of the small central square cut each side of the rectangle at two points, from which are drawn parallel oblique lines, two by two. The 'principal lines' of the composition are chosen from these—AA', BB', CC' and DD'. (Paris, Collection Heugel. Photograph by kind permission of Mr. J. Diéterle)*

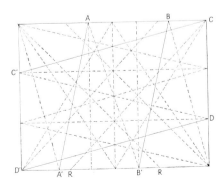

composed his pictures as the masters had done. The phrase already quoted— 'the immense influence the principal lines have upon a composition'— comes at the beginning of a very penetrating analysis of two engravings after Rubens: Delacroix takes a *Lion Hunt* (of which the original is lost[15]) and contrasts with it the *Hippopotamus Hunt* (original in the Munich Pinakothek) which is regularly inscribed upon the diagonals of the rectangle 'approximately in the shape of a St Andrew's cross with the hippopotamus in the centre'—lines which prolong 'a line of light'; and he notes clearly the concentration of the axes near the middle of the picture into a sort of star—a device he was to take up in turn in his *Hunt* pictures.

This concentration of axes, Rubens's way of using the armature of the rectangle, recurs constantly in Delacroix, beginning with the *Bark of Dante*, his first masterpiece—a fan of slanting lines which start from the middle of the top side and the middles of the right and left sides. The *Massacre of Scio* and the *Death of Sardanapalus* are composed similarly: the latter is divided into two symmetrical rectangles by a clearly visible vertical axis. The *Women of Algiers* are inscribed upon a diagonal, intersected by the line joining the middle of the left side to the middle of the base.

From the *Justice of Trajan* (1840) onwards, Delacroix showed a preference for the squares which are obtained by folding a shorter side on to a longer, and which overlap in the central area of the picture, as, for instance, in the *Entry of the Crusaders into Constantinople*, in a smaller version of the *Women of Algiers* (1849) and in the *Expulsion of Heliodorus*.

15. Max Rooses, *L'Œuvre de P. P. Rubens*, no. 1153 (reprod.).

Delacroix: Death of Sardanapalus. *In this, which is one of his finest compositions, the whole effect is one of equilibrium between opposites: light and dark tones, full and empty spaces, warm and cold tones, lights and shades. The construction is based on the armature of the rectangle. A few oblique lines start from points established by this scheme and group themselves at the top and bottom of the central axis. The large system of rays crossing the picture from left to right is delimited by the diagonals of the halves (vertical and horizontal) which start from*

In the *Liberty* (1830), though the influence of Géricault is clear, Rubens's example has made him adopt a composition that is full of life: to the lines of the rectangle it adds a dynamic triangle; this triangle is inscribed rather oddly upon the 9/16 ratio which sways over towards the right. It is unlikely that Delacroix chose this ratio consciously, for certainly he had no conceptual awareness of it; but his memory of pictures he had seen, guided by his great understanding for the implication of a subject, must have suggested it to him quite naturally.

The most individual characteristic of the compositions of Delacroix is their regular and balanced alternation of light and dark areas. This, together with the play of complementary colours, is the secret of the

the upper left-hand corner. So much for the framework of the picture plane. But to this is added a composition in depth: without realizing it, we are drawn into that imaginary space, into that marvellous equilibrium of women, slaves, horses and treasure gravitating about the bed on which Sardanapalus lies. (Paris, Louvre. Archives photographiques)

pictorial equilibrium to be found in most of his works. Here too Delacroix was a disciple of Rubens; but what, to the imagination of the great Flemish painter, was simply one effect among many others became for Delacroix a favourite means of expression. In the *Sardanapalus* the figures corresponding to one another along the symmetrical diagonals are opposed values, and this makes one half of the picture almost the negative of the other. In the sketch the linear arrangement is less strict, but this symmetry of contrasts can already be felt very clearly. The forms wheel, as in a Rubens sketch. In the picture itself, where more scope has been given to thought-out design, the classical spirit in Delacroix dictated to him a greater regularity: the curves are still dynamic, but they rise like a fountain from the bottom centre and expand in curves like foliage, dark on the left around the brightly lit horse's head, and bright around a dark patch to the right[16].

This alternation, already present in the *Massacre of Scio*, was to provide, throughout Delacroix's career, the musical melody and vibrant accompaniment to his battles, his Moorish horsemen, his large-scale compositions and his small sketches. In the *Heliodorus* it becomes a true, formal symmetry and creates a decorative arabesque.

16. A most interesting study of the pattern in this picture has been made by Marcelle Wahl, in her *Le Mouvement dans la peinture*, Paris, Alcan, 1936.

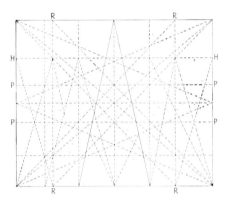

Delacroix: Entry of the Crusaders into Constantinople. *Rabatment of the shorter sides of the rectangle. The diagonals of the squares RR thus formed orientate the two groups in the foreground and give the principal horseman his movement. Long vertical lines, issuing from the points where the horizontals PP through the corners of the small central square intersect the diagonals of the two squares RR, divide the surface unequally and fix the positions of the lances and of the architecture. The points where the inner side of each of the main squares intersects the diagonal of the other give a horizontal HH, on which the horizon is placed, and many of the obliques which give the composition its rhythm end at this horizontal. (Paris, Louvre. Photo Giraudon)*

VII COMPOSITIONS IN SPACE

Up to now it has been from the point of view of geometry only that we have been studying the important problem—with which painters have been faced in every period—of depth: of how to express in one plane the third dimension, or rather to produce a transcription of it, an equivalent to it, in that plane. Every painter stumbles over this problem and has to find a solution. It is the price of any kind of representation or evocation of the outside world, and even of any pure creation: has not Cubism, more than any other school of painting, been haunted by the third dimension? And are not the abstract colourists of our own time thinking of it when they offer a negative solution? The problem is a difficult one and requires all the resources of painting to solve it—design, colours, science and technique, all is involved. No wonder, then, that it has its effect on composition.

Aerial perspective

This effect was not very marked in the Middle Ages. Then composition followed plane geometrical figures. All the painters were aware of the Pythagorean solids, but to present more than one aspect of these was not considered very suitable to the art of design.

Nonetheless, the crucial importance of sculpture during the four great centuries of the Middle Ages must be stressed: its effect on the stage-by-stage enrichment of painting in respect of depth was always decisive. Nature is so complex that painters always found it easier to fall back on that part of reality already digested by men's thought, the work of the sculptor, and sculpture could be all the more useful to the painter since it too, in the relief carvings, was 'telling stories'. So it came about that plasticity—though not yet depth—appeared in painting. Façades, and then the partitions between a choir and its ambulatory, themselves reliefs, stood out from the background. Giotto first, in painting, was to succeed in creating a similar space, a sculptor's space. His frescoes, as I have already pointed out, live between two parallel planes.

As for that microcosm which seeps in between the human figures in a picture by Van Eyck, it is as if a window has opened on to a dream

Antonello da Messina: St Jerome in his Study. *In this picture the third dimension is conveyed more by the light than by the perspective, which is broken by the saint's study. At the same time this study acts as a screen: it reflects back the light which enters through the great opening in the foreground, and it stops the light that filters in from the back. Because of the play of these two opposing sources of light, whose glimmering rays creep over the pavement and merge there, the lovingly described objects are sometimes stepping-stones, sometimes obstacles: the spectator's eye is meant to read the depth stage by stage only, till it reaches the ultimate horizon disclosed by the windows. (London, National Gallery. Photo Anderson)*

169

country, but the composition is not modified by it: it still falls plane. The vistas of the background play, to some extent, the part of those delightful glimpses of the countryside through the chinks of shutters in Memling's portraits. There remain to be considered those scenes which are set in the middle of an architectural whole, as in Van Eyck's *Virgin in the Cathedral*: here advantage is taken of the structural features of the building to accentuate the geometrical effect. One might say that, in this case, perspective is already playing its co-ordinating and decorative part.

Lastly in Italy, as we have seen (cf. p. 116), perspective, with its network, organizes and composes; but abuse of its linear diagrams soon had the effect of destroying, instead of producing, the perception of space, and the network remained in the plane of the picture. The third dimension really made its appearance—and very abruptly—with Piero della Francesca, thanks to 'aerial perspective', so called because, as Leonardo da Vinci tells us, 'through the differences in the air we can perceive the varying distances of various buildings which are cut off at the visual base by a single line[1].'

Piero della Francesca was certainly not the inventor of aerial perspective. It was everywhere at that moment, like a stretch of limpid water or a fine mist, in the miniatures of Fouquet, in the *Cœur d'amour épris*, in the pictures of Antonello da Messina. His *St Jerome in his Study*, in the National Gallery, gives an almost stereoscopic impression, which comes from the circulation of the light behind the objects and from the clear reflections on the pavements receding in perspective: it is not the perspective drawing but the air and the light that produce, in this picture, a physical sensation of space. Yet in most of the painters of that time the conquest of depth was only tentative, and the figures are still at the front of the stage: one has merely the impression that behind them a drop curtain has gone up.

Piero della Francesca was the first to attempt to take hold of the atmosphere: he tried to make it a part of his strict world of pure forms: cubes, spheres, polyhedra. The mathematician of the Pythagorean solids could not escape from this great endeavour—to introduce space among the perfect forms of reason. And so his simple and static figures bathe in air, but as though they had been poured into a crystal (cf. the *Flagellation* and the Arezzo frescoes). Piero gives us, in fact, an equivalent to the atmosphere, but an abstract one. And, to tell the truth, the whole enterprise was beyond the means of an Italian of the fifteenth century, for it presupposed a more refined, a more supple technique of painting, one that would be more capable of expressing the play of light. For this one must wait till Vermeer. The most skilled geometrical compositions by Piero della Francesca are those in which the background is shut off, as in the *Pala Brera*, where it is only a semicircle deep, a niche.

---

1. Leonardo da Vinci, *Treatise on Painting, codex urbinas*, translated by A. Philip McMahon, Princeton, 1956, vol. I, p. 101.

Leonardo da Vinci analyzed aerial perspective with an astonishing precision, and expounded scientifically what the French miniaturists, and after them Piero della Francesca and others, had expressed instinctively:

'Perspective is divided into three parts, of which the first deals only with the line drawing of bodies; the second with the toning down of colours as they recede into the distance; the third with the laws of distinctness of bodies at various distances[2]'.

Yet he used it somewhat in the medieval fashion, or rather, like those Chinese landscape artists who prefer the fantastic to the real.

The artists of the classical Renaissance did not really try to resolve the problem of space. Their space is often not very deep and is closed in by buildings, even when the painter is trying to make it take part in the construction of the picture and to incorporate the figures into it. Correggio is a case apart: his space is not large but he is perfectly at ease in it and, apparently without any suspicion of the difficulties, makes his figures move and have their being in a three-dimensional world.

Baroque space: depth, interlinking of planes and illusionism

With the Florentine Mannerists the problem of *depth* is at last formulated in a precise and theoretical way. Here again, as in the Middle Ages, sculpture exerts a great influence: the creator of statues was in the vanguard of Mannerism and, a little later, of the Baroque. Michelangelo had thoroughly stirred the sensibility of every artist, shaken up all routines and left his mark, for a long time to come, on all the arts. But the more modest artists also played their part: Benvenuto Cellini produced what were called 'multiple views' and inspired painters like Bronzino and Daniele da Volterra to emulation; they too tried to show more than one aspect of a subject simultaneously: full-face and profile, back and front. This was a *tour de force* soon surpassed by Giambologna, who replaced multiple views by a *contrapposto* in space. Mr. J. Holderbaum has given a vivid account of this competition between painters and sculptors[3] and has described with precision Giambologna's *contrapposto:*

'He conceives the torso as a gyrating nucleus from which the projections are emitted centrifugally... The raised left arm... projects from the central and bends clockwise in a way that is precisely complemented on the opposite side of the figure by the right leg, but the first can be fully perceived from only one side, the other only from the opposite side, and they are resolved into an equilibrium—by the familiar principle of asymmetrical balance—only in the mind, which must retain a number of impressions as it does themes in musical composition.'

The painters, in fact, would not rest until they had attained not merely the multiple views of Michelangelo and his pupils but a real equilibrium

2. Leonardo da Vinci, *Paragone*, translated by Irma Richter, Oxford, 1949, p. 25.
3. In an article in the *Burlington Magazine* for December 1956: 'A Bronze by Giovanni Bologna and a Painting by Bronzino.'

in all directions. It should be noted that this did not yet constitute an element in composition: the pure Mannerists composed in the picture plane, just as did the artists of the early Renaissance; they imparted a vibration to the forms, but these still moved only in a limited space, a sculptor's space (as in the Sistine ceiling). It was the Baroque masters who really transformed this sculptural *contrapposto* into a *contrapposto* in space.

Let us go back to Rubens's *Lion Hunt* in the Munich Pinakothek, already illustrated on p. 161 above. It is interesting to trace its ground-plan. Two figures are lying on the ground, their positions apparently determined

Delacroix: Battle of the Giaour and the Pasha, 1827. *Like Rubens, whom he so much admired, Delacroix used* contrapposto. *It was in his mind from his first picture onwards —from the* Bark of Dante, *in which one of the damned is seen full-face and the other from behind. Here the horsemen circle like Rubens's goddesses dancing round the two princesses. (Chicago, Potter-Palmer Museum. Photo Giraudon)*

by a circle about the central group. The one on the right is presented with the head towards us and the legs receding, and the other the opposite way. About them, there is another circle in space: to the right a dark-coloured horse leaping forwards with its head turned to the left, and another horse, white, in flight towards the background on the left, with its head turned towards the right. Thus in this picture, as in many others by Rubens, a complex *contrapposto* displays its counterbalancing S curves upon two planes; and the circles likewise turn at different inclinations, like wheels in some wonderful piece of clockwork. In this, Delacroix followed his spiritual master. The first version (1827) of his *Battle*

Delacroix: Battle of the Giaour and the Pasha, 1835. *This second version is more subtle. The interweaving of the bodies is close—a single whirlpool. The necks of the two horses, one white, the other black, form a knot. The* contrapposto *is established in the plane rather than in space. (Collection Baronne Gérard. Photo Bulloz)*

of the *Giaour and the Pasha* is a kind of tournament in space, the horse on the right being exactly the reverse of the horse on the left, so that they circle about each other. The far more fiery version of 1835 is also more individual: the circle is brought back into the plane of the picture, and the curve of the two men with their contrasted values turns about the knot formed by the two inversely contrasted horses' heads.

But there are other ways of *associating the background with the foreground* in a composition that is really conceived in depth. Let us return to Tintoretto, that master who has already given us the transition to the Baroque.

Parmigianino: Virgin and Child with Saints.
An instance of a figure used as a screen, placed quite near us: he would join us as another spectator if he turned his head. He forms a hyphen between the main subject and us. Degas took up again, considerably later, this use of figures cut off by the picture edge, but in a different spirit. (Florence, Uffizi. Photo Alinari)

Vasari: Frescoes in the Chancellery, Rome. *The rising perspective of certain ceiling-paintings gave artists the idea of painting in depth on walls as well as cupolas. Vasari, by a clever arrangement of illusionary steps, creates a curious theatrical transition between the painting and the spectator. (Photo Alinari)*

His love of oblique lines led him to use perspective in an entirely new way: it now digs into the picture like a wedge, drawing the figures in with it, drawing with it the very interest of the scene depicted—an interest which sometimes leads us far. Tintoretto's perspective associates the figures and objects of the foreground with planes at a great depth, by means of the movements, of foreshortenings, of the architecture or, sometimes, of long tables extending to the background. The foreshortenings invented by Correggio to produce an open ceiling, and subsequently used by the Mannerists insistently (until they began to exasperate critics like Dolce) in their ingenious combinations of simultaneous attitudes, were employed by Tintoretto to pierce the wall and make his figures go through into the third dimension. In his work the triangles and other figures shift and recede into depth, though at the same time still very much in evidence in the picture plane itself.

Bassano composed in the same way. There is a real opposition between these artists and the ones who have been called 'mural painters', such as Veronese, Puvis de Chavannes and Gauguin, who always make us feel the impenetrable surface of the wall on which the painting is situated.

It is interesting to observe that this problem of a connection between the planes was one that already preoccupied the Mannerists, and that they had found some rather original solutions for it. It is in their work that one meets with the quite new idea of trying to establish a transition between the fictional world of the painted scene and the outside world, between the figures and the spectator. Vasari, in his strange decorations for the Chancellery in Rome, invented staircases which descend from each painted scene into the room, and upon which there rest detached figures who are taking no interest in the scene represented and seem ready to leave that world of fiction for our own. Well before him, Raphael and his pupils had surrounded their frescoes with *trompe-l'œil* devices, imitation relief carvings, cameos and monograms. But here the invention is altogether more bold, and these flights of steps, intermediate between truth and fiction, make one think of those which a theatrical director, such as Gémier, would let down between stage and auditorium, so that his actors might sometimes mingle with the audience.

It was no isolated innovation. Apart from the direct imitations of Vasari's steps (Poccetti, Hospital of the Innocents, Florence), other Mannerists practised such transitions: in Parmigianino's *Virgin and Child with Saints* in the Uffizi there is a figure in the foreground who is cut off at belt level. The effect is somewhat surprising, but the intention is obvious: the man is quite close to us, between the spectators and the scene.

El Greco: Christ and the Soldiers. *By cutting some of the foreground figures off at half-length, El Greco makes the scene he is showing us more poignant: in the same way, cinema directors use 'zoom' shots, in which the movement of the camera towards the principal subject gives us the illusion that we ourselves are moving. (Munich, Pinakothek. Photo Bulloz)*

El Greco: Vision of the Apocalypse. *In El Greco the Byzantine remained alive. To mix large and small figures together was a current practice in the Middle Ages, for reasons of scale and hagiography: in this picture, under the influence of Northern Italy, it is used to lead the eye from plane to plane. (New York, Metropolitan Museum)*

El Greco took up again this device of a figure cut off halfway, in his *Adoration of the Shepherds* in the Church of San Domingo at Toledo; indeed one may see in this picture a direct reference to Parmigianino. In his *Christ and the Soldiers* at Toledo and in its other versions, the holy women are likewise cut off halfway, as are the donors in the *Crucifixion* in the Louvre. In other cases, a large figure in the foreground seems to be presenting the scene to us. El Greco takes this theme from Correggio[4], who in this was certainly the initiator; but he has made a striking transposition of it in the vast caryatid-angel of his *Vision of the Apocalypse* (New York, Metropolitan Museum).

4. Copy of the *Adoration of the Shepherds*, in Rome (Contini-Bonacossi Collection).

The favourite field for the evocation of space was, from the fifteenth century onwards, landscape painting. This developed chiefly in the North, but also in Italy, where a national genius of a more intellectual kind left its mark on it. One might describe the distinct characters of these two kinds of landscape painting by saying that, in the North, from the backgrounds of the Master of Flémalle and of Fouquet to the tremendous panoramas of Bruegel, it is as though a door were opening upon the countryside, or a fan, or a cone with its point at the eye of the painter, widening out to infinity. In Italy, on the contrary, the landscape painters were at first called 'perspective artists[5]', and were so haunted by the new science that in their case the cone seems to be the other way round: all the constructional lines of space, gathered into a bundle by the limits of the frame, converge to a single point, which for a long time was placed at the centre of the picture and later, even when it shifted to one side, still dug into the distance like the point of a sharp cone[6]. Compare Vermeer's *View of Delft* with a Canaletto: both are landscapes of cities by lagoons, but the conceptions are opposed. Vermeer might have chosen a canal, a vista piercing in or through: he preferred to take up his position outside the town, which extends like a strip between the water and the sky. Canaletto makes a Venice like a building, in which the vanishing points sink a long way in, draining away with them the complexity of the details.

These two attitudes remained distinct until the nineteenth century, although the Italian perspective artists, who went on repeating the same sort of thing, were forced to yield pride of place to Northern artists acclimatized in Italy. These achieved that perfect interlinking of the different planes which became and remained one of the principal qualities of the *paysage composé*. This genre, taking its impulse from Claude Lorrain and his rivals, yielded its most perfect examples in France (Joseph Vernet and the young Corot). René Huyghe[7] has clarified the characteristics of these compositions by a comparison between Corot's study for his *Bridge at Narni* from nature with the final picture: the harmonious succession of planes, separate and yet connected from the foreground to the infinite distance, is obtained by means of a few expert transformations of the real scene.

The *contrapposto* sets the figures pivoting about; but Roman Baroque went further and detached them completely from the wall. It too arose through sculpture, and its best expression is in the statues of Bernini. But well before Bernini it existed, in germ, in the work of Michelangelo,

5. Francesco di Giorgio Martini, *The Ideal City*, Palace of Urbino, and *History of St Benedict*, Uffizi. Jacopo Bellini, *Allegory* and *Presentation of the Virgin in the Temple*, drawings, Louvre.

6. 'Perspective, in dealing with distances, makes use of two opposite pyramids, one of which has its apex in the eye and the base as distant as the horizon. The other has the base towards the eye and the apex on the horizon.' (*Literary Works of Leonardo da Vinci*; ed. J. P. Richter, Oxford, 1939, vol. I, p. 153.)

7. *Discovery of Art*, pp. 213-214, figs. 196-197.

Gian-Battista Tiepolo and G. Mengozzi Colonna: Fresco in the Palazzo Labia, Venice. *In the work of most illusionist painters, perspective plays the chief part. But here perspective is reduced to the minimum. A flight of steps invites us into a vast chamber where the light-filled atmosphere is enough to create the illusion. (Photo Anderson)*

and in the Mannerist style as soon as this left the Florentine circle and settled in Rome.

In painting the new art made its appearance with the imitation statues of the Palazzo Farnese, in which Annibale Carracci, who as an easel painter was so apt to be solemn, attained a truly Baroque exuberance. The influence of sculpture transports us into space, and then the organic unity of the painting with the architecture keeps us there: Roman Baroque is a total art, uniting the three plastic arts so completely that we cannot conceive one of them without the other, or even tell which of them it is we are looking at. This is the triumph of *illusionism*, and (as I said at the beginning of this book) of monumental perspective at its perfection. Indeed painting became so wedded to architecture as in the end to betray it and to take its place. Seen from a certain point, from the point from which it is meant to be seen, is that cupola a real one or a false one? We cannot tell. In the Palazzo Labia in Venice, Tiepolo lent his skill to a fantasy of this sort: in the view of it here given, it is hard to know which part is real and which suggested by the painting. Evocation of depth has here reached its culmination. It has come to dominate painting entirely. Never would its hold be stronger. It creates illusion, it offers a dream world, yet with a concrete realism that troubles us and, as soon as we move, makes us dizzy. Composition, like everything else, is made subject to it and has become no more than a way of constructing the fictitious space.

Luminous space

Does this mean that we have attained the ideal of Piero della Francesca —space put at the service of the painter's abstract intention? It would be natural to think so. But the truth is that the painter of Baroque architectural fantasies remains a decorator: his whole conception is a scene painter's.

It is only in Vermeer that we shall find the dream of the geometer-humanist realized. His marvellous technique enabled him to express with the utmost precision *the quantity and quality of the light on a given surface in its exact situation relative to the source of the light and to the eye of the onlooker*. Vermeer's success is absolutely exceptional; so is his aim—few painters have thought of taking it as theirs. It was the result of the researches of a solitary and slow worker; each of his pictures is the solution of a problem. With a very small number of accessories—a chair, a table covered with a heavy cloth, a window—he receives or intercepts the light, which is reflected sometimes by a wide bare wall, sometimes by the cracks and shiny surface of a map placed in a glancing light. So he constructs that dressed stone, with its true water and proper gleam, which the great geometer of Arezzo had dreamed of, and he infuses it with the gentleness of the atmosphere of the North. Vermeer really is the painter of the third dimension. The distance between the objects has even ceased to be a matter of aerial perspective: it consists in a perfect consciousness of the conditions of vision, and so of the activity of the eye and its effect on the planes[8]; hence the impression of slight vagueness which seems to envelop

8. It is as if Vermeer had had advance knowledge of the thought of a theorist who, as we shall see later, had a great influence on Seurat: 'The idea of a difference in distance is brought out by a difference in the impression made on the organ of sight, independently of the blue air of the atmosphere which, as Arago has shown, does not alter the actual colour of objects except at considerable distances. In this way one will be quite simply made aware that the object is nearer than the background, and it will detach itself from that background. Also, if the object is an isolated one, the parts of it farthest from the eye will be less distinct than the nearer ones... This proves that an object represented in the foreground can be painted in such a way as not to hold up the eye of the onlooker or distract it from the principal object, which may be situated in the second plane...' (David Sutter, *Philosophie des Beaux-Arts appliquée à la peinture*, Paris, 1870, p. 292.)

Vermeer: Young Lady standing at the Virginals. *After establishing his geometrical space with the strictness we have noted in his Artist in his Studio, Vermeer set out to do the same for light. He leads it where it should go and organizes it, establishing a hierarchy of degrees of luminosity. In this he was certainly the forerunner of the modern film technique, using panels to reflect the light on to his figures—which would explain the peculiar luminosity of his shadows. The screen was perhaps the wall facing the windows, a wall which Vermeer never shows us (note the reflection on the back of the chair on the right). As for the orthogonal strictness of the scheme, which is based on the musical ratio 4/6/9, this surely makes one think of Mondrian. (London, National Gallery)*

some parts of the picture with air. In this way Vermeer acquired the power to make (in his *Young Lady standing at the Virginals*, London, National Gallery) a light-coloured face stand out against an equally light-coloured Cupid in a picture hung on the background wall, or again (in the *Young Woman with a Water Jug*, New York) a white veil against the white wall.

Each of his pictures introduces us so intimately into its world that we feel a kind of embarrassment: we seem to intrude. In the *Allegory of the Faith* (New York, Metropolitan Museum) we have stumbled on the scene and shall disturb it. The painter, in the Vienna picture of that name, is just about to turn and ask us what we are doing there. And this curious feeling of almost magical reality, which reduces us to silence, is produced by the most strict and completely intentional art, in which nothing is left to chance—neither the placing of the model, nor the position and proportions of a map: the beauty in it is pinned down by all its co-ordinates.

Other artists of Vermeer's period set themselves problems akin to his, yet these were more closely bound up than his with the techniques of perspective. The succession of screens which we find in the pictures of Pieter de Hoogh, leading us gradually towards the full light of a small garden, have surely a vague resemblance to the flats of a stage setting. But in his pictures the space is excavated by means of an enfilading view of diversely lit rooms and, as with Vermeer, depth is expressed by more than perspective: by the intensity of the light and its atmospheric content.

Imaginary space

This exact rendering of light was already to be found in the early works of a bold and confident young Italian who had arrived in Rome at a period when all artists went there in search of fortune—a lone wolf, a provincial, who at first seemed able to paint only half-length figures flanked by a still life. This young man was Michelangelo di Caravaggio.

At that time he was painting pictures of buxom girl lute players or of Bacchus in front of a basket of fruit. His work was solid like a Courbet, subtle like a Manet, and bathed in a light almost worthy of Vermeer. But there were few openings for a genre painter in Rome, and Caravaggio meant to astonish the world; so it was that he became the violent innovator whose influence on the great luminists of the North was so considerable. Caravaggio has brought us back to Italy, and I may be criticized for devoting so much space to the Italian school. But the Italians were responsible for all the abstract theories which form landmarks throughout the history of painting until the nineteenth century; and in so far as composition is intentional and thought out and not a matter of workshop traditions, Italy was its birthplace and the country where it acquired its most characteristic forms.

In the case of Caravaggio, as I have said, we have to do with a real innovator, and a violent one—or at least the violence of his second phase has caused him to be regarded as such: but this judgment needs to be modified.

He was not a self-taught artist: he came to Rome after having gleaned the lessons of the Lombard and Venetian painters. True, his character drove him to surprise and even to shock people, but he had learned his job like the other painters, from the same masters. At the same time he detested Mannerism, opposing to it a still-life painter's concrete feeling for the object. Finding the insipidities he was invited to paint ridiculous, he thought out afresh the religious subjects which had foundered in conventionality and, in doing so, opened the way to Rembrandt. But, as there was in him an element of mischief-making and lack of deference, he jostled traditions in the hope of causing a scandal. His spirit is that of a rebel, yet his composition is not revolutionary: taking his saints from the people, he shoves in our faces their feet and legs and the buttocks

Caravaggio: Entombment. *Lines starting from the upper right-hand corner seem
to draw the figures in a swaying movement
towards the lower left-hand corner, which in
a picture is the region of misery* (sinistra).
*The dynamic ratio a″ which, as we know,
groups the oblique lines in wide fans along the
diagonal, is used as framework for this composition. (Rome, Vatican. Photo Anderson)*

of their horses, but these heavy masses obey the most familiar designs:
the armature of the rectangle or the dynamic lines. The *Martyrdom of
St Matthew* is constructed on the 9/12/16 ratio (fig. *b′*, p. 156 above),
the Vatican *Entombment* on 4/6/9 (fig. *a″*).

In spite of this, Caravaggio's compositions are set apart by the passion he had for close-ups. Contrary to the customs of his time, he did not paint from drawings or sketches, but directly from the model. He painted what he saw; and this practice, handed on to the Northern schools, introduced quite new qualities into the art of painting. He himself remained always a painter of the object; his models, arranged close to him in his studio, became foreground figures, close-ups even, sometimes cut off by the frame. (Later, apparently as a counterblast to Caravaggio's imitators, Natoire[9] was to say: 'What is the good of painting from nature? Can nature supply middle and background figures?')

Along with the new way of presenting human figures there was a correspondingly new style of lighting. The young man from the provinces, as I have said, meant to astonish; and, to succeed in a city like Rome, saturated with painters, as is the Paris of our own day, it was essential to have a new idea. Caravaggio darkened his studio and threw the rays of a lamp, or of several lamps, on to his models, to awaken glows and reflections. Already, before him, Bassano had diffused a dark scene with coloured gleams of light, but always with a lyricism that was the opposite of Caravaggio's meticulous accuracy. Caravaggio was the originator of that dramatic use of light that was so much in vogue in the seventeenth century. In his work the object, of which he had such an acute sense, is isolated by the new method and becomes obsessive; but in the work of his Northern imitators, who had the minds of dreamers or visionaries, it becomes enveloped in something like a halo of light, which robs it of its reality.

To attempt to analyze pictures by Rembrandt may well be presumptuous. His way of composing a picture, like the texture itself, appears mysterious; it seems to escape from every kind of contingent factor. His technique consisted of continual retouching, of sheer work, of *cuisine;* and his conception was always supple, constantly changing, entailing such sacrifices of work already done that the final state of a picture or etching by him is often far removed from its starting point.

It was in etching that Rembrandt found his true expression, at least at the start. Gradually he transposed into painting the thrilling contrasts he had drawn from the copperplate, and these contrasts still kept pride of place on the canvas. Rembrandt did in fact learn, by the practice of engraving, to sacrifice details or secondary elements for the sake of the important figure, and he accustomed himself to heighten the centre of interest by means of light. And such was Rembrandt's love of light that in the end he became miserly with it: he used it as a stage manager often uses lighting: letting shadow occupy the whole stage and sacrificing the secondary characters, he steers the spectator's eyes to a point he has carefully chosen.

Formal composition, in Rembrandt, was simple and yet concealed. Bruegel apart, there is perhaps no other artist whom I have found so hard to decipher. But, as always with a great painter, it is from the work

9. Quoted by J. Charpier and P. Seghers, *L'Art de la peinture,* Paris, 1957, p. 308

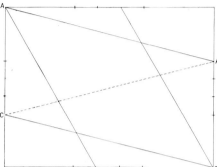

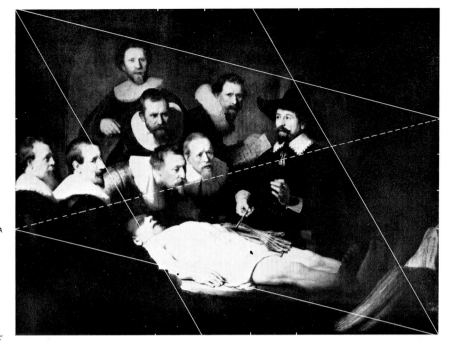

Rembrandt: The Anatomy Lesson of
Professor Tulp. *From four points, one on
each side of the picture, slanting lines are
drawn to the corners—two pairs of parallels.
The parallelogram AA' CC' is divided by a
diagonal into two equal triangles. Rembrandt
groups the portraits in the upper triangle,
and reserves almost the whole of the other
triangle for the corpse. (The Hague, Mau-
ritshuis. Photo Bulloz)*

itself that the schemes are gradually seen to emerge. It is, indeed, a curious
fact that Rembrandt's method, though more simple, is not unlike Bruegel's.
In some of Bruegel's pictures we observed parallel oblique lines starting
from points on the sides of the picture, selected from a division of each
side into nine. Rembrandt seems to content himself with four carefully
chosen points, one from each side; then, by a play of parallel oblique lines,
he obtains a parallelogram, which he sometimes cuts into two triangles.
This scheme is akin to the dynamic ratios. If we observe the points with
attention, we shall notice that they often produce a division of the central
third into three, which corresponds precisely with the familiar 4/6/9
ratio taken in both directions. Sometimes, but less often, the points
are further apart and correspond to the 9/12/16 ratio, again taken symmetrically.

The first scheme I have found in many of his pictures—in, for instance,
the *Anatomy Lesson of Professor Tulp* (The Hague), the Dresden *Portrait
of the Artist with Saskia*, the Leningrad *Sacrifice of Isaac* and the Louvre
Tobias and the Angel. Examples of a broader scheme, based on 9/12/16,
are the Leningrad *Danaë*, the Frankfurt *Blinding of Samson* and the Louvre
Bathsheba with its triangle of bright light inserted into a dark triangle.

This parallelogram situated on the diagonal was also used by Rembrandt
in many etchings, for instance in the *Jan Six* and the *Man Weighing Gold*.

What we find, in short, are the dynamic ratios recalled in a weakened
form, simplified by a master who was intent on stressing not the forms
so much as their transfiguration by light. Their recall should not
surprise us. Though Rembrandt did not visit Italy, others had done

Rembrandt: Blinding of Samson. *To the basic scheme, by which a chosen point on each side of the picture is used to form a parallelogram and this is divided into two triangles, Rembrandt adds further oblique lines which start from the four points or end at them: these oblique lines regulate the violent movements of the figures. (Frankfurt, Städelsches Kunstinstitut)*

so for him, Lastman, his master, in 1604, Terbrugghen from 1604 to 1614, Honthorst from 1610 to 1622; and the influence of the school of Caravaggio on Rembrandt (we find in him even themes taken from Caravaggio or from Honthorst) is so obvious that to insist on it is pointless. At the same time, like all the artists of his country, Rembrandt was little influenced by the Baroque. He was a great collector, and by preference his mind looked to the past; he had seen a great many old pictures and engravings, and remained faithful to stable, rectangular and symmetrical compositions in a spirit that was on the whole Classical or Mannerist.

Though a contemporary of Vermeer, Rembrandt's conception of art is wholly opposed to his. The Delft painter is the master of peaceful and sober life in full daylight. But Rembrandt is a magician with shadows: he draws the onlooker into deep darkness with a lantern in his hand, like his shepherd in the National Gallery *Adoration*, and throws its compassionate light on the sad spectacle of life.

The sense of equilibrium

Since depth was no longer suggested, as it had been in the Middle Ages, but was so rendered as to be directly felt, lines and coloured surfaces were replaced by *volumes*. As soon as forms are changed into volumes, we find that they acquire *weight*, and we cannot help experiencing a sensation of *equilibrium* or *disequilibrium*. And even if the composition is a dynamic one, even if a movement is indicated by the gestures of the figures, by the lines of their bodies and by the outline schemes which they obey, we like the masses to have a certain stability, to settle calmly within the limits of the picture. This reassuring impression is one on which we insist in the cases of architecture and sculpture, even when the materials and structural devices used make possible the most daring overhang. In painting, when the masses force themselves on the imagination, they act on us as if they were real solids, and the *contrapposto*, moving over from sculpture into painting, introduces there its demand for balance.

Just as we weigh things approximately in the hand, so the idea of 'balance' is a supple and subtle one, a matter not of calculation but of instinct. This is certainly what Poussin meant when he wrote to de Chambray that 'these parts are the painter's affair and cannot be taught[10]'. As is well known, he used to put this idea of mass to the test concretely, by modelling tiny figures and grouping them so as to get the direct sensation of equilibrium in space.

In proportion as the science of composition was lost, the part played by instinct increased. As we have seen, the extremely precise ideas of the theorists became more and more vague in the course of oral transmission. The musical proportions, for so long a reality in Italy, ceased to be more, to the Parisian Academy, than a confused memory of some influence of music on painting; the ideas of geometry were mixed up with perspective; and although the divisions of the rectangle remained, they lost their refinements. In the studios nothing at all precise was now taught about composition, which had degenerated to the use of a few devices, nor in the academies, where the lecturers lost themselves in literary analyses or side issues, wandering around on the outskirts of art (commentaries on iconography, ancillary branches of knowledge) because they no longer had any painterly doctrine; and the pupils clung to the ideas of equilibrium of masses and distribution of groups, since these are directly accessible.

10. Letter dated 1 March 1665.

'A group is an union of figures... they ought to be composed of an unequal number,' says Mengs in his *Practical Lessons upon Painting*[11]. And again he says:

'Who knew better than him [Raphael] how to equilibrate the compositions, to piramid the groups, and to give the contrast of an alternative motion to the members of the figures?[12]'...

And d'Azara, first editor of the 'Master's' writings, adds pompously:

'To piramid the groups, is to make the objects form a piramid, that is, that it has a greater base than point. And that in any other form but that in which they are composed, be it straight or circular, they will have a frightful effect.'

At the turn of the century Girodet took up the phrase and turned it to ridicule: 'According to the terms current in the schools at that time, it was always necessary to "*peloter*" and to "*faire pyramider la composition*[13]".'

Such are the confused expressions to which, in the end, the forgetting of geometry leads. Hardly anything was left but a certain visual memory, when the artist came under the spell of masterpieces made available through the collections of prints.

This equilibrium, judged by the eye rather than by calculations and measurements, was originally, it is true, an equilibrium of masses, as it was for the sculptor; but in painting its application was only to fictitious masses, essentially expressed by *shade* and *light*. Shadows and lights were means for the expression of volumes, certainly, but they were also a play of light and dark spots or patches on the plane surface of the picture. And so the equilibrium of values, that painterly expression of the play of volumes, becomes an equilibrium of spots or patches, such as the etcher seeks to realize on his inked plate.

A strange fact intervenes here: the whites and blacks do not have to be equalized in order to achieve counterpoise. The general practice of the great Venetians, according to Reynolds, was:

'To allow not above a quarter of the picture for the light, including in this portion both the principal and the secondary lights... Rembrandt... much less, scarce an eighth: by this conduct Rembrandt's light is extremely brilliant...[14]'

It is clear that the extent of the shade or of the light is in inverse ratio to its intensity. In Japanese prints a few spots of absolute black can perfectly counterbalance an entirely bright image without a single shadow. When the Impressionists, obsessed by the open air, excluded all the dark values from their palette, the equilibrium was disturbed and the result, in the long run, is a certain monotony.

11. *Works of Antony Raphael Mengs, First Painter to His Catholic Majesty Charles III*, with notes by Don Joseph Nicholas d'Azara; English translation, London, 1796: vol. II, p. 145.

12. *Op. cit.*, vol. I, p. 100 (from 'Description of the principal paintings of the royal palace at Madrid').

13. *De l'ordonnance en peinture*, Girodet-Trioson, *Œuvres posthumes*, Paris, 1829, vol. II, p. 226.

14. Reynolds, *Notes on the Poem 'The Art of Painting' by A. du Fresnoy*.

The ratio between light and dark areas, though it may vary from one painter to another and from one school to another, does therefore rest on a permanent basis. This can be clearly seen in our own day: the abstract painters who refuse to express volume but distinguish forms by contrasts of colour only, are in spite of everything led by their instinct for fundamental equilibria to set light tones and dark tones in opposition.

This instinct, formed or at least sustained by so constant a visual habit, has produced the same need for equilibrium in the field of *colour*.

It might seem, in theory, that equilibrium between colours must lead to the synthesis of the spectrum, to white—that is to say, must require the use of complementary colours in equal doses. Actually, nature rarely presents us with this absolute: some dominant tone is supplied by the atmosphere or the play of the light. And some Dutch painters have used colour moderately, or have even stuck closely to monochrome, precisely in order to avoid the instability of tones that threaten to break the unity of the light.

Viewed from this aspect, painters can be divided into two groups, or rather there are two attitudes towards colour. The aim of the *colourists* is a decorative equilibrium of tones, while that of the *optical* painters is to render as well as possible the modifications of colour offered to us by nature. These two tendencies have, at certain periods, been symbolized in the most striking way by two painters who can be set in clear opposition: thus, the purely colourist efforts of Poussin can be set against those of the man whom he called the anti-painter, the 'optical' Caravaggio. Delacroix the colourist, with his tremendous skill in the play of complementary colours, stands facing Courbet. Gauguin makes his pure tones sing by means of cunningly muted transitions of subdued tones, in contradiction to Seurat, in whose work the optical becomes scientific without, on that account, changing its aim. These clear-cut attitudes are rare. While Vermeer is an optical artist *par excellence* (a fact that does not prevent him from giving full value to colours), it would be true to say that so complete a master as Titian is haunted by the two types of research, whose union he embodied. In his *Bacchus and Ariadne*, to quote Reynolds again: 'To Ariadne is given (say the criticks) a red scarf, to relieve the figure from the sea which is behind her. It is not for that reason, alone, but for another of much greater consequence; for the sake of the general harmony and effect of the picture'[15]. (cf. p. 107)

We shall shortly see how first the nineteenth century, and then our own contemporaries, have endeavoured to solve the problems of space and colour.

15. Sir Joshua Reynolds, *Discourse* 8.

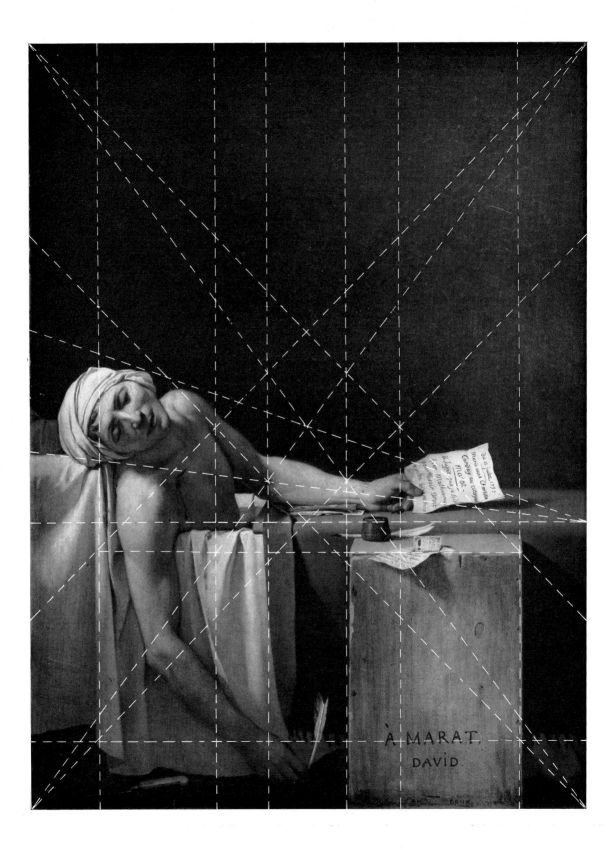

À MARAT

DAVID

VIII PICTURE FRAMEWORK IN THE NINETEENTH CENTURY

At the end of the eighteenth century, as we have seen, the schools no longer had anything to teach but insipidity and sentimentality. They were played out, when David came upon the scene, an artist who gave them an ideal once more and, with his young revolutionary blood, put life into the phantoms and the dead gods.

Everyone has stressed the miraculous effect of the time he spent in Rome. He left France as a pupil of Boucher, the decorator of Marie Guimard's boudoir; Rome dazzled him, 'removed his cataract', and from his second visit there he brought back *The Horatii*. In spite of the passage of time, which rubs out so many contrasts and makes so many violent controversies quite unintelligible, the novelty of this picture remains great. Was it the result, simply, of contact with the Antique? All the French painters at that time went to Rome; but they did not know how to use their eyes. David saw in the Roman bas-reliefs and sarcophagi very simple, angular compositions, fixed strictly in their rectangular frames and totally opposed to the *entrain*, the *chaleur*, the *membres cassés avec grâce* which were the shibboleths taught him by his master. But Poussin, too, had studied the works of the Greeks and Romans with passion, and this feeling for the frieze, this frontality, had been introduced by him into his work. Does this mean that David was a return to Poussin? His *Belisarius*, painted after his first visit to Rome, might make one think so: it has the same style of landscape painting and the same solemnity of mime—note the restrained gesture of the soldier. But *The Horatii* is quite another matter. Why? In the first place, the Roman atmosphere has changed: the scholarship has become less philosophical and more accurate. Greek things had come into fashion. But in addition, David was by nature bold, and it was he who would bring into painting that spare and grandiose style of which Boullée and, a little later, Ledoux were the courageous pioneers in French architecture.

The gradual affirmation of his originality can be seen very clearly even in the most superficial aspect of his work, in fact in his architectural backgrounds. The background of his Prix de Rome picture with its pilasters and Ionic columns, its friezes and griffons and its recessed bas-reliefs, is pure Louis XVI. In his *Belisarius* these same columns have their fluting eaten away by time, for David had now seen and fallen in

David: Marat. *In this picture, which is ruled by antique simplicity as this was understood at the time, all the orthogonal lines—for example, the upper edge of the bath—are tributaries of the small central square formed by the diagonals of the two squares that come from the rabatment of the rectangle's shorter sides. (Brussels, Musée des Beaux-Arts. Photo Giraudon)*

love with the Roman ruins. He retained those columns with their double-scrolled bases in his *Andromaque*. But already, in the *Portrait of Count Potocki*, he adopted the wall parallel to the picture plane, like a true background to a frieze, cold and bare. Yet a vestige of timidity made him trail some ivy over it, and in the *Andromaque* the wall is in shadow with a curtain falling across it. It was in the following year (1784), in *The Horatii*, that David came into the open; here, for the first time in French art, was someone presenting Doric columns, authentically Greek, with no bases; it should indeed be observed that the arcades in this picture belong to the architecture of Ledoux rather than to that of the Greeks or Romans. Finally, in his *Brutus*, David, encouraged by success, produced a regular Doric colonnade complete with entablature. The new style was taken up. His furniture, his coiffures were imitated: David set the fashion.

But let us go deeper: style is not made of settings and accessories, and it was by other things that David brought a new quality into composition. He did not for long retain the reserved mime of Poussin's figures: he came to like tense gestures, stressed by repetition. This is shown, already in the *Belisarius*, by the parallelism of the arms, then by that of the arms and legs of the three *Horatii* and even of their father, by that of the eagles and of all the human figures in the *Oath of the Army* (Versailles) and again by that of the arms in the *Leonidas*—the triple gesture of the young men holding out crowns. Horizontals are violently opposed to verticals: the orthogonal arrangement of the *Andromaque* (already present in germ in the Prix de Rome picture) is repeated exactly, though now stripped of all artifice, in the admirable *Marat*. In the *Brutus* the verticals and horizontals harden, while the women are inscribed in a triangle[1]. Tension of gesture, stiffness of basic lines, background shut off by a wall or curtain—by these means David always attempts to suggest a bas-relief striped with sloping lines that intersect. Unity is broken for the sake of a frieze-like composition in which the themes form a succession. This it was, chiefly, that was so new, it was this that was censured by the professors; and it explains the famous remarks made by Pierre, the Director of the Académie[2].

Was David's art really very new? If we study the framework of these pictures from the technical point of view, we shall at first be surprised by their extreme simplicity. In almost every case the armature of the rectangle suffices. Let us not forget, however, that the armature is not a style, but something from which different painters draw the most varied effects. David had the skill to select from it those lines which would powerfully stress his preference for parallels and right angles: he had a predilection

1. A frequent arrangement in his paintings: cf. the *Andromaque* and *The Horatii*. Note also the triangles formed by legs disposed scissor fashion.

2. 'Very well, sir,' he said in connection with the *Brutus*, 'go on! In your *Horaces* you have placed your three figures on the same line, a thing never seen since people began to paint. Now you place the principal person in the shadow... That's adding insult to injury. No doubt you were right, since the public finds it wonderful. But where did you ever learn that a composition can be made without using the pyramidal line?' (Jules David, *Le Peintre Louis David*, Paris, 1880, p. 57.)

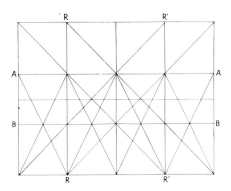

David: The Sabines. *The eighteenth century made frequent use of the rabatment of the shorter sides of the rectangle, and this was the favourite scheme of David, of his pupils and of many other artists in the nineteenth century. David uses it here with dry and scrupulous strictness: there is not a gesture, not a lance, whose direction is left to the inspiration of the moment. The rabatment of the shorter sides of the rectangle gives the sides R and R′ of the squares: these, where they cut the diagonals of the other square, determine the horizontals A and B. Together with the median axis these lines divide the canvas into twelve equal squares: a row of large triangles, each with a height of two of these squares, governs the movements of the figures. Obviously it is only when the two sides of the rectangle are in the ratio 3/4 that the rabatment of the shorter sides produces this regular division (cf. p. 45). (Paris, Louvre. Archives photographiques)*

for the squares obtained by rotating the shorter side of the picture on to the longer. In *The Horatii* he marked out the two squares thus obtained, and the point where their diagonals cross at the central axis determines the height of what is, in effect, a frieze adorned with a series of triangles. This kind of composition culminates in *The Sabines*, a picture with the geometrical strictness of a diagram: the shorter sides rotated on to the longer give two verticals on either side of the central division, so that the picture is divided into four rectangles; at the same time the height of the frieze (equal to half the longer side) is also derived from a similar rotation. All the movements of the figures and the details of the background are established upon the diagonals of the rectangles or upon the diagonals of the halves of the picture. In this composition there is an abuse of the diagonals that produces a certain monotony. The *Coronation of Napoleon* is composed upon the same scheme, but here the verticals are dominant and their stiffness gives this collective portrait an austere grandeur. The *Leonidas*—the worst and most laboured among these pictures that are results of a rather forced erudition—shows that after fifteen years David still stuck to his habits. It is curious to see that his pupils often adopted similar basic designs.

Two of those pupils are at the origin of the whole modern school: Ingres inspired the formal purists, the intellectuals, while Gros (who, under better conditions, might have been the French Goya) was the precursor both of Delacroix and of another spiritual family, that of Géricault and Courbet. Certain pictures by David already suggest Ingres, but they are still always plastic, haunted by statues and bas-reliefs.

Ingres: Romulus conquers over Acron. *(Paris, Ecole des Beaux-Arts. Photo Giraudon)*

It was chi
was carried
kind of dida
drawing, no
study for hi
Médecine): i
tion is the s
square (half
are simply t
only those d
what forced
all of which
ture, only t
marked: the
more perfect
pery, stresse
first one. It
to do their '
seen, the ba
reminders; b
imprison the

Girodet: Hippocrates; preparatory drawing. *Here the artist himself shows us his scheme. Its principle is the same as in David's* Sabines, *but the application is even more strict. There are twelve squares, of which eight compose a frieze. The diagonals of the squares of the frieze are the only ones used. No other oblique line is allowed to break the orthogonal* idée fixe. *In the picture itself the scheme is displaced towards the right, owing to the addition of a figure on the extreme left. (Paris, Ecole des Beaux-Arts. Photo Bulloz.)*

Girodet: Hippo
Artaxerxes; th
fields where the
their pupils are
studying the pu
secrets of their n

At that time the works of the Greeks and Romans were constantly reproduced in line engravings—a technique that is apt to be cold and didactic but sometimes, especially under the supple and sensitive hand of a Flaxman, yields a certain grace of contour. This hard thin art, closer to the cameo than to Praxiteles, was much liked, and in it both statues and charming scenes from the 'Etruscan' vases were given the same abstract purity. To a whole generation Antiquity, Greek art, meant this. This was the Antiquity of Ingres, very different from that of David. But Ingres was also 'Gothic', even eccentric, and was criticized for this by his contemporaries. He did not agree with these criticisms, and they made him angry. His gaze was centred on Raphael, and he did not realize that, through Raphael and by the very fact of being so permeated with him, he was becoming pre-Raphaelite. His Gothic is the Florentine Quattrocento, with its smooth modelling and its lightly drawn, pure contours.

The *Romulus conquers over Acron* (in the Ecole des Beaux-Arts) is the first large-scale painting by Ingres, and one of the finest. In it there is flagrant imitation of David's *Sabines* in certain details: the dead man lying on the ground is exactly the same as the one shown at half-length in David's picture (to which also the boys in the Ingres owe a great deal). But had not David taken over certain remains of Antiquity lock, stock and barrel? Ingres was only adopting from his master this unfortunate practice. It is chiefly in its composition that his picture comes close to *The Sabines*. Again the squares turn up: Ingres has here chosen a rectangle made of two squares side by side. The divisions at the half and quarters establish, by the play of the diagonals, the point on the median line on which the symmetrical axis of Romulus and the lance intersect; it is an example of the frieze *à la David*, realized as David himself might have dreamed of doing, for he never made any so perfect; and yet it is not certain that David would have liked this picture (which he is unlikely to have known). The modelling has a metallic incisiveness, making one think of the words of Baudelaire, clear-sighted as always: 'The hard and penetrating talent of M. Ingres.' In the last resort the picture is much too 'Gothic' to have pleased David (who never saw fully eye to eye with his pupil): there is in it a young man seen from the back, whose gentle shapeliness and meticulously distinct curls make him exactly like a page out of a Benozzo Gozzoli, while the boy next to him has the Botticellian charm which Ingres sometimes achieved.

His *Apotheosis of Homer* and his *St Symphorien* are also composed on squares; and it was in a conversation about the tedious *Jesus in the midst of the Elders*, painted at the end of his life, an unpleasing work in which the sedulous application of a method takes the place of inspiration, that Ingres himself revealed his way of going to work:

'He explained to us why the picture seemed to us so well constructed... "I began from the background, with the architecture. Once the lines were marked out, I called all my figures, one by one, and they came obediently to take their places in the perspective...[3]" '

3. Charles Blanc, *Ingres, sa vie et ses ouvrages*, Paris, 1870, p. 200.

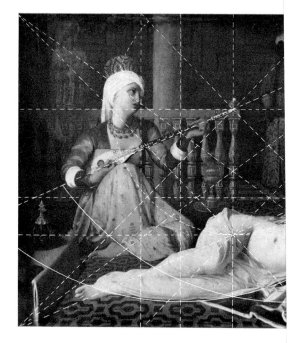

Géricault: Raft of the Medusa; sketch. (*Paris, Louvre. Archives photographiques*)

A very simple framework: the armature of the rectangle. As in several of Chardin's pictures, certain divisions (1/3, 1/4, 1/6) of the sides are selected, and a series of oblique lines are traced from these points. Here the chief part is clearly played by the points trisecting the top side of the picture.

Géricault: Raft of the Medusa; the finished picture. (*Paris, Louvre. Archives photographiques*)

A strang
on the s
like goo
I have
Raphael
are assoc
two arcs
lisque wit
of Ingres
ment lea
directly
tals. Th
governin
meet the
because i
lacking;
importan

David th
and since
tion Ing
faithful p
often sli

At the opposite pole from this method, let us take a look at Géricault's way of working. His *Raft of the Medusa* remains one of the finest examples —and perhaps the last one—of a truly classical composition. Among the many sketches and studies of all sorts that Géricault made for this picture, there is one (in the Louvre) which is, to all appearances, very elaborate: in it all the elements of the picture are already more or less in place, and the figures have the definitive gestures that embody the artist's idea and his sense of the drama. Everything is there, except the real order—indeed one might say that the expressive composition has been achieved, but not the formal composition. When he carried his sketch over to the canvas, Géricault proceeded to subject it to an extremely simple and strict frame-work taken from the armature of the rectangle. Seldom has a tracing been followed more faithfully. The shape of the raft, the direction of the mast, the axes of the figures, all are governed by lines that converge upon the halves, thirds and quarters of the sides; and, far from being skimped by this, the composition emerges magnified and covers the surface with an amplitude, an appearance of ease, not to be foreseen from the sketch. Where there was only a heap of bodies, there is now a complex of suffering human beings which compels our compassion, and out of its balanced counterpoise and secret symmetry there seems to rise a great tragic chant. Thus the painter is no more trammelled by the network he is obeying than a great poet is by the discipline of metre. One wonders if Victor Hugo would not have been able to tell this inspiring story more evocatively in verse than in prose[4].

Like the miniaturists of the *Psalter of Blanche of Castille*, Géricault is at ease within the geometry to which he subjects himself. And the process is the same one: invention, then harmonization, and, as final result, equilibrium.

Surprise effect

But in all that there were no really new discoveries in form. And, strangely enough, those who aimed at novelty and who really did modify the technique of painting, its language—or silence—and its effect upon our eyes, our spirit and our sensibility, these moderns, these innovators, for a long time did nothing to transform composition. It was precisely in this field that the studio routines, perhaps because they had become almost unconscious, proved most tenacious. The rotation (or 'rabatment') of the sides of the rectangle turns up yet again in the work of Delacroix, and more frequently in the works of his last period. In fact, Gros and Géricault went back to the classical painters, Delacroix to the Baroque, and even Courbet brought to this particular field of research less originality than is supposed. The *Burial at Ornans* is, like the *Coronation*, a collective portrait composed upon the verticals; Courbet may even have been conscious of

4. Cf. on p. 163 above, the words of Delacroix on this subject: 'I can distinguish poets and prose writers among painters...' (19 September 1847).

the resemblance. *The Artist's Atelier* is symmetrically counterpoised, and this arrangement is no new one. The artists of that time felt a real distaste for composition and the attitude of the Impressionists towards landscape painting is already present in Courbet's famous joke: 'When Jérôme stops, I paint a landscape.' Jérôme was his donkey.

Even Manet, who may be considered as the creator of modern painting, of that painting which is nothing but painting and possesses its end in itself—even Manet for a long time took no interest in composition. He followed, without the least scruple, the basic design of some famous picture: in the *Déjeuner sur l'herbe*, an engraving after Raphael; in the *Balcony*, Goya's *Majas on a Balcony*; in *Olympia*, the Urbino *Venus*.

Here it is perhaps necessary to make clear what was the real origin of the scandal which centred around the *Olympia*. Certainly it was not the subject of the picture; even though the young woman, so quiet and good in Titian's painting, has raised herself on her elbow and is giving us a bold stare. Nor was it even the boldness of that impenetrable mask and defiant gaze, for these things were already to be found in Goya's *Maja desnuda*. What was it then? In spite of the torrent of literature which was poured out for or against this woman, it must be recognized that the real cause of the scandal was a technical one—the complete absence of chiaroscuro. This brings us back to that crucial problem, depth, on which we have already spent some time. Manet's solution to it was a highly original one. If one tries to sum up the criticisms aroused by the *Olympia* at the Salon, leaving aside their intemperate language, what emerges is the picture's wan pallor and its flatness. Théophile Gautier, always so honest in his judgments, puts it admirably: 'The modelling is non-existent. The shadows are indicated by dark stripes of varying width[5].' This was Manet's essential contribution; he was putting forward, in this picture, what Maurice Denis later defined as follows: 'The picture is a plane surface covered with colours...' Degas understood Manet, but judged him with a sharp eye when he wrote: 'Manet... a playing-card with nothing printed on it...[6]' Was this woman found shocking because she was nude? But there are numberless nude women in the paintings of all periods. The truth is, she is not nude, she is unclothed. That is the impression she gave and that was voiced by Odilon Redon in a comment on her sister figure in the *Déjeuner sur l'herbe*[7]. She is unclothed because she is not, like the women of Titian and Rubens and all the others, clothed in chiaroscuro.

What gave Manet the idea of his *Olympia*, the cause of such a *scandale*? If I may hazard an explanation, it was the nudes of Utamaro; and the secret of the *Olympia* is perhaps contained in a juxtaposition which has not received all the attention it deserves—that of the sketch for the *Olympia*

Edouard Manet: Portrait of Emile Zola. *In this portrait of a writer whose frankness was already beginning to shock people, the qualities of the painting are of the same order, a frankness of execution with no concession to established procedures. Only the composition is still classical. (Paris, Louvre)*

5. Quoted by G. Bataille, *Manet*, Skira, 1955, p. 62.
6. Letter to Henri Rouart, 2 May 1882, in *Lettres de Degas*, Paris 1931.
7. 'There is one woman, in Manet's *Le Déjeuner sur l'herbe*, who will quickly put on her clothes again, for she is bored with her discomfort on the cold grass...' Odilon Redon, *A soi-même*, 14 May, 1888.

Daumier: Croquis musicaux, no. 16. The Orchestra during the Performance of a Tragedy; lithograph. *(Paris, Bibliothèque Nationale)*

Degas: Café-concert aux Ambassadeurs. *(Lyons Museum. Photo Bulloz)*

The drawings of Constantin Guys and the prints of Gavarni and Daumier revealed to Degas a new conception of art—one of profound realism, a genuine slice of life from the human comedy, a true poetry freed from the absurd idealism of that period. Degas saw what was to be learnt from it and, making full use of his solid grounding, looked about him with an entirely new sensibility.

with a Japanese print and, behind it, a reproduction of a Velasquez, in Manet's *Portrait of Emile Zola.*

Later, no doubt without realizing it, Manet came under the influence of Degas's method of composition, just as he was influenced by the Impressionists' technique of painting. He was also fond of surprising arrangements that excited the imagination by sending it astray, as in his *Bar at the Folies-Bergères,* and this was because Velasquez haunted him—Velasquez, whose contribution to the field we are studying consists chiefly in the surprise compositions, the unexpected and reversed arrangements of *Las Meninas* and *Las Hilanderas.*

The first profoundly original contribution of the nineteenth century to the basic arrangement of paintings was made by Degas.

He began his research in the field of portrait painting—a fixed formula if ever there was one. The portraits of Ingres, of Delacroix—and even those of Manet, with a square of light in one corner—did not, in their composition, differ from those of Tintoretto. Degas painted his *Woman with Chrysanthemums* (1865) and later the *Woman with a Vase* (1872) with the

Kiyonaga Women on a Terrace; print.
(Paris, Musée Guimet)

Degas: Woman taking a Bath; pastel.
(New York, Metropolitan Museum)

*In 1885 Degas said of the Impressionists:
'I have always tried to urge my colleagues to
seek for new combinations along the path of
draughtsmanship, which I consider a more
fruitful field than that of colour. But they
wouldn't listen to me, and have gone the other
way.' (Walter Sickert, Burlington Magazine,
November 1917.) Degas's classical grounding
did in fact make him more conscious of the
problems of composition than were his friends.
He did not, like some of his contemporaries,
use the new art of the Japanese print to extract
from it a technique based on a few facile
resemblances: he tried, on the contrary, to
understand and define the new plastic contribution of that art. In the print here reproduced
a whole milieu is evoked by means of three
geishas, three lanterns and some railings:
with a few women sitting outside a café Degas
achieves the same result.*

Degas: At the Café. (Paris, Louvre. Archives photographiques)

Utamaro: Woman Washing; print. (Paris, Musée Guimet)

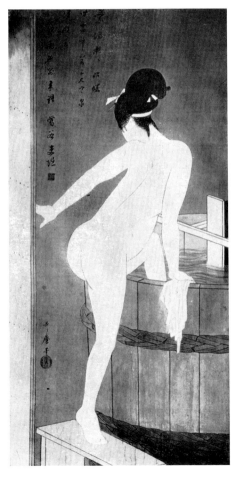

women sitting to one side and gazing elsewhere, while the principal subject is a bouquet of flowers[8]. The *Orchestras* (1868-72) are collective portraits whose compositions are more and more cut into. And from then onwards every picture of his displays a quite new layout, an exciting presentation of a subject that is itself unexpected. In this connection it would be impossible to stress too strongly the influence exerted by prints and by what was still a quite new invention, photography.

Artists had long made use of prints: the influence of these on the persistence of certain themes and certain methods of composition was indeed much greater than is ordinarily admitted. But these were reproductions of old pictures. In the nineteenth century the topical print, in the form of wood engravings or of lithographs, made its way into the newspapers and produced masterpieces[9]. The commonest scenes of everyday life were jotted down by Daumier or Gavarni, just as they were told by Balzac; but it did not occur to the painters to transpose them on to a canvas. And yet, what new life they brought with them! The expression 'layout' *(mise en page)*, which comes to mind immediately when one sees anything by Degas, shows that it is in the field of the book or the newspaper that one should look for his models—so much so that, to Degas's contemporaries, some of his subjects seemed to call imperiously for a caption. 'Here are women by the door of a café. There is one of them clicking her nail against her teeth as if to say: "There's more to it than that!" who is a poem in herself[10]'. So the great originator seems to be Daumier, who brought to the satirical topical print a profound originality, a way of cutting the scene off at surprising places and a bold distribution of blacks. He

8. 'For perhaps the first time in the history of painting, the portrait escapes from its abstract definition and mixes with life; the human being is no longer content to be a soul and a face, but is part of a *milieu* and moves past. He is not a permanent summing up of a whole life, legible in his past as in his future, but an instant of sensibility, made up of his momentary characteristics, of what he happens to be wearing that day, and of the setting, whether a room or some public place, in which the painter's eye has caught him as he passes or takes a brief rest.' H. Focillon, *La peinture des XIXᵉ et XXᵉ siècles*, Paris, 1928, p. 182.

9. Already, half a century earlier, Goya had studied the caricatures of his period and had profited not only from their virulence but also from their patterns. In his wonderful drawings one finds an original *mise en page* which owes a great deal to them.

10. G. Rivière, 1877, quoted by P. Cabanne, *Degas*, Paris, 1957, p. 113.

Guys, Gavarni and Daumier made Degas understand what resources everyday life— people at work, horse races, popular amusements, the theatre—can offer to a painter. He found much the same subjects in the Japanese prints, but with a supplementary originality, an alert pursuit of line and pattern, and in consequence a quite new and surprising mise en page, *which was often very beautiful. Degas saw in this a confirmation of his own researches into design. He may even have borrowed from Utamaro his favourite subject, the* Woman Washing, *a subject which appears in his work in about 1875, and which he painted again and again till the end of his life.*

Western taste had hitherto always required a painting to be justified by some pretext: women bathing must necessarily be Diana's companions; even Manet, when he painted Olympia, *had loaded it with literary associations. The Japanese print made European artists realize that a work of art could be created with the simplest subjects, and this while observing an incredible economy of means. What European artist could rival the poetic power which Hiroshige draws from a few lines suggesting rain? In* At the Theatre *Degas in turn aimed at the richest poetic evocation with the minimum of plastic signs. The lines of rabatment and their derivatives had hitherto been used to circumscribe and situate a figure:* *here Degas uses them to place an arm, a fan, or even simply a hand.*

Many of his pictures, like this Café-concert aux Ambassadeurs, *are composed on the rabatment of the shorter sides of the rectangle and on the diagonals* RE, EF *of the half-squares. There is nothing unusual about this scheme, and yet the composition strikes us as strangely new: this is because Degas does not merely show us the theatre, as Longhi had done, but by his bold placing of the frame he puts us right inside it. Everything seems unprepared, involuntary, and one might think the laws of composition had been swept aside; but Degas's strength lies precisely in his power to use these laws without letting it be seen.*

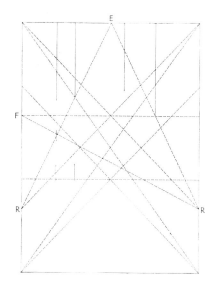

was the first to attempt, though with some loss of *verve*, to transpose these subjects of his drawings into painting. 'Just look at those washerwomen,' said A. Silvestre of a Degas, 'at a distance they look like a Daumier[11].'

Degas paid at least as much attention to the Japanese print as he did to the topical print. In this he was like Manet, but the lesson he found in it was different. What he tried to introduce into French painting from Japanese art was not the flat colours but the pattern, the sloping parallels of an unusual perspective, and also its spirit, which enabled it to say the most intimate things with such delicacy. In his *Woman with Dog* (Oslo), his *Dancing Lesson* (Philadelphia) and, later, in certain *Bathers* seen from the back, the pattern is as supple as a brush stroke. His way of cutting into the picture with vertical strips and his fondness for luminous globes like Japanese lanterns (cf. the *Chanson du chien* in New York and the *Café-concert aux Ambassadeurs* at Lyons) are to be compared with Kiyonaga, some of whose prints are known to have been in Degas's possession; and the same applies to the oblique parallels in *Absinthe Drinkers* and in *Dancers practising at the Bar*, etc., and again to his oddly cut-off figures, such as those in *At the Theatre* (Paris, Durand-Ruel)[12].

Lastly, it is not surprising that Degas should have liked photography and known how to profit from it creatively. He often spent a long time photographing whole scenes before painting them. As for snapshots,

11. Quoted by P. A. Lemoisne, *Degas et son œuvre*, Paris, 1946.

12. As we have seen already, the ideas of the masters are often expressed more insistently in the works of their pupils. Mary Cassatt, as a recent exhibition (Paris, December 1959) made plain, sometimes imitated Japanese prints very closely, applying their graphic technique to the expression of homely scene. Their surprising *mises en page* were always in her mind.

Degas: At the Theatre, pastel. *(Paris, Collection Durand-Ruel. Photo Bulloz)*

Utamaro: Woman having her Hair done; print. *(Paris, Musée Guimet)*

then possible only out of doors, he had seen some of these and they amused him: one comes upon the spirit of them in *At the Café* already mentioned (1877), and particularly in *At the Exchange* (1878), in which several gentlemen in top hats seem to have been caught unawares.

The wonderful thing about Degas is that he gets from all this a synthesis and is able to give weight to this new style. At first, his pictures are carried by their subjects: one could put captions under them. Then the subject disappears: a corner of a stage lit by the footlights, or a woman in her hip-bath—this is all he needs in order to realize his effects of disequilibrium, and of a singularly surprising selection. At the end of his life his art grows purer still: a few broken lines are now a sufficient starting point; he magnifies the colour and makes it radiate over surfaces that are scanned by straight lines at sharp angles.

Manet seized on this style (*At the Café-Concert*, 1874, Baltimore), and after him the Impressionists, though they let slip its calculated subtlety and kept only the love of the momentary. Degas's method was to work in his studio, and it was only through a great many tracings that he reached the definitive composition of a picture: this, in spite of its look of spontaneity, was exactly intended and the result of long labour. He would never have agreed that a picture should be 'a window open upon nature'.

The real window upon nature is the camera, opening its shutter and registering what it sees—a rather facile programme when one is painting a landscape. The Impressionists painted 'from life', and to them anything and everything was 'life'. In point of fact, since it was *light* they were in search of, they captured that chiefly upon waters: upon the Seine, or upon flooded or snow-covered plains. 'The Impressionist sits down on the bank of a river,' said Théodore Duret, paraphrasing Courbet, 'and paints a landscape.' With pictures containing human figures this method is less easy, and therefore the Impressionists treated such subjects less often; but in them too they strove for the momentary: Claude Monet shows his women running, Manet and Renoir their boatmen rowing past...

Renoir, however, did carry out some real compositions, though on rather traditional lines (his *Luncheon of the Boating Party*, in Washington, is constructed on the armature of the rectangle). The *Moulin de la Galette* is a conscious exercise in *dispersed composition*, and it is a masterpiece; but Renoir passed on to other things, and the idea had to wait for others to take it up.

The painters who may be called post-Impressionists paid more attention than the early Impressionists to composition, but continued to live on the acquisitions of the preceding generation. All the paintings of Bonnard and of Vuillard can be classed under the two formulae, *cut compositions* and *dispersed compositions*. Bonnard made no bones about his use of the scissors: taking up Degas's method, he would describe a whole scene and then cut, sacrifice parts of it and leave a striking fragment only. Dispersed compositions were obtained by a scattering of coloured and luminous spots and patches, which do away with the perception of space

and make a tapestry effect. Bonnard and, even more, Vuillard were masters of this. Without exactly going back to the wall, this art is closely akin, at least at its beginning, to the decorative art which that period prized. At the same time, since there is little contrast between the tone values, the effect is to suggest some lustrous, iridescent textile.

Geometry on the wall

These innovations did not supply a basis solid enough for the foundation of a future. A few wide-awake minds realized this—most of all Seurat. He did not simply try to establish the luminist technique upon a scientific analysis of vision[13], but strove tenaciously towards a new style of form and of distribution of forms: he succeeded in bringing back geometry into composition.

Was this a step backwards? The face of geometry is always the same. David, who thought he was doing something new, remained in fact close to the formulae of the past. What is miraculous in Seurat is his escape from repetition: it is as though he reinvented those large, quite naked places and those rigid verticals cutting across implacable horizontals. One seems to have never seen them before, for the style and technique with which he associated them were strange; yet the truth is that they were already to be found in the work of Puvis de Chavannes.

13. In this connection, see the quotation from Sutter referred to in note 8 to chapter VII above and the passage from Chevreul quoted below.

Puvis de Chavannes: Sacred Grove. *Puvis de Chavannes, in many of his pictures, decided on a division into eight both across and up and down; long oblique lines are then drawn from some of these divisions and create the rhythm. (Lyons Museum. Photo Giraudon)*

Puvis de Chavannes was not a product of the art school. He studied mathematics and prepared for the Polytechnique, then went to learn painting all by himself in Italy from the Florentine frescoes. His contact with the sources was therefore direct, and he rediscovered—was in fact perhaps the first to do so—that feeling for the wall, that respect for the wall, which (when not too puritan) is one of the healthy ideas of the nineteenth century. Puritan he was to some extent, but his discretion comes out chiefly in an intensely refined feeling for circumambient light. It was indeed his habit to go with his paint-box and take the tone of the shadow and light within the building he had been given to decorate. What painter has pushed the idea of an art bound up with architecture more strictly to its logical conclusion? His perspective is, in its way, as little classical as that of Veronese; and in a geometer like him this deliberate rejection of mathematical perspective is highly significant: the figures in the middle ground are too tall, and in particular the trees, which are given a monumental value, are too big. They are columns, or rather pilasters (for Puvis de Chavannes simplifies the modelling to the utmost). Like Degas, he worked on the basis of tracings, each time sacrificing some details. He was not a disciple of Ingres; he did not attempt such a precise formal composition. He does not belong to the line that runs from *L'Age d'or* through Degas's *Semiramis*. His drawing has more affinity with that of Millet.

But what must chiefly concern us is his geometry. Puvis de Chavannes has the air of a rather haughty independent. His geometry is not a residue of the classical formulae, but is conceived and thought out by a mind with a natural bent towards this kind of research. Let us look at his large-scale compositions in width, at his *Ludus pro patria* (Amiens) or his *Inter artes et naturam* (Rouen): the width as a whole is divided into two, then each half into two, and so on until there are eight equal parts. The picture surface is thus streaked with verticals which give the general tone of the composition; verticals and horizontals on dominants, stated with insistence; calm and clearly distinct, they suggest large spaces[14]. But that is not all: out of these eight divisions Puvis chooses the starting points of the long obliques which fill the whole picture with an uneven rhythm of broken lines and large triangles. This is how he constructs the *Sacred Grove* (Lyons), *Doux pays*, and even certain easel paintings, such as his *Autumn* at Lyons (a picture that is higher than it is wide), or the *Poor Fisherman*.

The decoration of the Sorbonne amphitheatre is a frieze of such length that he had to look for something else, for some means of cutting that continuous band into three and giving it a centre, without incurring the danger of monotony or making it into a triptych. What he did was to superimpose the length of the short sides upon the long four times, starting from the right, and take this as establishing a main division on

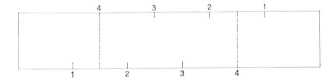

Puvis de Chavannes: Decoration of the large amphitheatre of the Sorbonne. *Four squares, obtained by the rabatment of the shorter side (the height), are placed side by side starting from the right, and four starting from the left: not only do the ends of these series divide the composition into three parts, but their overlapping creates a closer rhythm in the central part of the picture. (Paris. Photo Bulloz)*

the left—and to do the same from the left in order to fix a main division on the right. The resulting divisions are in fact very simple, but sufficiently concealed to avoid becoming obsessive.

Puvis de Chavannes is not much appreciated in our time; but justice demands that we should give him the credit for what is his real contribution, instead of adding it to the reputations of masters who are already so rich. He was, obviously, very fortunate: he was offered walls in profusion (though we must not forget the Pantheon is full of horrors!), whereas we can only dream of what a wall given over to Seurat would have been like, or a Pantheon wholly decorated by Gauguin...

14. The division of the sides of the picture into eight parts gives, at the 5/8 and 3/8, caesuras that are very close to the golden ratio; but since, as well as these, Puvis de Chavannes used other divisions into eight (6/8, 7/8, etc.), which have nothing to do with that ratio or its harmonics, I do not think we can, without straining the evidence, regard his compositions as based on the golden ratio. The same applies to Seurat.

Seurat: La Parade. *The most marked feature of this picture is a right angle formed by the top line of the balustrade and the vertical flat on the right: the horizontal is very close to the golden section, but the vertical is not. But if we subject this composition to the scheme produced by the rabatment of the shorter sides of the rectangle, we see at once that the two lines fall strictly at the intersection of the diagonals of the rectangle and the diagonals of the squares. At the same time, horizontals drawn from the upper and lower corners of the small central square give the positions of the figures or delimit the room they take up. This picture certainly bears out Sutter's phrase:* 'When the dominant is horizontal, a succession of vertical objects can be placed on it because this series will concur with the horizontal line, whereas a vertical line in isolation would create a second unity.' *(New York, Stephen C. Clark Collection. Photo Musées nationaux)*

Seurat did come from the art school, but from one whose only doctrine was that of Ingres. He was really a solitary. As Robert Rey has pointed out[15], what must have chiefly attracted him at the Ecole des Beaux-Arts was the Library. He read a great deal and, out of books disdained or read without attention by others, he drew the substance which his lucid and strict intelligence was to transform into a coherent system.

As early as 1878 or 1879, Seurat discovered Chevreul's treatise and found in it, among other things, the law of the simultaneous contrast of colours. What exactly does this law teach us?

'When two contiguous colours are seen at the same time, they appear as dissimilar as possible, both with regard to their optical composition and their depth of tone... The modifications of contiguous colours are precisely those which would result from the addition to each of them of the complementary of the contiguous colour... When colours are not of the same depth, that which is deep appears deeper, and that which is light appears lighter[16].'

This was the germ of Seurat's studies in optics. But his application to painting of the law of the simultaneous contrast of colours is only one aspect—and the one most open to differences of opinion—of that self-willed art of his, with its reliance on a precise and conscious conception of what art is[17].

15. *La Renaissance du sentiment classique*, Paris, 1931, p. 102.

16. M.-E. Chevreul, *De la loi du contraste simultané des couleurs et de l'assortiment des objets colorés considérés d'après cette loi*, Paris, 1st edition 1827, new edition 1889. (English translation: John Spanton, London and New York, 1859, pp. 9-10.)

Robert Rey has revealed a most important fact: Seurat had read with attention, pencil in hand, a certain article by David Sutter[18] and had extracted from it ideas on linear composition[19]. In this very curious article, which seems to take us back to Lomazzo, David Sutter stresses the importance of 'aesthetic lines', using examples taken from the bas-reliefs and paintings of Antiquity. Sutter's book *La philosophie des Beaux-Arts appliquée à la peinture* (Paris, 1870), which had come out some time before and was more general in character, was also, certainly, one of Seurat's bedside books. What do we find in it? To begin with this:

'Plutarch says: In the arts nothing that is done well is done by chance, and I know no work of art that has succeeded except through the foresight and science of the artist. They all constantly use rules, lines, measures, numbers.' (p. 74).

'A white figure rising against a black ground displeases the eye by the sudden opposition of the black to the white and the monotony of this opposition; the mass of black fights against the white mass; there is no unity. But if you light a part of that ground, the introduction of a subordinate white will produce a white unity. Similarly, if you place part of the figure in shade, the mass of blackness will become dominant, and unity will be restored.' (p. 139).

Have we not, in this law of black and white, the principle of Seurat's wonderful drawings and the secret of their unity? The book proceeds:

17. M. E. Souriau (*Y a-t-il une palette française*, in *Art de France II*, Paris, 1962) draws attention to the important part played by Ferdinand Plateau and the engineer Rosenstiehl in the neo-Impressionist researches into colour.
18. *L'Art*, 1880, vol. I, p. 74.
19. Robert Rey, *op. cit.*, pp. 127 ff.

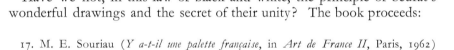

Seurat: La Grande Jatte. *In his love of exact geometry Seurat has chosen, here as with* La Parade, *to give the sides of the picture a proportion of 2/3. The divisions given by the armature of the rectangle therefore coincide with the rabatment of the shorter sides. The horizontal lines drawn through the upper and lower points of the small central square define, where they cut the diagonal of the rotated sides, a sixth of the total breadth, and where they cut the diagonal of the rectangle they define a quarter of that same length. In this way the scheme makes possible an asymmetrical composition: the right half is divided into three and the left half into two. The oblique lines* AB, CD, EF, GH, *which intersect upon the vertical axis, are sometimes used for their own sakes, and sometimes serve only to delimit the figures. (Chicago Art Institute. Photo Giraudon)*

Seurat: Models. *The woman who stands facing us in the axis of the picture is inscribed strictly within a vertical band lying between the glimpse of* La Grande Jatte *and the edge of the pictures on the wall. The other women, on either side, are governed by isosceles triangles, of which the one on the right is the stricter: its sides follow respectively the slope of her legs and the slope of the parasol, while the angle of the apex forms a niche for her head. On the left the geometry is more discreet: upon the triangle determining the group on* La Grande Jatte *is superimposed the triangle governing the woman who has her back to us; she sits, as though on a folding stool, on the crossed lines of a parasol and of the perspective of the low wall, which is underlined by a fan.* (*Merion, Penn., Barnes Foundation*)

The diagrams show a suggested analysis of the composition.

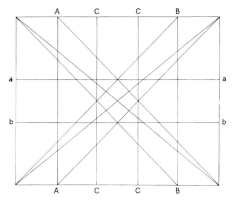

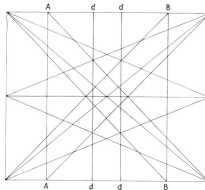

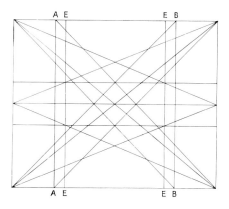

a) *Rabatment of the shorter sides of the rectangle establishes the two axes to left and right, AA and BB. The diagonals of the two squares thus obtained draw a small central square: a and b are the horizontals through its upper and lower corners and c, c the verticals through its right and left corners.*

b) *The four points of intersection, d, of the diagonals of the rectangle's horizontal halves and the diagonals of the squares govern the width of the central vertical band in the picture.*

c) *The two lines EE are the verticals drawn through the points where the diagonals of the halves intersect the lines a and b. The left-hand line EE is the axis of the woman on* La Grande Jatte.

d) The diagonals of each square cut the side of the other square at a point c′, *which determines two horizontals,* c′ c′, *one in the upper part of the picture, one in the lower. The upper one gives the base of the picture-frames on the wall and the apex of the right-hand triangle. These horizontal lines intersect the diagonals of the squares at the points* c c; *and where they intersect the diagonals of the picture as a whole they also determine the lines* EE.

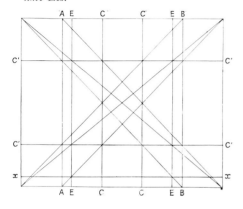

e) The triangles on either side of the picture are determined thus: the right-hand triangle goes from the bottom right-hand corner of the whole picture to the intersection of c′ c′ *with* BB *and from there to the lowest point of the vertical* c c; *the taller triangle on the left goes from the left-hand bottom corner to the top of* EE *on the left and from there to the bottom of the central axis; the smaller left-hand triangle goes from, again, the lower left-hand corner to a point on line* a a *and from there to the bottom of the vertical* c c. *A line* XX *drawn through the points where the diagonals of the square intersect the lines* EE *is also important.*

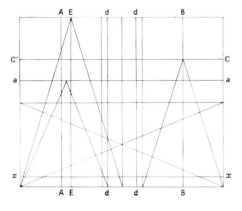

'When the dominant is horizontal, a succession of vertical objects can be placed on it because this series will concur with the horizontal line, whereas a vertical line in isolation would create a second unity.' (p. 207).

Seurat pondered over these ideas for a long time, and then formulated his conception of art in the well known letter of 28 August 1890, to Maurice Beaubourg. This letter is such a closely packed, carefully considered declaration of principles that every word in it is irreplaceable. I shall merely extract what is relevant to our subject:

'Art is harmony. Harmony is the analogy of contraries, the analogy of similars, in tone, shade, line, judged by the dominant and under the influence of a play of light in arrangements that are gay, light or sad. Contraries are..., as regards line, those that form a right angle.... Gaiety of line, lines above the horizontal; ... calm is the horizontal; sadness the downward directions[20]'.

To these ideas, expounded by Seurat a year before his death, all his pictures are faithful; and since Seurat was calm by temperament and did not give way to melancholy, he adopted by preference the horizontal dominant (as in *La Grande Jatte*, that 'succession of vertical objects').

As we have just seen, Puvis de Chavannes also loved the horizontal, the vertical and the right angle. He may have learned this simplicity from the frescoes of Benozzo Gozzoli. Seurat had not been to Italy; but the Ecole des Beaux-Arts, not long before he became a student there (in 1878), had acquired an important collection of a hundred and thirty-four copies after the old masters, chiefly the Italian ones, among which were two large fragments of Piero della Francesca's frescoes at Arezzo[21]. These copies were of real significance at a time when there was no such thing as faithful reproduction. They must surely have attracted the attention of a young artist whose affinity with Piero della Francesca was remarkable.

His large pictures (there are only seven, and each of them took him nearly a year's work) are visibly, almost obsessively, geometrical. In contrast to so many artists whom we have seen, in the classical centuries, trying to make guiding lines, which they regarded as too stiff and too tense, disappear as soon as they had served their purpose, just as a builder takes down his scaffolding when the building is finished, Seurat loved these lines. All his figures and objects bear the trace of the diagram; the parallels and perpendiculars are insistent. But the lines he stresses are, it must be clearly understood, derivatives—often unexpected ones, stressed precisely in order to produce surprise—not the primary elements of the construction, which are always the same and tend to make a picture monotonous.

20. These ideas of gay, calm or sad lines were taken by Seurat from his friend Charles Henry, who had expressed them in almost the same terms in his curious pamphlet, *Introduction à une esthétique*, Paris, 1885, pp. 7 and 11.

21. These copies reached the Ecole in May, 1874; the ones from Piero della Francesca are by the painter Charles A. Loyeux.

further to the left, and forms an axis of symmetry between the lamp on the left and the dresses of the dancing-girls. This shows, beyond any doubt, that Seurat gave most careful attention to the placing of the double-bass player; and in fact, in the picture itself, his axis is the vertical established by the intersection of the diagonals of the squares with the diagonals of the rectangle (the same vertical on which Watteau placed his Gilles). If we take this line as the axis of symmetry of the whole picture, it is curious to note how the double-bass player is enclosed between his left arm and a dancing-girl's leg, and her dress continues the pattern, while to the lamp on the left there are added two leaves, which form arcs and are arranged so that they answer symmetrically the arcs made by the dancing-girls' dresses. The odd shape produced by the magpie tail of the dancing man seems intended to echo the scroll of the double-bass, and there are many other correspondences. The flute on the left and two axes of the face on the right (with its curious mirror effect, the nose repeating the shape of the ear), and again, the same person's stick and the line marking the edge of the conductor's coat, would coincide if folded over on the same axis of symmetry. (Otterlo, Kröller-Müller Museum)

Seurat: Le Chahut. *This picture seems to be an application of Charles Henry's theory about ascendant lines creating a feeling of joy. But it should be noted that Henry attaches great importance to whether a line rises towards the right or towards the left: in this picture, curiously enough, most of them go towards the left; did Seurat mean by this to give a symbolic meaning to their direction, to add a harmonic of sadness to the joy? The jerky rhythm of the girls, the lines of force of the musical instruments, the wake left by the movement of the feet and the effect of trepidation given by the whole picture is like a prophecy of the Italian Futurist school. In this picture, yet again, the rabatment of the shorter sides of the rectangle supplies the main points for the general arrangement.*

In the chalk study for this picture (Paris, Collection Gourgaud) the double-bass player is to the right of the central vertical axis; in the painted study (London, Home House Trustees) he is slightly to the left; and in the final study (Buffalo Museum) he is even

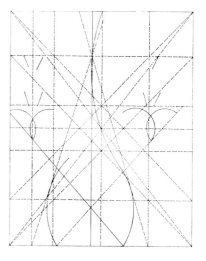

Seurat: Circus. *The same solutions are found in nearly all the pictures of Seurat, who was one of the most short-lived of artists; but in his last big picture, the* Circus, *the beginnings of a new development can be felt. In the painted study for it (in the Louvre) the clowns—for there are two of them—seem to be holding an arc which occupies almost the whole of the lower part of the composition. In the final picture there is only one clown, and all that is left of the arc is a small segment in his right hand. This causes the static appearance of the sketch to be replaced by movement. The composition illustrates Kandinsky's reflections on the effect of the way in which geometrical figures are placed in a picture (a triangle resting on its base strikes a calmer, stiller note than the same triangle standing on one of its corners; cf. p. 237 below): upon a background of straight lines parallel to the frame of the picture, Seurat has placed a sloping, almost square rectangle which seems guided by the clown's hand; and to this unstable balance he adds a sort of Catherine-wheel effect, a suggestion of arcs on the sides of the square, arcs whose prototype is the crescent held by the clown. The clown is really juggling with M. Loyal, the acrobat, the equestrienne and the horse. This scheme is in fact very simple and is, yet again, established by the rabatment of the shorter sides of the rectangle. The network of orthogonals and obliques which is still visible in places through the thin touches of colour, and in which M. Henri Dorra (in his* Seurat, Les Beaux-Arts, *Paris 1959) sees a principle of composition, is in my opinion simply a trace of squaring-up. (Paris, Louvre. Photo Bulloz)*

Seurat did what has been done in all periods (and more than ever since David): he slewed the shorter sides round on to the longer and traced the crossing diagonals of the two squares thus obtained, inscribing in the centre of the picture a small square balanced on one of its corners; the horizontals and verticals from the corners of this small square and the intersections of diagonals give the essential points in the picture and establish its divisions, within which Seurat often places acute-angled triangles[22].

As we follow him from one picture to another, we can see how he brings his secret framework nearer and nearer to perfection. *La Grande Jatte*, through its proportion of two to three, is divisible into six equal squares, whose diagonals coincide with those of the rotated smaller sides: the scheme is still a very simple one. The next picture, *Models*, in which a part of *La Grande Jatte* is again seen, is, together with the latter picture, the most charming of Seurat's canvases, the one in which a kind of benevolence—if not tenderness—is present, not yet frozen into a harsh irony; in which, also, the geometry is more discreet and the women have not been transformed into automata. Nonetheless, it is quite easy to see that the three women at the sides are inscribed in triangles and the woman at the centre upon a vertical band. How did Seurat establish that band and those triangles? Here, already, the construction is less obvious. *La Parade* is characterized by a key point, precisely determined (it is where a diagonal of the rectangle crosses a diagonal of one of the squares), which engenders, by means of its projections on to the sides, a clearly visible rectangle. In *Le Chahut* Seurat uses the rabatment of the shorter sides together with intersections of certain diagonals. Finally, in the *Circus*, the vertical axes are no longer visible: they serve as starting points, but disappear entirely from the composition, which includes only horizontals, obliques and curves.

Our illustrations give detailed analyses of his principal pictures. I believe that in this way I have shown Seurat's rigorously logical procedure. 'No detail is placed at random,' wrote Sutter in the article which Seurat read with such attention. And while all that Girodet or Guérin could

22. In accordance with the method adopted at the beginning of this book, I have tried to rely on written evidence contemporary with the artist and especially, whenever possible, the writings of the artist himself. In the letter to Beaubourg, Seurat expounds his conceptions of painting, in which Sutter's theories occur cheek by jowl with those of Chevreul, Charles Henry, Helmholtz, Maxwell and Rood; and he does so in order to claim publicly a pioneering status for his ideas. Seurat is particularly susceptible on this point: he considers that he is the first to have applied scientific theories to painting. But, touchy as he was about the ownership of his aesthetic ideas, Seurat does not mention the use of the divine proportion, to which Charles Henry had certainly drawn his attention since he himself explained its principles in his *Introduction*, though recognizing the primacy of the Germans in this field of research. We are justified in believing that, if he had been responsible for reviving the golden number, Seurat would have claimed that honour and given prominence to it in the letter to Beaubourg. That certain lines in his compositions fall close to the golden section is very possible—this is true of many pictures at all periods; but one or two lines at or near a ratio do not necessarily prove that the composition was constructed upon that ratio. The detailed analyses which I give should be enough to show what I mean.

make from geometrical designs was a series of stiff, starched figures, Seurat performed the miracle of taking Sutter's advice literally in work which retains the freshness and purity of the early Renaissance.

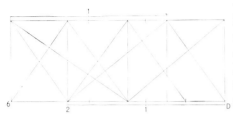

Seurat was the opposite of a rebel. His friends indeed reproached him with being 'a school man' and found it compromising to be hung near him. The attitude of Gauguin was the very opposite. He was a rebel through and through. He was delighted when Degas called him, one day, 'the lone wolf without a collar'[23]. But a wolf has cunning, too. Lacking real culture (as he willingly admitted), he nonetheless took from the past all he needed, greedily and secretly like the wild animals. He detested that official success, Puvis de Chavannes. He kept saying that

Gauguin: Whence come we? *When the rectangle is wider than two of the squares placed side by side, several solutions are possible. In this great mural painting Gauguin uses the method employed by Puvis de Chavannes at the Sorbonne (p. 209 above). The two squares, taken from the right, give the axis of the idol; the mid-line of the second square taken from the left situates the main standing figure. The chief oblique lines, running to the ends of these two axes, establish all the other figures, which are inscribed along these sloping lines with an almost naïve strictness. (Boston, Museum of Fine Arts. Photo Bulloz)*

he himself did not work from tracing to tracing—not he! When his masterpiece, *Whence come we? what are we? whither do we go?*, was exhibited in 1898, he was told that the allegory was not clear, and the allegories of Puvis de Chavannes were thrown in his teeth. Puvis again! Defending himself, Gauguin said that he did not paint allegories. He loathed the literary, banal, too facile allegories of Puvis. And yet he added: 'I admire him as much as you do and more, for different reasons. (Don't be angry, with more knowledge)'[24]. What were these reasons? He does not say. His pictures must do the talking.

Let us, then, pay attention to *Whence come we? what are we? whither do we go?*, since it was this wonderful picture that gave rise to the question. Let us try to forget about the title—if that is what it is—and about

23. Gauguin, letter to A. Fontainas, March 1899.
24. From the letter quoted above.

the 'subject', which the critics complained of not being able to read clearly. The picture is balanced, complete and closed: in it we are far from both Baroque dynamism and the cut compositions of Degas; the symmetry is evident, but not too strongly stressed; the existence of a geometrical framework is clearly apparent. The idol, that secret presence, will give us the key: its distance from the right-hand side is double the picture's height. Taking up afresh the method of Puvis de Chavannes, Gauguin has slewed the shorter side on to the longer to form squares. The great width of the picture has made him decide to double this square (Puvis had repeated it four times at the Sorbonne). That is how Gauguin determined the position of his idol, the key to the picture. Then he took the same squares from the left, but, to avoid monotony, placed the upright naked figure halfway across the second square and not at its end. All the other figures are on oblique lines connecting these essential points. From this we can understand very well that Gauguin had his reasons for admiring Puvis, but they were technical reasons of which the critics could have no inkling and he was not anxious to speak. Once again Focillon shows himself clear-sighted and finds the right words to describe a relationship which should be neither denied nor exaggerated:

'In the Polynesian sacred wood the ordered and peaceful inspiration of Puvis de Chavannes lives anew; but the nobility of humanism here gives place to the nobility of strangeness. The lovely naked body stretching up to pick a spray from the tree does not undulate like the serene figure

Gauguin: Tahitian Girl. *(Moscow, Pushkin Museum. Photo Giraudon)*

Puvis de Chavannes: Tamaris. *(Collection Bonnières)*

These two figures are very close to each other. Gauguin disliked the allegorical pretexts of Puvis de Chavannes, but had a great admiration for the plastic and rhythmic expressiveness of his pictures. Is this a case of involuntary reminiscence? (Photo Bulloz)

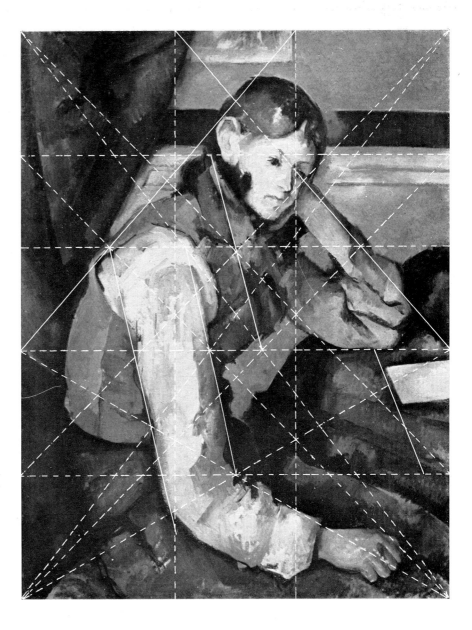

Cézanne: Boy with the red Vest. *It was on the diagonals of the squares obtained by rabatment of the rectangle's shorter sides that Cézanne established the composition of some of his portraits—the* Gustave Geffroy, *the* Vollard, *etc. In the* Boy with the red Vest *there are, in addition to a selection of* these diagonals and oblique lines directly derived from the normal framework (notably the large triangle in the upper part), certain noticeably parallel oblique lines which help to establish the equilibrium. (Zurich, Bührle Collection. Photo Giraudon)

Cézanne: Le château noir. *Poussin has already supplied us with examples of the use in a landscape of a whole network of lines at right angles. In this picture Cézanne establishes on the intersections of the diagonals of the squares the vertical or horizontal lines that give his landscape its rhythm. (Winterthur, Oskar Reinhart Collection)*

of *Autumn;* he rises like some unknown god, with firm stance and slim thighs, on a coral reef'[25].

'Strangeness' is certainly the characteristic quality of Gauguin. Some have tried to contrast his symbolism with the art school allegories and to connect it with the great tradition of earlier ages. But this would imply association with esoteric beliefs from which, I think, Gauguin stood aloof. The word 'symbolism', used as the name for a school, must not mislead us: it is more true to say that Gauguin, like Goya, had the sense of mystery, or even, since in him cleverness was blended with instinct, the art of mystery.

Cézanne, too, is apt to be taken as an isolated artist who tried, all alone and with rugged strength, to rediscover the classical grandeur. But he was, in fact, a familiar of the masters, a constant visitor to the Louvre, and he had patiently studied the Venetians (especially Tintoretto), the French classical painters, the Baroque painters (including Delacroix) and, finally, Courbet and the Impressionists, before he withdrew alone to the depths of the country near Aix. All this culture matured within an original and observant intelligence, mistrustful of spontaneity. He did not, like his friends, look out for the momentary and fugitive; even in his landscapes painted from nature he always constructed a solid painting,

25. Focillon, *op. cit.*, p. 288.

braced by a framework, supported on a scheme, just as did those masters who worked at leisure in their studios. In his work, as we have seen in the case of other nineteenth-century painters, the verticals and horizontals, together with the right angles they form where they touch or intersect, are the preferred lines, to which must be added the counterpoise of the obliques. His *Château noir* is inscribed between the verticals and obliques derived from the rabatment of the sides (division into five vertical and three horizontal bands, with parallel obliques), just as Hobbema's *Avenue, Middelharnis*, for instance, also followed the armature of the rectangle closely. If Cézanne shows four trees rising, they will be very nearly parallel and equidistant. All his work was marked by a constant preoccupation with composition. The culmination of this effort is his *Bathers (Grandes Baigneuses)*, which he took up again and again during eight years and left unfinished. The *Bathers (Petites Baigneuses)*, the *Card Players* and some of his portraits are stages in this constant research, in which he inscribes simplified volumes and tense forms within the secret play of curves, lozenges and pyramids, to form compositions that are static and closed.

In Cézanne the geometry never expresses depth: never does he make direct use of the diagonals of the rectangle, which inevitably create perspective[26]. And it is through this absence of linear perspective that Cézanne's landscapes so often bring to mind the buildings in those of Poussin.

26. On the representation of space in Cézanne's pictures, cf. the next chapter.

Hobbema: The Avenue, Middelharnis. (London, National Gallery. Photo Bulloz)

Van de Cappelle: Ships on the Estuary. (London, National Gallery)

It is amusing to find how these pictures by Hobbema and Van de Cappelle, one a landscape and the other a seascape, follow what is clearly the same scheme, based on the armature of the rectangle.

IX SOLUTIONS OF THE PROBLEM IN CONTEMPORARY PAINTING

Painting is a language. Up to Cézanne, painters used familiar words: it was upon recognizable elements of the outside world that they imposed their personal syntax. To get a picture, they projected the forms of their intellect on to the diversity of things. This made the work of art a synthesis, towards which all the resources of the art were called to co-operate.

With and after Cézanne, there comes a great change: the novelty of the means brought into action by him directed attention to the components rather than to the synthesis. Painting literally exploded, and the painters of the twentieth century found themselves face to face, some with the problem of the third and even of the fourth dimension, others with harmonies of pure tones, and others again with the geometrical lines that govern composition in a plane.

These researches have profoundly modified the very vocabulary of painting. The recognizable elements have been replaced by forms which are sometimes allusive, sometimes purely geometrical, sometimes even fortuitous, yet are still signs and still bring us a message, especially when they are organized by an intellectual principle.

The third and fourth dimensions

At this point we return to the problem of space, that obstacle so difficult to pass, for it greatly complicates the linear framework, whatever may be the solutions adopted. Those adopted by the moderns are really new ones.

Let us begin with the *luminous* evocation of space. Manet shocked people by expunging the chiaroscuro, but he still stressed certain volumes with a dark line; and indeed he was too versatile to stick to the same method for long. The practice of painting out of doors led the Impressionists, on the other hand, to do away with black, and soon all they sought to represent of the object was its various chromatic aspects, light and shade. Starting from the same premises, Cézanne restored the object in its concrete presence, its immediate volume, its density, by analyzing and loading the local tone, and then transforming this through the colour of the inci-

Jacques Villon: Boire à la Chimère. *Jacques Villon is alone or almost alone, in our time, in taking up again the old medieval method: a secret diagram serves as framework to each of his pictures. (Paris, Galerie Louis Carré)*

223

dence of light[1] and atmosphere[2]. 'When the colour is given its richness,' he said, 'the form gets its fullness... The contrasts and relationships of tones—that is the secret of modelling[3].' Thus he obtains, all together, colour, volume, unity of light and unity of shade.

Differences of planes are reduced by Cézanne to a minimum, and he expresses them by means of oppositions of which Sutter gives an excellent analysis:

'It is principally by looking at the rough ridges of a building that one can see the means which nature uses to bring out objects and make them stand out from one another. A luminous ridge is made to stand out against the sky by a line of a darker blue than the mass of the sky, and a dark ridge is made to stand out by a luminous line in opposition to it[4].'

1. For Cézanne: 1) light is tinged with orange and, by virtue of this, transforms the local tone of the object on which it rests; 2) shade is blue—another transformation of the local tone. To pass from orange to blue, there will be red-violet modulations, then violet-blue modulations of the local tone; or else, going the other way round the chromatic triangle, yellow-green and green-blue modulations: Cézanne chooses one or other of the two ways, never both together.

2. 'Nature, to us men, is more in depth than in surface; hence the necessity of introducing into our vibrations of light, represented by reds and yellows, a sufficient amount of bluish tinges to make the air felt.' Letter from Cézanne to E. Bernard, 15 April 1904.

3. E. Bernard, *Souvenirs sur Paul Cézanne*, Paris, 1925, 4th ed., p. 39.

4. *Philosophie des Beaux-Arts appliquée à la peinture*, Paris, 1870, p. 242. Already Leonardo da Vinci had said: 'Each colour shows more distinctly where there is proximity to the one in contrast to it than it does in the centre of its own area.' (*Treatise on Painting*, codex urbinas; translated by A. Philip McMahon; Princeton, 1956.

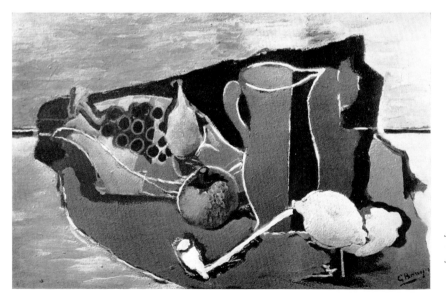

Braque: Still-Life. '*With a still-life, we have to do with a tactile, even manual space, which one may contrast with the space in a landscape—visual space. The still-life makes the sense of touch take part in the conception of the picture. It ceases to be a still-life as soon as it is out of arm's length. In tactile space you measure the distance that separates you from the object, while in visual space you measure the distance that separates things from each other.*' (Propos de Braque, *in* Verve, *VII, nos. 27-28, p. 71*) *(Private Collection. Archives photographiques)*

Picasso: Guernica. '*There is no such thing as figurative and non-figurative art. All things appear to us in the form of figures. Even in metaphysics the ideas are expressed by figures, so you can easily see how absurd it would be to think of painting without the imagery of figures. A human being, an object, a circle, are figures; they act on us more or less intensely. Some are nearer to our sensations and produce emotions that touch our affective faculties; others address themselves more particularly to the intellect. One must accept them all, for my mind has as much need of emotion as my senses have.*' (Picasso, 1930-1935; Éditions 'Cahiers d'art', Paris, 1936) (*New York, Museum of Modern Art, Photo Giraudon*)

When tones have been carried to their maximum sonority, Cézanne suggests the planes by means of their ridges and by using complementaries of the light tone (as in *La Carrière Bibémus*). He probably knew Sutter's ideas, either directly or through friends.

Cézanne's exciting technique for expressing contrasts of planes was simpler and easier to hand on than was his sharpness of vision. The Cubists kept this in mind and, by reducing the law of contrasts to the *accentuation of the ridges* (a sign of depth rather than an expression of it), they produced an interplay of the planes of dislocated objects.

It was also in the work of Cézanne that they found the essence of their doctrine: in some of his still-life paintings, and even in some of his landscapes, Cézanne already seems to be placing himself at several different points of view. The first Cubists, Braque and Picasso, extracted all its possibilities from this multiplicity of points of view. Simplifying the other problems in order to dig as deeply as possible into this one, analytical Cubism showed a mistrust of colour and presented a broken vision of volumes. 'A man like Picasso studies an object as a surgeon dissects a cadaver[5]'. Each part of the dissected object is brought firmly on to the picture plane, and there they are all juxtaposed and the surface is turbulent with a huddle of ridges that suggest a recession into space.

5. Guillaume Apollinaire, *Les Peintres cubistes*, Paris, Athéna, 1913, p. 14. (English translation: Lionel Abel, *The Cubist Painters...*, etc., *Documents of Modern Art*, vol. I, New York, 1949, p. 13.)

La Fresnaye: Conquest of the Air. *La Fresnaye bases the linear architecture of his picture on the golden proportions dear to his master Sérusier, but the initial strictness of the framework is only partially carried out: a point of intersection and the slope of an oblique line give the artist enough to go on in balancing his composition. (New York, Museum of Modern Art)*

Others, on the contrary, sought to express the third dimension by means of *colours*. They too were going back to Cézanne, who seemed the inexhaustible source of all the modern researches.

La Fresnaye studied what Cézanne had called 'delimitation of objects when the points of contact are tenuous, delicate'—that is to say, the transitions, those slight interruptions in the contour of a volume which still never completely stands out against the field, whatever the light.

For Delaunay, Cézanne's phrase 'The edges of objects escape towards a centre situated at our horizon' was, as early as 1906, the starting point of researches into the alterations produced by light in the contour of objects. Delaunay had also noticed that certain tones seem to advance or to recede in accordance with what lies next to them and with their importance or intensity. But it was in vain that he denied the reality of contour. He could not stop his chromatic circles from organizing themselves upon diameters and chords and from suggesting lines as well as depth.

To the third dimension the Italian Futurists decided to add a fourth: that is to say, they claimed to represent *duration*, in the form of movement. This truly Italian idea had already been responsible for the Baroque: at that time it had expressed itself through the hidden dynamism of the geometrical network. In the work of the Futurists dynamism, a symbol of modern life, became the very theme of art: the objects, which had been so painstakingly studied by the Cubists, were unable to resist this whirlwind and broke up into fragments, as in Severini's dancing girls, Boccioni's houses, etc. 'We are going to put the spectator at the centre of the picture,' said Carrà; the spectator would no longer move around the object, but the whole world, life, would move around him. Thus the painter's rapid notations would become a juxtaposition of successive visual images during the development of a collective movement. One can clearly see, in this, the influence of the photographs of movement taken at the beginning of the century.

Composition, in the works of these Latin artists, is still to a great extent linear: the diagonals are imperious and repeated oblique lines, either parallel or radiating like fans or lighthouse beams, stress the shift of the forms. These are lines of force or 'line-forces' (as in Boccioni's *Dynamism of a Street*, 1910, or Balla's *Pénétration dynamique d'une automobile*, 1913); their tendency is towards a quasi-cinematic notation of movement. In France, in the works of Villon and his brother Marcel Duchamp, the expression of this tendency inclined more to synthesis.

Pure colour

The Fauves were very little concerned with the dimensions of space, and for their group the essential problem was set by a different component of painting: pure colour. They went so far as to do away with all indication of volume in order to leave for colour its full power of expression. This line of research can be traced back to Manet, and to Gauguin (more to his words than to his work, in which the muted tones make the brilliant colours sing), to the Nabis, who were dazzled by the famous 'talisman'[6] —but principally to Van Gogh. The Fauve group was formed in 1905: Van Dongen and Matisse were the only members who continued to work along that line, which to them was not a passing fashion but a natural means of expression.

Preoccupation with colour does not exclude an interest in composition. This is particularly clear in the work of Matisse, who indeed has left us an example exceptionally well suited for analysis. He was given, once in his life, the opportunity to carry out a large-scale monumental composition, *The Dance* (Barnes Foundation, Merion, U.S.A.). Let us examine his method of working: it is certainly an individual one, and could prove misleading. As he himself said:

'In the end I took three five-metre canvases, the same size as the wall, and one day, armed with a stick of charcoal on the end of a long piece

Delaunay: Hommage à Blériot. *Study of the way in which forms are destroyed by light led Delaunay to paint pictures that are purely chromatic. This picture, nonetheless, is constructed on a network of slanting lines which is based on the armature of the square. The lines start from the top left-hand corner and go towards the bottom right-hand corner. (Paris, Collection Cazel. Archives photographiques)*

6. The 'talisman' was a study executed by Sérusier in the autumn of 1888 at Pont-Aven, under the eyes of Gauguin. He showed it to his colleagues at the Académie Julian on his return. In it pure tones were juxtaposed, and the result was an appearance of intense brilliance.

Matisse: The Dance; first state. *(Musée de la Ville de Paris; copy by C.B.)*

of bamboo, I set to work to draw the whole thing at one go. In me it was like a rhythm that carried me. I had the surface in my head.' Nonetheless, he adds immediately:

'But when the drawing was done, when I began to lay on the colour, I had to change all the forms I had planned. I had to fill it all in and see that the whole remained architectural. At the same time I had to keep in close association with the masonry, so that the lines should resist the enormous jutting blocks on which the arches rested, and should—what is more—drive through them and have enough impetus to join up with

Cézanne: Bathers (Grandes Baigneuses). *On the rabatment of the shorter sides of the rectangle Cézanne superimposes an elaborate play of curves, with their centres on the horizontals and verticals derived from the intersection of the diagonals of the squares (that is to say, from the corners of the small central square standing on its point). These well devised curves must have inspired Matisse in his preliminary work for* The Dance. *(Philadelphia, Museum of Art. Photo Bulloz)*

one another. To compose with all that on my hands and still get something that would live, would sing, I could only grope my way, ceaselessly modifying my compartments of colours and my blacks[7].' This passage is important because it is simple and sincere and because it describes with precision the processes of creation in a master who was both spontaneous and deliberate. At one and the same time he lays down the double aim—unity of the whole and its adaptation to a building divided into

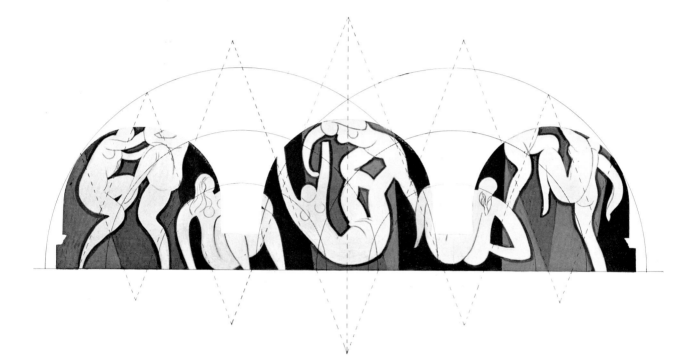

Matisse: The Dance, final state. *In this second version of* The Dance *there is added to the radiation of the bands a double play of parallel oblique lines forming a series of triangles. A series of curves centred on the places where the arches of the building descend to the wall counterbalance the weight of these and give the movement of the figures its rhythm. (Merion, Barnes Foundation. Photograph taken in the artist's studio and available by kind permission of Madame Duthuit)*

sections—and the means he found for attaining it: a great radiating rhythm of 'lines that drive through the blocks with enough impetus to join up with one another'. This impetus is more clearly felt in the first version[8]. In the second, which was the result of many studies, the figures are small, more rounded, and they obey the architecture more closely and respect its scale more completely, but the initial impetus is still expressed by bands that start from the bottom and blossom outwards like rays of the sun, while, on the contrary, the axes of the dancing girls converge towards the top. Interlaced arcs can be guessed at beneath the forms, controlling their leaps. Thus we can see the artist, face to face with his wall, following

7. Conversations with Matisse, published in *Paris, les Arts et les Lettres*, 19 April 1946; quoted by G. Diehl, *Henri Matisse*, Paris, Tisné, 1954, p. 85.
8. In the Musée des Beaux-Arts de la Ville de Paris.

229

Matisse: Decorative Figure on an ornamental Background. *This sculptural figure submits with docility to the armature of the rectangle: diagonals and perpendiculars regulate every detail by their secret play. In this way the inner rectangle is established—as regards the verticals, at the points where the diagonals of the vertical halves of the picture intersect those of the horizontal halves, and, as regards the horizontals, by the intersection of the diagonals of the horizontal halves and those of the quarters. This is rather exceptional in the work of Matisse: his compositions were usually made up of equilibrium rather than geometry. (Paris, Musée d'Art moderne. Archives photographiques)*

his impulse and throwing on to the surface the lines of a theme which he has matured over several years, and then indefatigably digging it up again (did he not paint the *Roumanian Blouse* eleven times?) until the hidden network gradually comes to its final definition.

Matisse must, in this, have been guided by what was perhaps an unconscious memory, certainly a predilection: Cézanne's *Bathers (Grandes Baigneuses)*. He loved that picture, and possessed a preparatory study for it in which the composition was already sketched[9]. In spite of the essential difference between their frames, the rhythms are closely similar. In *The Dance* the melody of the curves develops upon severe harmonies formed by the oblique bands of the background, like that of the *Bathers* on the branches of the trees; but these triangular radiations with the apex at the top were still, in Cézanne's picture, static, whereas Matisse's bands explode skywards. The figures in *The Dance* have also less rigour than those of Cézanne: this is because they give rise to the scheme instead of falling in with a pre-existent diagram. Here let me quote Kandinsky:

'...Cézanne's *Bathers*, a composition in a triangle (the mystic triangle). Such build-up in geometric form is an old principle which was finally abandoned, because it led to stiff academic formulae which no longer possessed any inner sense or any soul. Cézanne's application of this principle gave it a new soul... In this case, the triangle is not an aid to harmony of the group but the accentuated artistic aim... Cézanne, with full justification, alters the human figure. He not only makes the entire figure point to the head of the triangle but also individual parts of the body are constantly driven, more and more strongly from the bottom to the top, as by an inner impulse. They become lighter and lighter until finally they expand visibly[10].'

In *The Dance* we can see how Matisse organizes his flat colours and his patterns. All his pictures are at once free and thought out: the most cursive and carefree lines, the most abrupt touches, are controlled, in his work, by a completely lucid mind.

The other Fauves extinguished their youthful ardour and chose, each one, his path. Derain, who was one of the stalwarts of the group between

9. This study is now in the Musée des Beaux-Arts de la Ville de Paris.

10. W. Kandinsky, *Über das Geistige in der Kunst*, Munich, 1912. (English translation: Hilla Rebay, *On the Spiritual in Art*, New York, Solomon R. Guggenheim Foundation, 1946; Footnote on p. 50.) As Kandinsky has rightly noted, the human in this picture subjects itself to the demands of geometry, in accordance with the rules now familiar to us.

Derain: Last Supper. *Two approaches to creative work lie open to an artist. One is to take up what his immediate predecessors were trying to do and carry it further, as in the case of Seurat completing Impressionism, of the Cubists developing the discoveries of Cézanne, of the Fauves drawing the conclusions suggested by Van Gogh. The other is to aim at perfection and, with that aim, stand out from one's period and study the masters of earlier times: this was Poussin's approach. It is also the one adopted by Derain when he centres all his efforts upon composition, trying to make it calm and balanced and therefore inevitably rediscovering the principles of the masters. In this picture the intersection of the diagonals of the rectangle and those of the squares determines the axis of the Christ. The table occupies the space between the median horizontal and the horizontal which passes through the side of each square at the point where it intersects the diagonals of the other square. When Cézanne had chosen a scheme, he was sometimes influenced by it to the point of distorting the object. Derain sought in the masters the art of using a scheme with discretion. (Private Collection. Photo Seuil)*

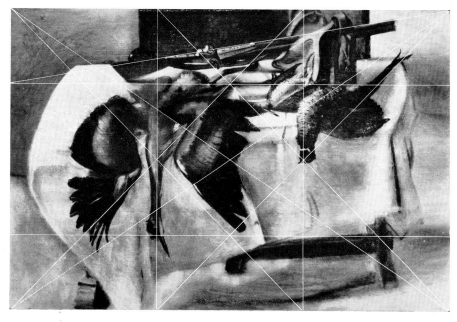

Derain: Still-Life. *The most complete liberty seems to dominate this still-life; and yet the picture obeys the classic rules of still-life painting as Oudry conceived it, and the rabatment of the shorter sides of the rectangle is rigorously applied. (Pittsburgh, Carnegie Foundation. Photo Jean Gilbert)*

231

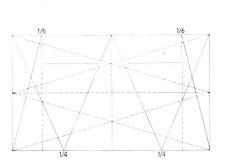

Dufy: Le Bel Eté; tapestry. *The multiplicity of small details makes, in this work, a perfect subject for tapestry; and yet this dispersion obeys the simplest design derived from the armature of the rectangle: the quarters, halves and thirds of the halves. (Paris, Galerie Louis Carré)*

Rouault: Stella Vespertina. *Axis of symmetry strongly marked. Horizon on the intersection of the diagonals. Perspective of the road following the diagonals of the lower square. (Paris, Galerie Louis Carré)*

1901 and 1907, later abandoned pure colour: 'It is a dyer's theory,' he told Vlaminck. He turned his whole research in the direction of a constructional art, imbued with grandeur and consciously faithful to the disciplines of the past.

Raoul Dufy adds to his charming spontaneity a feeling for the wall, whenever he has occasion for it: he then raises the horizon to the top part of the canvas, taking the plane of the landscape back to the plane of the wall, as Bruegel had done. His geometry is simple, or rather, is a symmetry: a central axis accompanied by vertical bands of colour. But always—and his secret lies there—the interest is distributed equally throughout: Dufy possesses the art of the dispersed composition.

Though in temperament at the opposite pole from Dufy, Rouault sometimes obtained verticality of plane by the same method, by re-erecting perspective, which then becomes one with the axis of symmetry. But instead of attempting a scattering, his aim is always a greater density.

In this way these artists who had started as Fauves became thoughtful, deliberate painters, very much at ease within the old geometrical forms, which they simplified to the utmost and used to express a completely modern personality.

In the same period the German Expressionists were creating a true romantic art of painting—perhaps the only one that has succeeded in being a spontaneous projection of the self by means of profoundly modified natural

Rouault: *Though the texture of his pictures was very different, Rouault's method of working reminds one in some ways of Matisse. Both artists took up the same picture again as many as ten times, Rouault working on the same canvas, Matisse taking a fresh one or obliterating and starting again. In the case of these indefatigable researches it is hard to guess at the process of creation: did they start from a scheme, or is the scheme the final result of their thinking?*

Rouault: 'Miserere', plate XLVI. 'Le juste comme le bois de santal parfume la hache qui le frappe.' *The two axes governing the composition of this plate are the verticals drawn from the corners of the small central square formed by the diagonals of the two overlapping squares. A large circle has its circumference running through the points where these diagonals and these verticals intersect. (Photo Hurault)*

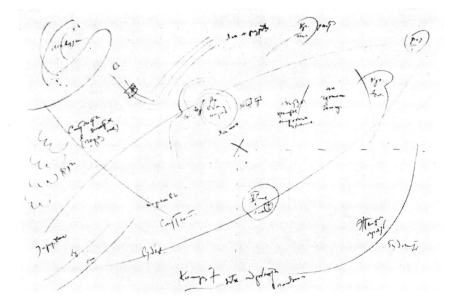

Kandinsky: 'Composition VI'; study and
finished picture. *The median axis is marked
by a cross, and the development in the form
of a broken spiral is indicated by three segments
of curves intersecting two by two. The breaks
are even more marked in the picture itself,
but the general arrangement remains the same.
(Paris, Collection N.K.)*

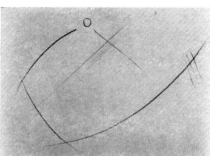

Kandinsky: 'Composition VII'; study and finished picture. *The diagonal creates a rising movement. This slanting line from the bottom left-hand corner to the top right-hand corner is stressed by two arcs. In the final picture it is broken by lines at right angles to one another which frame, so to speak, the central focus. In the sketch this centre is only indicated by a cross, joined to the sides by two dotted perpendiculars. (Moscow, Tretiakov Gallery)*

elements. For this purpose they used the purely aesthetic discoveries of the Fauves and, like them, adopted pure colours, though for purposes of suggestion. The principle of distortion was admitted as an axiom: it could be taken very far, was indeed practically subjected to no limits, because the forms taken from nature were not there for the sake of exploring nature, but for the sake of revealing, by allusion, the artist's own tendencies, his sentiments, passions, aspirations or melancholy. A Russian, brought up on the decorative wealth of his native land, stands out from this group as vitally important for our enquiry, Wassily Kandinsky.

In 1910, at the moment when his individuality was really finding itself, he wrote *On the Spiritual in Art*, a theoretical book which is essential to the understanding of his painting in its different phases. In it the idea that *forms have a sense or content proper to them*, an idea that comes more naturally to German thought than to the French conception of art, takes on an exceptional vigour: every form is considered to be the outward manifestation of a content; it must manifest in the most expressive manner 'the innermost content of the form.' (p. 47). In spite of appearances this is no longer Expressionism: Kandinsky's thought goes much further, and in this book of his we are able to follow his whole evolution in the direction of the abstract—an abstraction that remains, nonetheless, 'expressive' and strangely alive.

'Today the artist cannot progress exclusively with purely abstract forms, as these forms are not sufficiently precise. Limiting oneself to the unprecise, it deprives one of possibilities, excluding the purely human and, therefore, weakening the power of expression.' (p. 48).

But at the same time the abstract form is felt as a clean, precise, well-defined form, and its apparent poverty changes into an inner enrichment. These abstract forms attracted and fascinated him more and more, and are to him 'beings' which, though purely abstract, possess their own life, their own influence, and make their own value felt. Such 'are a square, a circle, a triangle, a rhombus, a trapezoid, and innumerable other forms becoming more complicated with no mathematical designation. All these forms occupy space in the realm of the non-objective.' (p. 48). Between the material and the abstract 'lies the endless number of forms in which both elements are contained and where either the material or non-objective predominates.' (p. 48). Thus, in spite of his striving after cold logic, the artist reveals his secret tendencies, his exceptional gift for creating something alive. And Kandinsky was a great visionary.

After his youth as an Expressionist and a Fauve, this evolution of Kandinsky towards the abstract divides into two periods:

Between 1910 and 1920 his canvases exhibit forces which cross the picture obliquely, from left to right, about nuclei that suggest a world of nebulae, of galaxies—a kind of magma subjected to slow but violent impulses. Sometimes there are also strange beasts, quite unrelated to reality, which move about with the abruptness of slipper animalcules. These, clearly, are the beings that 'pullulate' and justify that word 'organic' which always came into Kandinsky's mind when he wished to suggest the concrete.

In about 1921 or 1922 the forms crystallize into rigid elements—circles, triangles, squares—but the translatory movement is maintained until about 1925 when, as the artist grew older, a more static quality, a striving for calm and equilibrium, became dominant.

Throughout this evolution Kandinsky was a deliberate artist who submitted exuberant gifts to the strict control of a mind with a bent for construction: the real man was already there in his analysis of Cézanne's *Bathers*. Nothing in his tumultuous work is left to chance. Two preparatory sketches dating from the first period (1913) show us how far, even then, his impulses were subjected to a precise construction. Later on, by a sort of reaction against himself, he chose sharp, cutting, sword-like forms; and at other times the circle, which had become the field of a microscope, enclosed the agitated movement of his creatures within narrow bounds. 'Composition is twofold,' he tells us, composition of the whole, and composition of the various parts subordinated to the whole. The total composition is a form: the objects, whether real or abstract, will bend to that form, 'they will be that form'. At the same time the isolated elements are modified by combining with one another, or simply by their orientation.

'This is called movement. For example, a triangle directed upwards has a quieter, more steadfast, stable appeal than the same triangle set obliquely on its side.' (p. 53).

Kandinsky: Sur Blanc. *In his second period Kandinsky makes use of the lines of classical armatures, and following them obediently or turning gently aside in one way or the other, he creates a sort of instability. But this instability is not disconcerting because it is never far from the fixed lines of the frame that formed its point of departure. (Paris, Private Collection. Photo Seuil)*

It is clear from this that, to Kandinsky, the displacement of the lines was essential. In this second phase of his work it was the only means he had retained of recreating life. The composition used the perpendiculars and diagonals as its support. Not in order to establish itself on them: on the contrary, to take off from them. Arrows, lances, triangles seem to indicate to us the armature of the rectangle, but also to escape from it and launch themselves out of its network. Symmetrical pictures, such as his *Conversation* (1926), are rare.

237

Odilon Redon: Germination; *and* In a Dream (1879). *(Photo B.N.)*

Irrationalism

Already in the nineteenth century a profoundly original artist, Odilon Redon (born in 1840), had discovered the limits of consciousness and those vital forces which often escape from it:

'My gifts have led me into the world of dream; I have suffered the torments of the imagination and the surprises which it gave me through my pencil; but I have guided and controlled those surprises in accordance with organic laws of art which I know, which I can feel, to the sole end of obtaining in the spectator, through subtle attraction, all the evocative, all the seductive power of uncertainty, close to the confines of thought[11].'

This attitude was at that time an isolated one, and it made Odilon Redon a being set apart; but it gradually gained strength and has become one of the strangest characteristics of our generation. A stream seems to be welling up and spreading, of irritation against reason: what reason illuminates appears too well known, and one soon tires of it; the really marvellous must be what reason leaves in the shade! In point of fact, the enrichment of painting at the beginning of this movement was intoxicating; but it was not long before this enterprise began to disappoint, and its contribution became less and less communicable. It is easy to see why.

The forms of reason are what is most universal in human beings: they impose a language accessible to all. It can be understood and handled sometimes more easily, sometimes less, but there is still only one intellectual language, only one geometry, only one logic. True, the world of tendencies and of semiconscious or unconscious association of ideas has its 'archetypes', but the expressions of these are, in their concrete structure, as varied as the individuals themselves. By means of them it is possible to inject a perpetual novelty; but it must be recognized that art is difficult to transmit if it is not based on anything general: images that are too individual remain mere curiosities, cold and without response.

On this strange path I can only mention a few landmarks. One of them was a great artist from a *milieu* very close to that of Kandinsky. Paul Klee sought, under an appearance of free and easy charm, to express the invisible, 'that whole universe of which the visible is only an isolated example'. He was not an abstract artist, nor was he an 'informal', but a magician who transformed all concrete allusions into signs. He was a great lover of music and seems to have been, for a long time, pursued by the image of musical staves and notes. The lines of the stave haunt very many of his drawings and paintings, as for instance the *Pavilion of Women* (1921) and *Cool Breeze* (1924). Flowers, birds' heads *(Twittering Machine)* or women *(In the Meadow)* suggest notes which the colours make sing. These

11. *A soi-même*, 1867-1915, Paris, 1922.

Odilon Redon: Lithographs. *When we dream we lose our critical sense. The works of Odilon Redon are poetic dreams in colour, and they escape from any known idea of composition: they make one think of flowers coming out.*

Paul Klee: In the Meadow. *Paul Klee compared composition to a tight-rope walker who keeps his balance by moving his pole successively to right and to left. He distinguished three kinds of balance: of sizes, of values and of colours. Apart from this general law which prevails throughout, his work seems to* me to fall into four periods: first the *crystalline or prismatic compositions, made up of large or small elements (magic squares);* then the coralline *compositions, with their organic, articulated and sinuous development;* thirdly the descriptive fairy *compositions (fishes, flowers, etc.); and lastly the 'script'* compositions (musical or ideographic notation). In the Meadow *is a coralline composition, with a more or less vertical median axis as its fulcrum of balance. These flower-women seem subject to the laws of the growth of flowers—the large ones keep the small ones at a distance. The harmony in distortion between the vertical and horizontal elements is so subtle that it is difficult to say which are dominant. The figures remind one also of musical notes arranged on a double stave. (Locust Valley, Connecticut, Willard-Johnson Collection. Photo Giraudon)*

Paul Klee: Air-Tsu-Dni. *Composition of the script type. Klee, who was a musician, had certainly been struck by the grave beauty of certain pages of musical scores, and with his sensibility and logic he set to work to explore all their plastic possibilities. This picture is also affected by the square and its armature: the series of small verticals in the lower part reduces the design to a square, the division of which into four gives the composition its axes. (Berne, Hans Meyer Collection)*

239

Paul Klee: Flourishing Port. *Taking as his starting-point the genetics of forms, which was the basis of his teaching, Klee became more and more deeply concerned with the symbolism of objects or of living creatures. He created for his use a kind of script, whose 'characters' seem related to the Glagolitic alphabet. This succession of signs inserted into one another is in truth a script which, like poetry, allows its message to be read. The composition is balanced: it gains architectural quality from the fragmentary straight lines and their right angles, and life from a few circles. (Basle Museum)*

are ideograms, symbols: 'The symbol..., an image concentrated in the mirror of the spirit and yet identical with the object[12].'

Paul Klee delights in placing these signs within a network of horizontals and verticals, or about a central point, or even on either side of a definite axis of symmetry—naïve compositions that express the same childlike freshness as his epigrammatic and witty drawings.

Towards 1934 the musical stave disappears, and the signs, in black or dark colours against coloured backgrounds, become a writing (*Secret Writing*, 1934; *Script*, 1940; *Flourishing Port*, 1938). In one of his last pictures, the *Kettledrummer*, the sign even stands alone, stating its own existence, and the note which has been struck bursts out as a red patch.

Surrealism carried the research on into the irrational. Beginning as a literary movement with a philosophical cast (exemplified in the experiments with automatic writing) it sought to violate the customary laws of thought and morality. It was more a 'mental subversion'[13] than a plastic revolution. This meant that it had trouble in finding a painterly form, and composition was clearly not its major preoccupation. It did, however, make possible the blossoming of several highly original painters. Chirico did not do away with the traditional plastic frameworks, but by a displacement of the vanishing points and points of distance he modifies the perspective, making it nightmarish. By means of great shadows suggesting

12. Goethe, *Essay on the Painting of Philostratos.*
13. Mesens, quoted by Marcel Jean in his *Histoire de la peinture surréaliste*, Paris, éd. du Seuil, 1959, p. 77. This book is a complete study of the Surrealist movement.

day's end, he renders the essentially human space of classicism menacing, and creates, with the help of unaccustomed cultural reminiscences, a highly novel and attractive poetry. Joan Miró recalls Kandinsky's formal 'beings', those fantastic slipper animalcules peopling his dimensionless world. Finally, Max Ernst contrived to produce a seductive and refined art, while concealing within his pictures a secret and bitter feeling, destructive of both social and artistic conventions. I have, however, made it my rule not to deal with the work of painters still developing.

Emigrating to America in 1940 and meeting there the refugees from Central Europe, the Surrealists brought to those disorientated artists their technical innovations and inventions. From this arose that strange school of painting which the Americans have called—according to the various

Joan Miró: Painting. *Miró started from a Surrealism tinged with Fauvism, but gradually drew away from this and, while retaining a brilliant palette, created a strange world peopled with forms which, though unreal, seem alive. In this picture the armature of the rectangle can be made to supply a valid explanation of the way in which they are placed. (Philadelphia Museum of Art)*

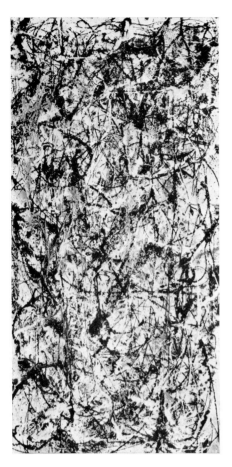

Jackson Pollock: Cathedral. *Jackson Pollock was the originator of a way of pictorial thinking in which gesture is the primary element. At the same time, painting turns away from the closed and realized form in order to penetrate into the wider world of the potential. It is gesture, in fact, that has given rise to those allusive forms, those successive or simultaneous structures, those aimed segments, etc. from among which the choice is never completely made. In this complex world, however, the constructional activity remains awake: Pollock himself sometimes insists on a rhythm; at others he leaves to the spectator—a new Leonardo—the freedom to intervene and to project on to the painting, along with his emotion, constructional schemes that were implicit in the gesture. Composition becomes choice. (Dallas Museum)*

groups—*action painting, abstract Expressionism, tachism,* etc. Its most famous representative is Jackson Pollock. He took up Max Ernst's technique of 'oscillation' (setting a paint-filled funnel to swing about over the horizontal canvas) and rechristened it *dripping,* but did away with the automatic movement and 'acted' through rapid, sensuous spurts of paint, which move back and forth under the impulse of a kind of vital rhythm, yet never go outside the frame. Side by side with the delicate relationship of the colours, the exuberance of his line and the vitality of his calligraphy succeed in expressing a new romanticism in painting, which comes from a violent exteriorization of the painter's self. Yet it is clear that Pollock does not wholly escape from plastic composition: one may judge of this from his use of verticals in *Cathedral* (Dallas Museum) or from the rhythms of his *Blue Poles* (New York, Ben Heller Collection).

Geometry

Other painters, more modest, consider that their tumultuous and irrational self is of interest to nobody and that their impulses must be disciplined if they are to turn into works of art. Kandinsky, as we have seen, realized that only geometry could render the dynamism of which he was possessed accessible to all. Geometry has still its faithful followers. The purism that today isolates each of the components of painting leads these inevitably to confine themselves within the picture plane and to make the play of forms occur exclusively in the two dimensions of the canvas.

This *plane vision* was already to be found in the work of Braque and Picasso as soon as they had passed the stage of analytical Cubism. They quickly tired of following literally Cézanne's advice to treat nature by means of the cylinder and the cone. In 1912-1913, in the period of synthesis, a period richer in suggestion, they provoked the reflex of cognition by presenting only characteristic parts of the object reduced to the plane. In some of their *collages* they did away with the support of concrete elements, such as the table on which the objects are arranged, and presented them as though pinned to the wall, with no depth. Round about 1927 Fernand Léger returned to this idea, though with more insistence on plastic realism. But with him it was not a systematic method: compositions massed towards the centre and putting no weight on the base, as for instance his *La Joconde aux clefs* or *Les Belles Cyclistes,* are matched by such weighty groups as *Les Loisirs.* When he came to project these suspended masses upon a wall, they tended to destroy the stability of the monument.

Juan Gris, that lucid and logical Spaniard, detected an antinomy between all interpretations of the third dimension and linear geometry: he preferred to do away completely with the awkward concept of depth.

'And I insist on flat forms, for to consider these forms in a spatial world would be more a sculptor's business. I will go so far as to say that the only possible painterly technique is a kind of flat, coloured architecture[14].'

This sets the painter free to employ all his powers in the research after pure form. Painting has become well and truly an experiment: it is necessary to separate the elements, to decant them, keeping always in mind the obsessive search for purity—at one time pure colour and now pure form. In the words of Juan Gris:

'Geometrical figures and forms subjected to a vertical axis have more gravity than those whose axis is not definite or not vertical... We can see that all this can even form the basis of a pictorial architecture. It would be the painter's mathematics, and only this mathematics can serve to establish the composition of the picture. Only from this architecture can there arise the subject—that is to say, an arrangement of the elements of reality caused by that composition.'

Here, in contrast to the classical method analyzed elsewhere in this book, the subject arises from the architecture and the idea is derived from the lines that engender it.

Léger: Les Loisirs. Here Léger draws near to the Douanier Rousseau: the same frontality, the same static quality. In addition to the armature of the rectangle, a hidden circle organizes the composition. Léger's predilection for this geometrical figure is well known. (Paris, Musée d'Art moderne. Archives photographiques)

14. Lecture by Juan Gris to the *Groupe d'Etudes philosophiques et scientifiques* at the Sorbonne, 15 May 1924; quoted by D.H. Kahnweiler, *Juan Gris, sa vie, son œuvre, ses écrits,* Paris, Gallimard, 1946. (English translation: Douglas Cooper, London, 1947.)

Léger: Les Belles Cyclistes. Léger saw Poussin's Rape of the Sabines *as 'a battle of straight lines and curves'. Up to 1925 his painting applied this theory (for example,* Les Disques, Le Grand Déjeuner*). Later on, he abandoned the 'tubist' style: the straight lines became sinuous and volumes less schematic. This picture has a composition based on the circle with a pentagon inscribed. (Chicago Art Institute. Photo Giraudon)*

Juan Gris: Guitar and Flowers. *Each of the Cubists had his own problems. Gris was not concerned with the third dimension —he avoided it systematically. On the other hand, linear mathematics made its presence more and more felt in his work. This canvas, a hymn to geometry, is based on the armature of the rectangle: diagonals of the rectangle, diagonals and sides of the horizontal halves, of the vertical quarters and of the horizontal and vertical sixths. (New York, Museum of Modern Art)*

It should be noted that Juan Gris nearly always says 'architecture', not 'geometry'. By doing so he is introducing a value judgment: 'All architecture is a construction, but not every construction is architecture...' His conception is very close to my own idea of the frameworks of pictures. When Gris says 'mathematics', what he has in mind is 'the painter's mathematics', and he takes care not to give it an exaggerated strictness.

Some modern painters, on the contrary, delight in basing their work on measurements and on constructions with the compasses, which almost take us back to the Middle Ages. In this connection one fact in particular deserves our attention: the quite new interest in the *golden number*, the use of which had gone out of fashion and the theory of which had come to seem so remote.

One may well ask where this revival of the golden number among artists and theorists originated. The use of that ratio had become, as we have seen, a more and more confused and almost instinctive studio practice. It was the German theorists at the beginning of the nineteenth century who unearthed the concept and studied it in precise detail, in particular by examining its use in the Egyptian monuments. The neo-classical school of Cornelius and Overbeck, which, being German, had in it a much stronger tendency to abstraction than had that of David, delighted in the incommensurable numbers $\sqrt{2}, \frac{1 + \sqrt{5}}{2}$. Through Father Didier (P. Lenz) these numbers became the essence of the famous 'Sacred Measures', the artistic creed of the Benedictine monastery of Beuron[15]. The French artists became aware of the sacred measures through Sérusier, to whom they were revealed in 1897, when on a visit to Prague he saw his friend Verkade, a novice of Beuron. As soon as he was back from Prague, he began to expound these principles: 'I have spent several days in Paris,' he wrote to Verkade[16], 'and, as you can imagine, have talked a great deal about your measures... I have talked a great deal to all our friends.' From 1908 onwards Sérusier was one of the principal teachers at the Académie Ranson, where he taught his pupils these principles, lucidly restated in his *ABC*, which came out only in 1921[17]. Ghyka, who had a thorough and direct knowledge of the German philosophical writings, explained and resumed the doctrine of the golden number a few years later[18].

Geometrical construction of the square roots of the prime numbers.

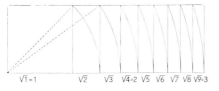

$\sqrt{1}=1$ $\sqrt{2}$ $\sqrt{3}$ $\sqrt{4}=2$ $\sqrt{5}$ $\sqrt{6}$ $\sqrt{7}$ $\sqrt{8}$ $\sqrt{9}=3$

15. Beuron, in South Germany, on the Upper Danube.

16. Maurice Denis gives these details and quotes a number of letters in his study of the life and work of Paul Sérusier, which forms the preface to a new edition of Sérusier's *L'ABC de la peinture*, Paris, Floury, 1942. The letter quoted here is on page 75 of this.

17. In 1905, Sérusier had translated Father Didier's *Zur Ästhetik der Beuroner Schule*, Vienna and Leipzig, n.d. (*L'Esthétique de Beuron*), but this was no more than a general exposé, a preliminary statement.

18. Ghyka, *Esthétique des proportions dans la nature et dans les arts*, Paris, Gallimard, 1927. — *Le Nombre d'or, Rites et rythmes pythagoriciens*, Paris, Gallimard, 1931.

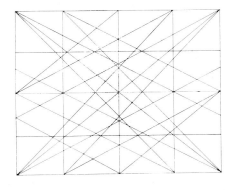

Jacques Villon: Un Atelier de Mécaniques. '*Painting is based upon perspective, which is nothing else than a thorough knowledge of the function of the eye. And this function simply consists in receiving in a pyramid the forms and colours of the objects placed before it. I say in a pyramid, because there is no* object so small that it will not be larger than the spot where these pyramids are received into the eye. Therefore if you extend the lines from the edges of each body as they converge you will bring them to a single point, and necessarily the said lines will form a pyramid.' (Literary Works of Leonardo da Vinci, ed. J.P. Richter, Oxford, 1959, vol. I, p. 139)

Villon took this paragraph as his artistic creed. Like his Mécaniques, this picture is composed on the rabatment of the shorter sides of the rectangle. *(Paris, Galerie Louis Carré)*

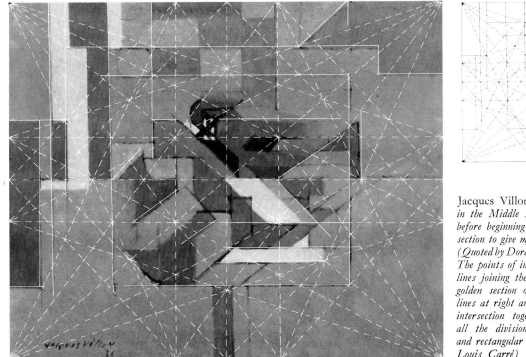

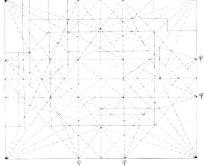

Jacques Villon: L'Oiseau empaillé. '*As in the Middle Ages they offered up a prayer before beginning to paint, I rely on the golden section to give myself a preliminary assurance.*' (Quoted by Dora Vallier, Cahiers d'Art, 1957) The points of intersection of the several oblique lines joining the corners of the picture to the golden section of its sides, and the straight lines at right angles which join these points of intersection together, enable us to establish all the divisions of this strictly rectilinear and rectangular composition. *(Paris, Galerie Louis Carré)*

Jacques Villon: Mécaniques. '*When I am making direct studies my drawings follow the inner movement, that inner line of the object which, like a tightened cord, gives it its unity. I make, in fact, an analysis from nature, so as to have time to think... My next preoccupation has been rhythm.*' (*Quoted by Dora Vallier, op. cit.*). *This picture is divided into three parts by the rabatment of the sides: each of these three bands has its own rhythm, given by the dia-gonals of the rectangle and of the square. Quite recently, Jacques Villon was kind enough to give me confirmation of this: '*This division of the surface into three parts (not always equal) is very important to me, for it corresponds with the synthesis of space. Already in my initial drawing I choose my three planes. I imagine that the colours are transparent and so capable of being modified by superimposition. The first division to the right or left will be the first plane; in it the principal design will be asserted. The second plane, being the harmonic hinge of the picture, may occupy the whole surface of the canvas. Then comes the third plane. The first plane will influence the general plane and will be influenced by it in the part where it is super-imposed. The same will be true of the third part, which will be subject to the influence of the main plane. But this harmonic hierarchy in space will always be determined by the first plane.*' (*Paris, Galerie Louis Carré*)

Sérusier claimed to be 'the father of Cubism' because Roger de la Fresnaye had been one of his pupils. Certainly the taste for the golden number permeated the Cubist circle, most strikingly in the cases of Villon and André Lhote. Jacques Villon and his brothers Marcel and Raymond Duchamp, together with Gleizes and Picabia, organized in October 1912 the *Salon de la Section d'or* and Villon says that the whole idea of the Salon was his. Villon, who is both a subtle, sensitive colourist and a severely constructional painter, has never ceased to base his pictures lovingly upon a strict architecture both in the plane and in space, as our illustrations show.

The Cubists and their theories tend to lead us astray from our subject: to them, composition was not always a major problem, their attention being absorbed by the creation of a graphic language. Yet some of them

André Lhote: L'Escale. *(Musée de la Ville de Paris. Photo Bulloz).* '...Upon this radiating scheme of objects wholly reduced to their plastic music, a number of slight decorative features here and there lay their explicit embroideries. These are the rigging of the ships, the windows of the houses... and many other textual signs, which will allow the spectator's eye to identify the mingled forms.' *(André Lhote, Parlons peinture, Paris, 1946, p. 35)*

had also an acute concern for syntax. This was certainly true of André Lhote: that great theorist and writer, who refused to separate composition and painting, who was an enthusiast for the golden number and who set himself to show the connection between the Cubist experiments and tradition, is surely allied to Cézanne, whose desire was to unite Impressionism with the constructional painters of the past by 'painting Poussins from nature'.

But the French painters never dared to go as far into pure geometry and the strict use of the golden section as did the cold and pitiless Dutchman Piet Mondrian. His thinking had matured in a *milieu* rich in researches into the problems of art, from which were to emerge the great Dutch architects in the group that took the name of 'la Nouvelle Plastique' and in 1917 started the small review *De Stijl*, whose influence was far-reaching. In 1920 Mondrian published in that review a series of dialogues on *Natural Reality and Abstract Reality*: in these he expounded the austere but logical

Charles Bouleau: Composition on the Dynamic Ratios 9: 12: 16. *(Photo Marc Vaux)*

247

Mondrian: Painting I. *Mondrian takes the large square as his starting-point and divides it by means of the diagonal AC and by EF, a parallel to two of the sides, which passes through point S, the golden section of the diagonal. The major segment AS, gives us the side of a small square, which obeys the same scheme as the first and is placed on this, but with the positions reversed: the diagonal A'C' will fall on EF while E'F' will fall on the original diagonal AC, the points of intersection coinciding. These steps result in an orientation of A'B'C'D' at an angle of 45° to ABCD, and in its fitting exactly upon the first square. The thickness of the black lines is in the ratio 3, 4, 5. (New York, Museum of Modern Art)*

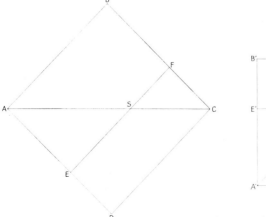

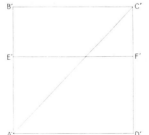

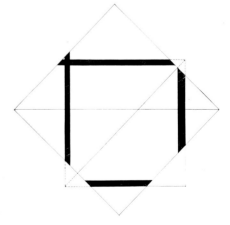

principles which were the result of his reflections. These dialogues, now available in French and English[19], are divided into seven scenes; each scene starts with a Dutch landscape, horizontal and calm under a moon or a starry sky. The dominant impression is repose; and this is what art must seek: spiritual repose. 'Repose becomes plastically visible through the harmony of relations'—these being of three kinds: *relations of position*, *relations of proportion* and *relations of colour*.

'Relations of position' lie 'not in the *size* of lines and planes, but in the *position* of lines and planes with respect to each other. The most perfect instance is the right angle, which expresses the relation between two extremes.'

Thus duality—what Mondrian calls 'one plus one'—is necessary to the orthogonal relation, which will be presented solely in the plane, since 'modelling of any kind makes the picture too material'.

The right angle determines the 'primordial relation', but in the multiple (which 'we are not obliged to think of as multiple') it ceases to be a unity and is broken up, giving rise to rhythm, which changes with the inequality of the relations.

At the same time Mondrian gives his preference to the straight line because 'the straight line is the "fulfilment" of the curve'.

At the beginning of the fourth dialogue there is a mill, which extends its arms in a cross. Mondrian immediately warns us against anything that may remind one of a subject, and even against the use of any form such as the cross, 'to which we so readily associate a particular and somewhat literary idea'. This brings us to the culminating point of the doctrine: the 'inner vision' within all things is individual, and it is essential to attain the general, the universal. Mondrian is definitely opposed to the Expressionists and to the painters of the subconscious, who express their own reality and not 'abstract reality'.

Dialogues V to VII are principally concerned with the new art in its handling of space, and here there occur those applications to architecture which were destined to have so wide an influence.

And so, with exceptional intransigence, Mondrian confines his aim to the expression of the constants of the human spirit. The application of these principles in his pictures from 1921 onwards was equally intransigent. It brought Mondrian to the pure scheme or diagram, and is a kind of extreme confirmation of this book's whole line of research into the frameworks of pictures. Whether the lines do or do not serve to delimit a form, we must, if we wish to apply our disciplines strictly, recognize that the scheme already contains in itself the very principle of beauty. Nobody before Mondrian had dared to try to prove this. He, by elimination, arrived at one kind of scheme only, a scheme that embodies the supreme satisfaction, repose. His most fully realized pictures depart from symmetry; everything in them takes place through bands that cut or intersect, through rectangles, and through the thickness of lines: 'relations of position', the

19. Michel Seuphor, *Piet Mondrian, sa vie, son œuvre*, Paris, Flammarion, 1956; *Piet Mondrian, Life and Work*, London, Thames and Hudson, 1957.

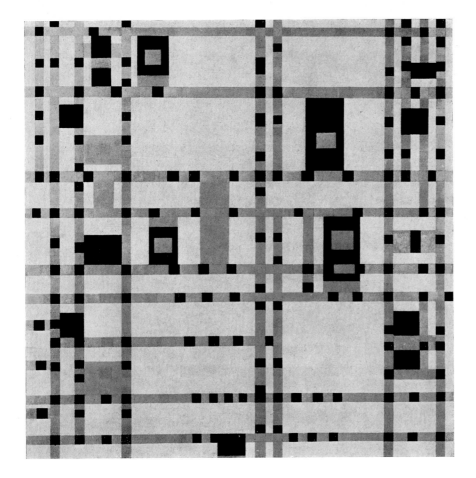

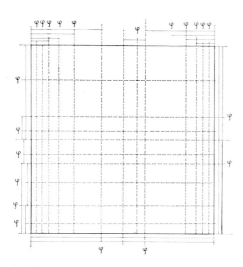

Mondrian: Broadway Boogie-Woogie.
*The horizontals and verticals which make up
this picture are nearly all in the golden ratio.
As regards the verticals, the first segments
thus obtained are redivided in turn by the
ratio and so on, as many as six times. As
regards the horizontals, the ratio is taken
and redivided sometimes towards the top,
sometimes towards the bottom. The lines
given by the composition limit the painted
band, sometimes on one side, sometimes on
the other. I think the artist's purpose in
this was to give the picture a certain suppleness.
(New York, Museum of Modern Art)*

right angle and the parallels; 'relations of proportion', simple divisions and the golden number; 'relations of colour', discreet and sonorous harmonies of unshaded tones; all these relations broken, now and then, by the rhythms of multiplicity. One thing alone matters—to create through rigid mathematics a superior beauty, the pure work of the spirit, rejoicing the intellect of the spectator through the eye. And this explains what is, in fact, a very curious instance of the wheel coming full circle, a sort of delayed vindication: Alberti's architectural plans had given artistic directives and criteria of beauty to the painters of his time, and Mondrian's pictures give to the architects of today guidance in the organization of their façades.

Mondrian: Composition with Two Lines. *The picture is a square standing on one point. In it two lines begin to form another square. How is this done? On the large square* ABCD *the diagonals and median lines are* drawn. *We get four small squares, whose side* AE *will be the major of a golden ratio* A'E'F. *On the length* AF *thus obtained a new square* A'FGH *is constructed. To place this second square in the first, Mondrian* superimposes *the golden sections* E' *and* E" *on the diagonals of the large square,* AC *and* BD, *making the former cross at the intersection of the latter. This gives him his final scheme. (Amsterdam, Municipal Museum)*

CONCLUSION

This book has not attempted to provide a complete history of pictorial composition. There are a great many artists who are not mentioned in it, but this does not mean that they disregarded the laws of construction. Somewhat like a navigator, I have been trying to take bearings, and to this end I have analyzed a large number of paintings. Although only two or three pictures by a given artist are dealt with in this book, I have always tried to study the artist's complete production: close study of a single canvas is not enough to determine a painter's individual manner, for each artist has a favourite type of composition, in which his period, his studies and his own temperament are reflected. When the moment came to choose from among the many analyses in my portfolios, I tried to present only works that had not yet been studied in a similar way.

Originally I grouped these observations under the title *Charpentes*—Frameworks. Others prefer to speak of geometrical tracings, and Sutter of aesthetic lines. These various terms express the same idea. Artists have constantly applied their intelligence to giving organization to forms, harmony to lines. In the West they have been subjected, in addition, to the imperatives of the frame and of symmetry, even when they ended by breaking them. The internal construction of a picture has varied in complexity from period to period: sometimes it has been reduced to the elementary data of the picture's shape (for instance, the diagonals of the rectangle); but even complexity has been obtained by the simplest means.

Let me now attempt to sum up the results of our enquiry. In the first place, I have been constantly on guard against the insidious and frequent temptation to misuse such words as 'numbers', 'music' and 'laws of harmony'; these words are generally vague and ambiguous.

Numbers are of very limited use in painting. If we leave aside the distinction between even and uneven numbers, and also such arrangements as do not involve more than a few elements which can be counted at a glance without any calculation, numbers did not really come into the plastic arts until the fifteenth century, with Alberti's doctrine. The use of numbers in painting is a delicate matter, and it characterizes a period when painters worked always with meticulous application; the division of a length into nine equal parts, for instance, though not difficult, requires a good deal of care. As we have seen, these methods fell into oblivion, notwithstanding the visual habit which prolonged their use for some time, and for all the efforts made to revive them by the Baroque painters.

The words '*music*' and 'musical proportions' and 'musical harmony' must therefore be used in a precise sense, in the same sense in which they were understood by the Renaissance artists. The most exact term would be 'ratios of consonance'. But after these ratios had been abandoned, or even totally forgotten, artists and writers on art still went on using the words, which they found in the old treatises. And indeed, painters are always haunted by the idea of music—it offers them comparisons and metaphors. What one finds in texts such as Coypel's is a complex blend of these memories and analogies; and in our own time, also, some painters have sought out the company of musicians and meditated on the resemblances between painting and music: Kandinsky speaks of the 'sound' of a form, and Paul Klee is attracted by the symbolism and beauty of musical notation.

The rest is *geometry*—and sometimes very simple geometry.

It is in the Gothic period that one finds artists using the diagrams that are most tricky to work out; they start from regular polygons which require considerable strictness in their construction. These figures, more often than not inscribed in the frame, serve as support for an apparently inexhaustible fantasy. But painters soon grew tired of these difficult constructions and constantly sought to simplify the framework suggested by geometry. Hence the highly significant success of Dürer's short book, in which he treats of how to construct a pentagon '*with the opening of the compasses unchanged*'.

A single angle of the compasses was one too many: painters did not like using the compasses. They came to prefer 'snapping' the diagonals of their pictures with a chalk line[1] and using the natural divisions of the rectangle which, given by the points of intersection of the diagonals, required no instrument other than a cord for the marking of certain lines or the reproduction of certain lengths. On this basis all sorts of permutations and combinations were tried: one variant of which painters were especially fond was the 'rabatment', or rotation, of one side of the rectangle upon another, together with the use of the intersecting diagonals of the two squares thus obtained. It is a method which comes so naturally that artists have used it in all periods; but its employment seems to have become general in the nineteenth century.

Sérusier was well aware of the difficulty of tracing certain diagrams when he began to study the mathematics in use at Beuron. 'I have gone back to the sacred measures... I confess it is not all plain sailing, and I get rather confused,' he wrote to Maurice Denis[2], who could not help laughing at Father Didier with his proportional compasses always in his hand.

---

1. 'Take all your measurements, carefully, snapping lines first, getting the centres of the spaces..', Cennino Cennini, *Il libro dell'arte*. (English translation by Daniel V. Thompson Jr.: *The Craftsman's Handbook*, Yale, 1933, p. 43.)

2. *Op. cit.*, p. 76.

The reserve shown by younger artists towards the golden proportion is a proof of the difficulties met with in applying it; and this reluctance has encouraged me to make my examination of composition throughout the different historical periods in complete freedom and without any preconception in favour of the golden number. Our analyses have, I think, shown how greatly the solutions adopted have varied according to individual temperaments, schools and periods. I have always tried to find the simplest scheme and to stick to it.

A confrontation of many different works, such as this which we have undertaken, always brings out the arbitrary character of certain oppositions of tendencies. Of, for instance, the current distinction between abstract and figurative art. In some of Gustave Moreau's water colours the whole of the Kandinsky of the first period is already contained. And surely, in the purity of Mondrian, one finds once more the strictness of medieval composition. Is the freshness of Paul Klee any less than that of Fra Angelico?

I should add that, as a partisan of geometrical construction, I am delighted when I see it become, sometimes, the actual form which the picture presents to the view, but this does not make me think that geometry is everything in painting. The work of art draws its enrichment from the tension between its various components.

In conclusion I should like, if I may, to say this: what we have learned about construction in art is not valid only for art. In earlier centuries, over against a precise, strict and analytical art, there existed empirical techniques: mathematical thinking, which was one of the glories of man, would have disdained in those days to stoop to the work of perfecting the crafts, but it did, on the other hand, feel itself very close to the search for the beautiful. Today mathematics, through mechanics, have permeated and moulded our life to such a degree that many people have set up, in opposition to them, an art of negation and revolt, an extended expression of the self, a new romanticism or, perhaps, a simple explosive reaction of the individual against the tightening vice of conformism.

'This labour (of the spirit) is so strenuous that sometimes the mind can do no more. All that it then seeks or needs is to relax, to lose willingly all sense of form, to accept passively whatever may flow up to it from the ocean-depths of life. The mind, at such a time, believes that it can find rejuvenation in mere brute instinct, in the admission of fugitive impressions... it overturns the checkerboard of logic. And yet these riots and tumults have no object other than the invention of new forms...[3]'

Mathematics, even in becoming more and more nearly all-pervasive, remain bound up with the search for the beautiful. Sometimes—in parallel, as it were, with works of art—one finds in the shape of a ship or an aero-

3. Henri Focillon, *La vie des formes*, Paris, P.U.F., 1955, 4th edition. (English translation: Charles Beecher Hogan and George Kubler, *The Life of Forms in Art* (part of the series, *Yale Historical Publications: History of Art*), Yale, 1942; p. 52.)

plane the amazing revelation of a beauty too often concealed from the eyes of most people by utility or function. The artist should bring out this beauty, render it visible to everyone, and in its presence keep the freshness of approach of the men of the fifteenth century, with their admiration for 'that great variety of figures, manifold in their origins and forms, yet bound together harmoniously in one symphony[4]'.

4. Pacioli, *op. cit.*, ch. VI.

LIST OF ILLUSTRATIONS

SELECT BIBLIOGRAPHY

Ancient and Renaissance Writers

L. B. Alberti. *De re aedificatoria*, Florence, 1485. French translation by Jan Martin, Paris, 1553. English translation by James Leoni *(Ten Books on Architecture)*, London, 1726, 1739, 1755 and Tiranti, 1955.

— *Della pittura (De pictura*—this was the title of the original Latin manuscript). Venice, 1547. English translation by J. R. Spencer, London, 1956.

Boethius. *De musica*, Venice, 1491-92. German translation by Oscar Paul, Leipzig, 1872.

Cennino Cennini. *Il libro dell'arte* (1437 or earlier); text edited by Daniel V. Thompson Jr., Yale, 1932; English translation by the same *(The Craftsman's Handbook)*, Yale, 1933.

F. Colonna. *Hypnerotomachia Poliphili*, Venice, 1499. French translation *(Le Songe de Poliphile)*, Paris, 1546.

J. Cousin. *Livre de pourtraicture*, Paris, 1571.

A. Dürer. *Underweysung der Messung...*, Nuremberg, 1525 (revised edition 1538).

— *Vier Bücher von menschlicher Proportion*, Nuremberg, 1528. French translation by L. Meigret Lionnois, Paris, 1557.

— *Briefe, Tagebücher und Reime*, ed. Thausing, *Quellenschriften*, Vienna, 1872.

— *Records of the Journey to Venice and the Low Countries*, Boston, 1913.

Euclid. *Elements*, ed. Isaac Todhunter, London (Everyman's Library), 1933 and reprinted.

Marsilio Ficino. *Opera*, Basle, 1576.

F. Giorgio. *De harmonia mundi totius*, Venice, 1525.

Leonardo da Vinci. *The Literary Works*, compiled and edited from the original manuscripts by J.P. and I.A. Richter, London, 1883 and 1938, 2 vols.

— *Paragone: a comparison of the arts*, translation with an introduction by I.A. Richter, London, 1949.

— *Treatise on Painting* (codex urbinas latinus 1270), translated and annotated by A.P. McMahon, 2 vols., Princeton, 1956.

G. P. Lomazzo. *Trattato dell'arte della pittura*, Milan, 1584 and 1844. English translation (of the first five books only), *A Tracte containing the Artes of curious Paintynge Carvynge and Buildinge*, by R[ichard] H[aydocke], Oxford, 1598.

— *Idea del tempio della pittura*, Milan, 1590.

— *Traité de la proportion naturelle et artificielle des choses*. Plates by Hilaire Pader, Toulouse, 1649.

L. Pacioli. *Summa de arithmetica*, Venice, 1494.

— *Divina proportione*, Venice, 1509. Editions: Winterberg, *Quellenschriften*, Vienna, 1889; and *Fontes Ambrosiani* XXXI, Milan, 1956.

A. Palladio. *I quattro Libri dell'Architectura*, Venice, 1570.

Piero della Francesca. *De quinque corporibus regularibus.* Editions: Winterberg, *Repertorium für Kunstwissenschaft,* 1882; and Mancini (from the codex vaticano-urbinate no. 632), 1913.

— *De prospectiva pingendi.* Editions: Winterberg, Strasburg, 1899; and G. Nicco Fasola, Florence, 1942.

S. Serlio. *Tutte l'Opere d'Architettura,* Venice, 1584. English translation, *The second Booke of Architecture, made by Sebastian Serley, entreating of perspective...,* London, 1611.

G. Vasari. *Le Vite de' piu eccellenti Architetti, Pittori e Scultori Italiani, da Cimabue insino ai tempi nostri,* Florence, 1550; revised and enlarged, 1568. English translation by A.B. Hinds (Everyman's Library), London, 1949, 4 vols.

Villard de Honnecourt. *Album,* Paris, Bibliothèque Nationale, Ms. fr. 19093. Editions: Lassus and Darcel, Paris, 1858; R. Willis, London, 1859; H. Omont, Paris, 1927; and H.R. Hahnloser, Vienna, 1935.

— *De architectura,* Rome, 1486.

Vitruvius. *(Architecture ou Art de bien bastir).* French translation by Jan Martin, illustrations by J. Goujon, Paris, 1547.

F. Zuccaro. *L'Idea de' Pittori, Scultori et Architetti...,* Turin, 1607.

Modern Writers

J. S. Ackerman. '*Ars sine scientia nihil est: Gothic theory of architecture at the cathedral of Milan*', *Art Bulletin,* June, 1949.

G. Apollinaire. *Les peintres cubistes,* Paris, Athéna, 1913. English translation *(The cubist painters: aesthetic meditations)* by L. Abel, New York, 1944 and 1949 [*Documents of Modern Art,* vol. I].

R. Bacou. *Odilon Redon,* Geneva, Cailler, 1956.

J. Baltrusaitis. *La Stylistique ornementale dans la sculpture romane,* Paris, Leroux, 1931.

— *Anamorphoses ou perspectives curieuses,* Paris, O. Perrin, 1955.

— *Réveils et prodiges, le gothique fantastique,* Paris, A. Colin, 1960.

G. Bataille. *Manet,* Geneva, Skira, 1955. English translation by A. Wainhouse and J. Emmons, New York, 1955.

E. Béothy. *La Série d'or,* Paris, Chanth, 1932.

E. Bernard. *Souvenirs sur Paul Cézanne,* Paris, R.-G. Michel, 1925-26.

Charles Blanc. *Ingres, sa vie et ses ouvrages,* Paris, 1870.

— *Grammaire des arts décoratifs,* Paris, 1882.

Sir A. Blunt. '*Thesis summarized*' in *Bulletin de la Société d'histoire de l'art français,* 1933, p. 125 ff.

— *Artistic Theory in Italy,* 1450-1600, Oxford, 1940, London, 1956.

C.-E. Briseux. *Traité du Beau essentiel dans les arts...,* Paris, 1752.

P. Cabanne. *Degas,* Paris, Tisné, 1957.

J. Charpier and P. Seghers. *L'Art de la peinture,* Paris, Seghers, 1957.

A. Chastel. *Art et humanisme à Florence au temps de Laurent le Magnifique,* Paris, P.U.F., 1959.

M.-E. Chevreul. *De la loi du contraste simultané des couleurs...,* Paris, 1827, 1839 and 1889. English translation by John Spanton *(The Laws of Contrast of Colour...),* London, 1857, 1859, 1883.

Sir K. Clark. *Landscape into Art,* London, 1948.

— *Piero della Francesca,* London, Phaidon, 1951.

Colloque Nicolas Poussin, publié sous la direction d' A. Chastel, Paris, C.N.R.S., 1960, 2 vols.

P. Coremans. *L'Agneau mystique au laboratoire, les Primitifs flamands*, III, Antwerp, 1953.

A. Coypel. *Discours prononcés dans les conférences de l'Académie royale de peinture...*, Paris, 1721.

J. David. *Le Peintre Louis David*, Paris, 1880.

E. Degas. *Lettres*, edited by M. Guérin, Paris, Grasset, 1931. English translation by M. Kay, Oxford, 1947.

E. Delacroix. *Journal*, edited by A. Joubin, Paris, Plon, 1932, 3 vols. English translation (selection) by L. Norton, London, Phaidon, 1951.

M. Denis. *Nouvelles Théories...*, Paris, Rouart et Watelin, 1922.

G. Diehl. *Henri Matisse*, Paris, Tisné, 1954.

B. Dorival. *Les Etapes de la peinture française contemporaine*, Paris, Gallimard, 1946, 3 vols.

H. Dorra and J. Rewald. *Seurat*, Paris, *Les Beaux-Arts*, 1959.

P. du Colombier. *Histoire de l'art*, Paris, Fayard, 1942.
— *Les Chantiers des cathédrales*, Paris, Picard, 1953.

C.-A. du Fresnoy. *L'Art de peinture* (translated from the Latin), Paris, 1668, 1673. English translations, London, 1695 (with preface by Dryden), and York, 1783 (with remarks by Reynolds).

M. Emanaud. *Géométrie perspective*, Paris, Doin, 1921.

A. Félibien des Avaux. *Entretiens sur les vies et les ouvrages des plus excellents peintres*, Paris, 1666-1685.
— *Conférences de l'Académie royale de peinture et de sculpture pendant l'année 1667*, Paris, 1669.

F. Fénéon. *Les Impressionnistes en 1886*, Paris, Publications de la Vogue, 1886,

H. Focillon. *La Peinture aux XIXe et XXe siècles*, Paris, Laurens, 1928.
— *La Vie des formes*, Paris, Leroux, 1934; 4th edition, Paris, P.U.F., 1955. English translation *(The Life of Forms in Art)* by C.B. Hogan and G. Kubler, New Haven, 1942, New York, 1948.
— *L'Art d'Occident*, Paris, A. Colin, 1938.
— *Piero della Francesca*, Paris, A. Colin, 1952.

A. Fontaine. *Conférences inédites de l'Académie royale de peinture et de sculpture*, Paris, Laurens, n.d.

Dr Funck-Hellet. *Composition et nombre d'or dans les œuvres de la Renaissance*, Paris, Vincent-Fréal, 1950.

M. Ghyka. *Esthétique des proportions dans la nature et dans les arts*, Paris, Gallimard, 1927.
— *The Geometry of Art and Life*, New York, Sheed and Ward, 1946.
— *Le Nombre d'or. Rites et rythmes pythagoriciens...*, Paris, Gallimard, 1931, 2 vols.

E. Gilson. *Painting and Reality*, London, Routledge, and New York, 1957.

A.-L. Girodet-Trioson. *Œuvres posthumes*, Paris, 1829.

W. Grohmann. *Paul Klee*, London, Lund Humphries, and New York, 1954.

P. Guadet. *Cours de perspective*, Paris, Vincent-Fréal, 1929.

G. Habasque. *Le Cubisme*, Geneva, Skira, 1959. English translation by S. Gilbert, Skira, 1959.

L. Hautecœur. 'Les proportions mathématiques et l'architecture', *Gazette des Beaux-Arts*, December, 1937.

Ch. Henry. 'Introduction à une esthétique scientifique', Paris, *La Revue contemporaine*, 1885.
— *Cercle chromatique*, Paris, 1888.

F. Hoffstadt. *Gothisches A.B.C. Buch, das ist Grundregeln des Gothischen Styls für Künstler und Werkleute*, Frankfurt-am-Main, 1840[-45]. French translation *(Principes du style gothique à l'usage des artistes et des ouvriers...)*, Frankfurt-am-Main, 1847.

J. Holderbaum. '*A Bronze by Giovanni Bologna and a Painting by Bronzino*', *Burlington Magazine*, December, 1956.

R. Huyghe. *Dialogue avec le visible*, Paris, Flammarion, 1955. English translation *(Discovery of Art)* by Norbert Guterman, London, Thames and Hudson, 1959.
— *L'Art et l'âme*, Paris, Flammarion, 1960. English translation *(Art and the Spirit of Man)* by Norbert Guterman, London, Thames and Hudson, 1962.

M. Jean and A. Mezei. *Histoire de la peinture surréaliste*, Paris, Ed. du Seuil, 1959. English translation *(History of Surrealist Painting)* by S.W. Taylor, London, 1960.

Jordan. '*Der Vermisste Traktat des Piero della Francesca über die fünf regelmässigen Körper*', *Jahrbuch der Kgl. Preuss. Kunstsammlungen*, I, 1880.

H. Jouin. *Conférences de l'Académie royale de peinture...*, Paris, 1883.

D.-H. Kahnweiler. *Juan Gris, sa vie, son œuvre, ses écrits*, Paris, Gallimard, 1946. English translation by Douglas Cooper, London, 1947.

W. Kandinsky. *Über das Geistige in der Kunst*, Munich, 1912. English translations: by M.T.H. Sadler *(The Art of Spiritual Harmony)*, London, 1914; and by Hilla Rebay, *(On the Spiritual in Art)*, New York, 1946.

H. Lapauze. *Ingres, sa vie et ses œuvres, Paris*, 1911.

J.-P. Lauer. *Le Problème des pyramides d'Egypte*, Paris, Payot, 1952.

P. Desiderius Lenz (Father Didier). *Zur Ästhetik der Beuroner Schule*, Vienna and Leipzig, n.d. French translation *(L'Esthétique de Beuron)* by P. Sérusier, Paris, 1905.

A. Lhote. *Parlons peinture*, Paris, Denoël et Steele, 1936.
— *Traités du paysage et de la figure*, Paris, Grasset, 1958. English translations by W.J. Strachan: *Treatise on Landscape Painting*, London, 1950; *Figure Painting*, London, 1953.

F. M. Lund. *Ad Quadratum: a study of the geometrical bases of classic and medieval religious architecture...*, printed by order of the Norwegian Parliament, London, Batsford, 1921, 2 vols.

E. Maillard. *Du Nombre d'or*, Paris, Tournon, 1943.

A. Malraux. *Saturne*, Paris, La Pléiade, 1950. English translation *(Saturn, an essay on Goya)* by C.W. Chitton, London and New York, 1957.

H. Martin. *Les Joyaux de l'Arsenal*, I: *Psautier de Saint Louis et de Blanche de Castille*, Paris, n.d.

J. Meder. *Die Handzeichnungen*, Vienna, Schroll, 1923.

A. R. Mengs. *Opere*, edited by J.N. d'Azara, Parma, 1780, 2 vols. English translation, London, 1796, 2 vols.

P.-H. Michel. *La Pensée de L.-B. Alberti*, Paris, 1930.
— *De Pythagore à Euclide*, Paris, 1950.

J. Nicolle. *La Symétrie dans la nature et dans les travaux des hommes*, Paris, La Colombe, 1955.

Paillot de Montabert. *Traité complet de la peinture*, Paris, 1829, 9 vols.

E. Panofsky. '*Die Entwicklung der Proportionslehre als Abbild der Stilentwicklung*', in *Monatshefte für Kunstwissenschaft*, 1921, p. 208. English translation *(The History of the Theory of Human Proportions as a Reflection of the History of Styles)* by E. Panofsky in *Meaning in the Visual Arts*, Garden City, N.Y., Doubleday, 1955.
— *The Life and Art of Albrecht Dürer*, Princeton, 1955.

Les Peintres futuristes italiens: Catalogue of exhibition, Paris, Bernheim jeune, 1912.

Ch. Picard. *Manuel d'archéologie grecque: la sculpture, période classique*, Paris, Picard, 1939.

Ch. Picard and G. Fougères. *L'Acropole*, Paris, Morancé, 1910 ff., also 1929, 1932.

A. Pozzo. *Prospettiva de' pittori* et *architetti*, Rome, 1717.

O. Redon. *A soi-même, journal 1867-1915*, Paris, Floury, 1922.

R. Rey. *La Renaissance du sentiment classique dans la peinture française à la fin du XIXe siècle*, Paris, *Les Beaux-Arts*, 1931.

Sir Joshua Reynolds. *The Complete Works*, Bohn's Standard Library, London, 1846.

— *The Discourses*, London, 1924.

M. Rickert. *Painting in Britain, the Middle Ages*, London, Penguin, 1954.

M. Rooses. *L'Œuvre de Rubens*, Antwerp, 1886-1892.

F. von Rziha. *Studien über Steinmetz-Zeichen*, Vienna, 1883.

L. Schwob. *Réalité de l'Art*, Lausanne, Rouge, 1954.

M. Serullaz. *Les Peintres impressionnistes*, Paris, Tisné, 1959. English translation *(French painting: the Impressionist painters)* by W.J. Strachan, Paris, 1960.

P. Sérusier. *L'ABC de la peinture, avec une étude sur P. Sérusier par Maurice Denis*, Paris, Floury, 1942.

M. Seuphor. *Piet Mondrian, sa vie, son œuvre*, Paris, Flammarion, 1956. English translation *(Piet Mondrian, Life and Work)*, London, Thames and Hudson, 1957.

P. Signac. *De Delacroix au néo-impressionnisme*, Paris, Floury, 1911.

E. Souriau. *La Correspondance des Arts*, Paris, Flammarion, 1947.

— *La Structure de l'œuvre d'art*, Paris, Centre de documentation universitaire, 1956.

— '*Y a-t-il une palette française?*', in *Art de France*, II, Paris, 1962.

W. Stechow. '*Dürers Bologneser Lehrer*', in *Kunstchronik*, 1922, p. 251.

D. Sutter. *Philosophie des Beaux-Arts appliquée à la peinture*, Paris, Morel, 1870.

— '*Les Phénomènes de la vision*', in *l'Art*, 1880, I, pp. 74 ff.

D. Vallier. '*Villon*', in *Cahiers d'Art*, 1957.

L. Venturi. *La Pittura contemporanea*, Milan, Hoepli, 1948.

A. Verdet. *Fernand Léger*, Geneva, Cailler, 1955.

E.-E. Viollet-le-Duc. *Dictionnaire raisonné de l'architecture française du XIe au XVIe siècle*, Paris, 1858-1868.

M. Wahl. *Le Mouvement dans la peinture*, Paris, Alcan, 1936.

G. Wildenstein. *Chardin*, Paris, *Les Beaux-Arts*, 1933.

Edgar Wind. *Pagan Mysteries in the Renaissance*, London, Faber, 1958.

R. Wittkower. *Architectural Principles in the Age of Humanism*, London, Tiranti, 1949 and 1952.

H. Wölfflin. *Kunstgeschichtliche Grundbegriffe...* 6th edition, Munich, 1923. English translation *(Principles of Art History)* by M.D. Hottinger, London, Bell, 1932.

INDEX OF NAMES